Research and Practice in Applied Linguis

General Editors: **Christopher N. Candlin** and **David R. Hall**, Linguistics Department, Macquarie University, Australia.

All books in this series are written by leading researchers and teachers in Applied Linguistics, with broad international experience. They are designed for the MA or PhD student in Applied Linguistics, TESOL or similar subject areas and for the language professional keen to extend their research experience.

Titles include:

Dick Allwright and Judith Hanks
THE DEVELOPING LANGUAGE LEARNER
An Introduction to Exploratory Practice

Francesca Bargiela-Chiappini, Catherine Nickerson and Brigitte Planken
BUSINESS DISCOURSE

Christopher N. Candlin and Stephen H. Moore
EXPLORING DISCOURSE IN CONTEXT AND ACTION

David Cassels Johnson
LANGUAGE POLICY

Francesca Bargiela-Chiappini, Catherine Nickerson and Brigitte Planken
BUSINESS DISCOURSE, SECOND EDITION

Alison Ferguson and Elizabeth Armstrong
RESEARCHING COMUNICATION DISORDERS

Lynne Flowerdew
CORPORA AND LANGUAGE EDUCATION

Sandra Beatriz Hale
COMMUNITY INTERPRETING

Geoff Hall
LITERATURE IN LANGUAGE EDUCATION

Richard Kiely and Pauline Rea-Dickins
PROGRAM EVALUATION IN LANGUAGE EDUCATION

Marie-Noëlle Lamy and Regine Hampel
ONLINE COMMUNICATION IN LANGUAGE LEARNING AND TEACHING

Annamaria Pinter
CHILDREN LEARNING SECOND LANGUAGES

Virginia Samuda and Martin Bygate
TASKS IN SECOND LANGUAGE LEARNING

Norbert Schmitt
RESEARCHING VOCABULARY
A Vocabulary Research Manual

Helen Spencer-Oatey and Peter Franklin
INTERCULTURAL INTERACTION
A Multidisciplinary Approach to Intercultural Communication

Cyril J. Weir
LANGUAGE TESTING AND VALIDATION

Tony Wright
CLASSROOM MANAGEMENT IN LANGUAGE EDUCATION

Forthcoming titles:

Anne Burns and Helen de Silva Joyce
LITERACY

Sandra Gollin and David R. Hall
LANGUAGE FOR SPECIFIC PURPOSES

Marilyn Martin-Jones
BILINGUALISM

Martha Pennington
PRONUNCIATION

Research and Practice in Applied Linguistics
Series Standing Order ISBN 978–1–403–91184–1 hardcover
978–1–403–91185–8 paperback
(*outside North America only*)

You can receive future titles in this series as they are published by placing a standing order. Please contact your bookseller or, in case of difficulty, write to us at the address below with your name and address, the title of the series and the ISBN quoted above.

Customer Services Department, Macmillan Distribution Ltd, Houndmills, Basingstoke, Hampshire RG21 6XS, England

---

Language Policy

David Cassels Johnson
Washington State University, USA

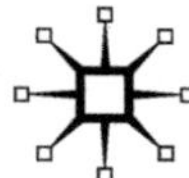

First published 2013 by
PALGRAVE MACMILLAN

Palgrave Macmillan in the UK is an imprint of Macmillan Publishers Limited, registered in England, company number 785998, of Houndmills, Basingstoke, Hampshire RG21 6XS.

Palgrave Macmillan in the US is a division of St Martin's Press LLC, 175 Fifth Avenue, New York, NY 10010.

Palgrave Macmillan is the global academic imprint of the above companies and has companies and representatives throughout the world.

Palgrave® and Macmillan® are registered trademarks in the United States, the United Kingdom, Europe and other countries.

ISBN 978–0–230–25169–4 hardback
ISBN 978–0–230–25170–0 paperback

This book is printed on paper suitable for recycling and made from fully managed and sustained forest sources. Logging, pulping and manufacturing processes are expected to conform to the environmental regulations of the country of origin.

A catalogue record for this book is available from the British Library.

A catalog record for this book is available from the Library of Congress.

Typeset by MPS Limited, Chennai, India.

For Nancy, Rebecca, and Tom

Contents

List of figures and tables xi

General Editors' preface xiii

Acknowledgements xv

Part I Laying the Groundwork: Definitions, Theories, and Concepts

1 What is language policy? 3
- 1.1 Definitions 4
- 1.2 Types 9
- 1.3 Example language policies 12
  - 1.3.1 A brief history of English language policies 12
  - 1.3.2 Indigenous languages and policy 16
  - 1.3.3 Oil production and language policy in Equatorial Guinea 20
- 1.4 Discussion 24

2 Theories, concepts, and frameworks: An historical overview 26
- 2.1 The origin and development of early language planning scholarship 27
- 2.2 Expanding frameworks and conceptualizations in the 1970's and 80's 30
  - 2.2.1 Dell Hymes' sociolinguistics 30
  - 2.2.2 Critical (socio)linguistics 32
  - 2.2.3 Expanding frameworks in language planning and policy 33
- 2.3 Critical language policy (CLP) 39
- 2.4 Ethnography of language policy 43
- 2.5 Reversing language shift and linguistic imperialism 47
  - 2.5.1 Reversing language shift 47
  - 2.5.2 Linguistic imperialism 49
- 2.6 Ecology of language 51
- 2.7 Educational language policy 52
- 2.8 Discussion 55

Part II Findings

3 Example studies 59
3.1 Marilyn Martin-Jones 60
3.2 Feliciano Chimbutane 64
3.3 Florence Bonacina 69
3.4 Angela Cincotta-Segi 75
3.5 Francis M. Hult 80
3.6 Lin Pan 82
3.7 Dafna Yitzhaki 85
3.8 Shannon Fitzsimmons-Doolan 88
3.9 Discussion 91

4 Findings 95
4.1 Appropriation vs. implementation 96
4.1.1 Finding #1: Language policy agents have power 98
4.1.2 Finding #2: Language policy power is differentially allocated among *arbiters* and *implementers* 100
4.2 Language policies as instruments of power 101
4.2.1 Finding #3: Governing bodies use language policies for control 102
4.3 Language policies as instruments of empowerment 103
4.3.1 Finding #4: National multilingual language policies *can* and *do* open spaces for multilingual education and minority languages 103
4.3.2 Finding #5: Local multilingual language policies *can* and *do* open spaces for multilingual education and minority languages 105
4.4 The multiple layers of policy text, discourse, and practice 105
4.4.1 Finding #6: Top-down and bottom-up are relative 108
4.4.2 Finding #7: Macro multilingual language policies are not necessarily enough 108
4.4.3 Finding #8: Local multilingual language policies are not necessarily enough either 109
4.4.4 Finding #9: Meso-level language policies matter 110
4.5 The nature of language policy text and discourse 111
4.5.1 Finding #10: National language policies are not necessarily ideologically consistent 111

4.5.2 Finding #11: Policy intentions are especially difficult to ascertain 113
4.5.3 Finding #12: Language policy language constitutes its own genre 117
4.6 Conclusion 117

Part III Researching Language Policy

5 Research approaches and methods 121
5.1 Early language planning work 121
5.2 Historical-textual analysis 124
5.3 Political theory and the law 128
5.3.1 Judicial decisions and the courts 129
5.3.2 Language policy and political identity 132
5.3.3 National identity, citizenship, and language 133
5.3.4 Constitutional and statutory interpretation 137
5.4 Media discourse and LPP 140
5.5 Ethnography of language policy 144
5.5.1 Definitions, benefits, and challenges 144
5.5.2 Method 149
5.6 Discourse analysis 152
5.6.1 Critical discourse analysis 154
5.6.2 Intertextuality, interdiscursivity, and recontextualization 158
5.6.3 Criticism of CDA 164
5.6.4 Linguistic anthropology and speech chains 166
5.7 Discussion 168

6 Educational language policy engagement and action research (ELPEAR) 170
6.1 Action research 170
6.2 Language policy action research 174
6.2.1 The language policy action research cycle 175
6.2.2 Features of language policy action research 178
6.3 ELPEAR examples 180
6.3.1 Neville Alexander and PRAESA 180
6.3.2 Rebecca Freeman 184
6.3.3 Richard Hill and Stephen May 186
6.4 David Corson's model for critical policymaking in schools 188

6.5 Language policy engagement: Creation 190
6.5.1 Macro-level language policy creation 192
6.5.1.1 Engaging politicians 194
6.5.1.2 Grassroots organization and political activism 195
6.5.1.3 The courts 197
6.5.1.4 Engaging the media 198
6.5.2 Micro-level language policy creation 206
6.6 Language policy engagement: Interpretation 210
6.7 Language policy engagement: Appropriation 212
6.8 Discussion 213

7 Research direction(s) and model projects 215
7.1 Topics and contexts 216
7.2 Access and positionality 220
7.3 Research questions and organizing data collection 224
7.3.1 Creation 224
7.3.2 Interpretation 232
7.3.3 Appropriation 236
7.4 Data collection and analysis 239
7.5 Example analyses 253
7.6 Discussion 259

Part IV Resources

8 Further resources 263
8.1 Books 263
8.2 Journals 265
8.3 Professional organizations and conferences 267
8.4 Organizations and projects concerning language policy and education 267
8.5 Example language policies 268
8.6 Electronic mailing lists which feature LPP information 269
8.7 Websites 269

References 271

Index 290

List of figures and tables

Figures

5.1 Fairclough's model of discourse analysis (2010: 133) 156

6.1 The action research spiral 172

6.2 Relationships between macro, meso, and micro educational language policy 193

Tables

1.1 Language policy types 10

2.1 Haugen's (1983: 275) model of language planning 28

2.2 Kloss's and Wiley's policy orientations framework (adapted from Wiley 2002: 48–49) 35

2.3 Language policy orientations in educational language policy 38

2.4 Ethnographies of language policy 46

5.1 Hornberger's integrative framework for language policy and planning goals 122

5.2 Research outline for comparative studies of language planning (Fishman *et al.* 1971) 126

5.3 Data collection for ethnography of language policy 151

5.4 An interdisciplinary method for analyzing language policy 168

6.1 Terminological history of "Ebonics" 199

6.2 Some popular myths about language (education) 206

7.1 LPP topics according to discipline 216

7.2 LPP contexts according to topic 218

7.3 Countries receiving little or no attention in the LPP literature to date 218

7.4 Creation activities 225

7.5 Interpretation of LPP: Activities and data sources 233
7.6 Appropriation of LPP 237
7.7 Analyzing goals 244
7.8 Primary data collection methods for LPP processes 247

General Editors' Preface

Research and Practice in Applied Linguistics is an international book series from Palgrave Macmillan which brings together leading researchers and teachers in Applied Linguistics to provide readers with the knowledge and tools they need to undertake their own practice-related research. Books in the series are designed for students and researchers in Applied Linguistics, TESOL, Language Education and related subject areas, and for language professionals keen to extend their research experience.

Every book in this innovative series is designed to be user-friendly, with clear illustrations and accessible style. The quotations and definitions of key concepts that punctuate the main text are intended to ensure that many, often competing, voices are heard. Each book presents a concise historical and conceptual overview of its chosen field, identifying many lines of enquiry and findings, but also gaps and disagreements. It provides readers with an overall framework for further examination of how research and practice inform each other, and how practitioners can develop their own problem-based research.

The focus throughout is on exploring the relationship between research and practice in Applied Linguistics. How far can research provide answers to the questions and issues that arise in practice? Can research questions that arise and are examined in very specific circumstances be informed by, and inform, the global body of research and practice? What different kinds of information can be obtained from different research methodologies? How should we make a selection between the options available, and how far are different methods compatible with each other? How can the results of research be turned into practical action?

The books in this series identify some of the key researchable areas in the field and provide workable examples of research projects, backed up by details of appropriate research tools and resources. Case studies and exemplars of research and practice are drawn on throughout the books. References to key institutions, individual research lists, journals and professional organizations provide starting points for gathering information and embarking on research. The books also include annotated lists of key works in the field for further study.

The overall objective of the series is to illustrate the message that in Applied Linguistics there can be no good professional practice that isn't based on good research, and there can be no good research that isn't informed by practice.

CHRISTOPHER N. CANDLIN and DAVID R. HALL
Macquarie University, Sydney

Acknowledgements

Who knows how everyone we meet influences what we do and write? T.S. Eliot wrote that immature poets imitate; mature poets steal (often erroneously cited, but perhaps improved, as "bad poets imitate but good poets steal"). If this is true, and if the goal is to be a mature poet, then I am proud to have stolen from the best, three of whom are listed in my dedication because they have been my primary sources of guidance and inspiration. I could not have done this without them, or at least, the "this" would be totally different and not as good. Further, if Bakhtin is right and nothing we say is completely original, filled as it is with intertextual and interdiscursive connections to others and to the past, then the list of individuals who helped make this book possible is truly innumerable. I will attempt to enumerate them anyway.

I first want to thank my editors Chris Candlin and David Hall. If this book is at all good, it is due in large part to their intense critique, helpful suggestions, and constant encouragement throughout this lengthy process. They have pushed me to be comprehensive and innovative and I cannot thank them enough. If the book is at all bad, on the other hand, that's all me.

Next I want to thank my colleagues, co-authors, and compatriots Francis Hult and Eric Johnson. Francis and I have maintained an ongoing dialogue about many of the issues discussed in this book for about a decade now. These conversations do not always have an obvious discernible or demonstrable impact but the book would not and could not be the same without them. Eric and I have a newer relationship but our ongoing collaboration and research on language policy in Washington State has engendered findings and concepts that are on display throughout the book.

In Chapter 3 I wanted to showcase interesting new language policy research projects that incorporate innovative concepts and research methods and offer intriguing findings. I believe this small collection of studies demonstrates some of the new and exciting directions in the field. In the process of reviewing this work, however, I became inspired by it and was able to make connections throughout the book. Some of the authors I know well, some I don't know at all, but I would like to thank all of you, especially those of you – Marilyn Martin-Jones, Angela

Cincotta-Segi, Florence Bonacina, and Francis – who sent me electronic (and hard!) copies of publications.

Other collaborators and colleagues have contributed in diverse ways – email conversations, conference presentations and discussions, advice, and inspiration – and some have been kind enough to send me copies of their publications. I would therefore like to thank the following scholars who have inspired and assisted me: Harold Schiffman, Terri McCarty, Terence Wiley, Brian French, and, finally, Jim Tollefson. While writing, I thought about Jim's ideas often, especially his book *Planning Language, Planning Inequality*, and my goal was to live up to it.

I also am deeply indebted to all of the educators who I have worked with. Their tireless dedication to improving educational opportunity for linguistic minorities is a constant inspiration. The U.S. tends to be portrayed as a monolingual country but there are plenty of talented, creative, and innovative educators working to preserve multilingual education in U.S. schools. They often work in very difficult political, educational, and financial situations and they need our support with all of the above.

Part of the research for this book was funded by grants received from Washington State University and the College of Education therein, for which I am very grateful. I would especially like to thank my WSU colleagues Pam Bettis, Dawn Shinew, Tom Salsbury, and Joy Egbert, who have been incredibly supportive and make it a pleasure to come to the office.

Finally, I would like to thank my family: My parents, whose encouragement is indomitable (although they won't read a lick of this and I don't blame them); Brinda, who has always been supportive and tolerant of my ivory towering; and finally to my kids, Devi and Mira, who are a constant source of joy and inspiration: I definitely could have written this book without you. In fact, I probably could have written two in the time this one took because you are black holes, into which time and energy and (day)light are sucked and obliterated. Of course, our universe could not exist as it does without black holes.

Publisher's note

Part I

Laying the Groundwork: Definitions, Theories, and Concepts

1
What is language policy?

Chapter outline

1.1 Definitions
1.2 Types
1.3 Example language policies
1.4 Discussion

The natural first question is: What is language policy? The question is commonly asked in books on the topic but concrete definitions are less common than discussions of language policy in terms of types, goals, or examples. This chapter will take both approaches by first examining and synthesizing definitions already in circulation and then looking at some example language policies to see how these definitions hold up. Complicating the question is the relationship between language policy and the term that preceded it, *language planning*. Most would agree that language policy and language planning are closely related but different activities. Some argue that language planning subsumes language policy (Kaplan and Baldauf 1997) while others argue that language policy subsumes language planning (Schiffman 1996). For the title of this book, the term *language policy* is adopted for two reasons: (1) terminological simplicity, and (2) within accepted definitions of language planning, there is an assumption that some agent(s) makes a plan intended to influence language forms or functions, yet, there are many examples of language policy that are not intentional and/or not planned. However, throughout much of the book I will use *language planning and policy*, often referred to as LPP, both out of respect for the tradition of research that gave rise to the field (language planning) and because the two fields have, for all intents and purposes, coalesced into one (Hornberger

2006a). The historical trajectory of these terms will be discussed in more detail in Chapter 2.

1.1 Definitions

Five definitions of language policy may help us arrive at an appropriate synthesis. The first is from Kaplan and Baldauf (1997) who argue that a language policy is part of the larger process of language planning:

Quote 1.1 Kaplan and Baldauf

The exercise of language planning leads to, or is directed by, the promulgation of a language policy by government (or other authoritative body or person). A language policy is a body of ideas, laws, regulations, rules and practices intended to achieve the planned language change in the societies, group or system.

(Kaplan and Baldauf 1997: xi)

Kaplan and Baldauf portray language policy as a set of laws or regulations or rules enacted by an authoritative body (like a government) as part of a language plan. Certainly, what Kaplan and Baldauf describe here *is* language policy but other activities can be considered language policy as well. Language policies do not need to be enacted by an authoritative body – they can emerge from a bottom-up movement or grassroots organization – and not all language policies are intentional or carefully planned.

Quote 1.2 Harold F. Schiffman

[L]anguage policy is primarily a social construct. It may consist of various elements of an explicit nature – juridical, judicial, administrative, constitutional and/or legal language may be extant in some jurisdictions, but whether or not a polity has such explicit *text*, policy as a cultural construct rests primarily on other conceptual elements – belief systems, attitudes, myths – the whole complex that we are referring to as *linguistic culture*, which is the sum totality of ideas, values, beliefs, attitudes, prejudices, religious strictures, and all the other cultural 'baggage' that speakers bring to their dealings with language from their background.

(Schiffman 1996: 276)

Schiffman's primary argument is that language policy is grounded in linguistic culture and examining one without the other is "probably futile, if not simply trivial" (Schiffman 1996: 5). Captured within this definition are both explicit policies enacted by a polity but also policy as a cultural construct, which relies on the implicit language beliefs, attitudes, and ideologies within a speech community. He further argues that, too often, elements within the linguistic culture (language use, attitudes, etc.) are portrayed as an outcome of language policy "when it is clear that they are elements *underlying* the policy. That is, conclusions are drawn about supposedly causal relationships between language and policy that seem to me totally turned around" (Schiffman 1996: 3). The point about causal relationships is important and careful language policy research should not make causative claims about policy creator intentions, policy language, and policy outcomes without clear evidence. We should not *a priori* attribute language and educational practices to policy since they could have arisen without, or in spite of, any policy support.

Quote 1.3 Bernard Spolsky

A useful first step is to distinguish between the three components of the language policy of a speech community: (1) its language practices – the habitual pattern of selecting among the varieties that make up its linguistic repertoire; (2) its language beliefs or ideology – the beliefs about language and language use; and (3) any specific efforts to modify or influence that practice by any kind of language intervention, planning, or management.

(Spolsky 2004: 5 [numbering mine])

Spolsky (2004) distinguishes between three components of what he calls the language policy of a speech community (Quote 1.3). Each of the tripartite set of components is explained in detail in the first chapter of Spolsky's book. The third part of the definition references traditional conceptualizations of intentional language planning and policy development (*language management,* in Spolsky's terms, 2009) and is contrasted with the first two components – practices and beliefs – which are not necessarily planned or intentional. As he says, language ideology is "language policy with the manager left out, what people think should be done" (Spolsky 2004: 14). The idea that language policies are engendered by the beliefs and ideologies within a speech community is very similar to Schiffman's notion of the close connection between language policies and linguistic culture. The difference seems to be that, while Schiffman avers that language policy is grounded in language beliefs and ideologies, Spolsky portrays such beliefs and ideologies *as* language policy. As well, he includes language practices, not occurring as a result of, or resulting in, language policies, but as language policies *in and of themselves*.

> **Quote 1.4 Teresa McCarty**
>
> I have characterized language policy as a complex sociocultural process [and as] modes of human interaction, negotiation, and production mediated by relations of power. The 'policy' in these processes resides in their language-regulating power; that is, the ways in which they express normative claims about legitimate and illegitimate language forms and uses, thereby governing language statuses and uses.
>
> (McCarty 2011b: 8).

McCarty offers a unique definition based on a sociocultural approach, also described as New Language Policy Studies (McCarty, Collins, and Hopson 2011), and views language policy not simply as "top-down" or "bottom-up" but multi-layered and, similarly to Schiffman and Spolsky, while she recognizes official government texts as potential language policies, she is more interested in how language policy is produced in human interaction and negotiation. Policies regulate language use and are evident in the "everyday ideologically saturated language-regulating mechanisms that construct social hierarchies" (McCarty *et al.* 2011: 339). This definition also includes an important critical perspective, portraying policies as mechanisms that produce power asymmetries.

A critical conceptualization of policy is at the fore of Tollefson's (1991) definition, which positions "language policy" within critical theory:

> **Quote 1.5 James. W. Tollefson**
>
> [L]anguage planning-policy means the institutionalization of language as a basis for distinctions among social groups (classes). That is, language policy is one mechanism for locating language within social structure so that language determines who has access to political power and economic resources. Language policy is one mechanism by which dominant groups establish hegemony in language use.
>
> (Tollefson 1991: 16)

Tollefson (1991) implemented an invaluable critical conceptualization into language planning and policy research that has proven to be very influential. His approach is influenced by critical theory and draws on the work of Habermas (e.g. 1973), Giddens (e.g. 1971), and Foucault (e.g. 1979), among others. As his definition makes clear, Tollefson views language policy as a mechanism of power, which institutionalizes language hierarchies that privilege dominant groups/languages and denies equal access to political power and economic resources. A later re-formulation (2013b: 27) emphasizes how language polices create systems of inequality but also how they *resist* such inequality. His critical language policy (CLP) approach is taken up in a number of places in this book, but particularly in 2.3.

These definitions create some challenges for the field. Traditional notions of *policy* portray it as something that some governing entity or polity enacts and when we hear the word "policy", we tend to think about government policies or laws or some type of regulation that comes from on high. Yet, as Schiffman and Spolsky point out, language policies exist across many different layers or levels, from official governmental law to the language practices of a family for example (see King and Fogle 2006 on family language policy). Further, policies can be official regulations enacted by some authoritative body (Kaplan and Baldauf) as well as unofficial principles and cultural constructs that emerge within a community (McCarty, Schiffman, Spolsky). Spolsky argues that "language policy" encompasses both beliefs and ideologies about language as well as language practices. One is left to wonder, however, if all language ideologies and practices are actual language policies. Does subsuming language ideology and language practices under the umbrella term "language policy" mean that whenever an individual has an attitude about language or produces an utterance, those beliefs and actions, *in and of themselves,* are language policies? These definitions highlight the important connection between language ideologies and language policies (e.g. McGroarty 2013); for example, a policy can emerge from particular language ideologies, a policy can engender language ideologies, or a policy can be interpreted and appropriated in ways that depend on language ideologies. However, it still seems helpful to distinguish between language ideology and language policy as distinct, albeit interconnected, concepts.

Another challenge is considering whether all modes of human interaction – i.e., language practices – constitute actual policies? Are all patterns in conversations, utterances, and interactions language policies? McCarty (2011b) appears to distance herself from this position by asserting that the 'policy' is the language-regulating mechanism within the language practices. How do language practices described as language policies differ from established terms already in use like *norms of interaction* (Hymes 1972b) or *discourses* (Foucault 1978)? Are they one and the same thing? (see Bonacina 2010, and discussed in this volume, section 3.3 who argues that they are.) Language practices are influenced by, products of, producers of, and instantiations of language policies but unless a part of the interaction results in a policy (e.g. a teacher utters a declarative speech act, which has the effect of policy, like "Only English can be used for this activity!"), the value of conflating all language practices as language policies is not clear. For example, at the dinner table, a parent might clear their throat when a child uses forbidden language with the intention of reprimanding and/or warning the child. While the clearing of the throat expresses, or instantiates, the policy, the act and the policy are still separate things. The policy (don't use language X at the dinner table) precedes the other (clearing of the throat) and the existence of the latter relies on the former since the policy could exist with or without the speech act while the pragmatic content of the speech act would be meaningless (or at least, not have the meaning "don't use language X") without the policy.

Finally, regarding a critical conceptualization of policy, while it is important to recognize the power of language policies to marginalize minority and indigenous languages and their users, language policies can also have the opposite effect, specifically when they are designed to promote access to, education in, and use of minority and indigenous languages. Thus, critical conceptualizations need to be balanced with the recognition that language policies can be an important, indeed integral, part of the promotion, maintenance, and revitalization of minority and indigenous languages around the world (even if this has not been the trend, historically). This aspect of policy needs to be further promoted if we are to be successful in protecting threatened languages and promoting the educational and economic rights and opportunities for indigenous and minority language users. The balance between structure and agency in LPP research – between a critical conceptualization of policy as a mechanism of power and a grassroots understanding of the power of language policy agents to interact with policy processes in unique and unpredictable ways – is a theme I will return to throughout the book.

Based on these definitions, I offer the following:

> **Concept 1.1 Language policy defined**
>
> A *language policy* is a policy mechanism that impacts the structure, function, use, or acquisition of language and includes:
>
> 1. Official regulations – often enacted in the form of written documents, intended to effect some change in the form, function, use, or acquisition of language – which can influence economic, political, and educational opportunity;
> 2. Unofficial, covert, de facto, and implicit mechanisms, connected to language beliefs and practices, that have regulating power over language use and interaction within communities, workplaces, and schools;
> 3. Not just products but processes – "policy" as a verb, not a noun – that are driven by a diversity of language policy agents across multiple layers of policy creation, interpretation, appropriation, and instantiation;
> 4. Policy texts and discourses across multiple contexts and layers of policy activity, which are influenced by the ideologies and discourses unique to that context.

An increasingly diverse and broadened group of definitions offers innovative new perspectives on what can be considered language policy, but it remains to be seen whether they will open the door to newer kinds of creative language policy research that inform the field in substantive ways or whether they, instead, will stretch the definition of "language policy" so far that all sociolinguistic research that examines language attitudes and practices will be considered language policy research. If so many concepts, phenomena, and processes are considered "language policy", the question may arise: What *isn't* language policy?

1.2 Types

As well as a general definition, it is useful to delineate the various types of language policies and sets of dichotomies (Table 1.1). While these terms are often used in the literature, they are defined and used in different ways and thus the model in Table 1.1 is offered as a starting point and heuristic, not a definitive framework. Language policies can

Table 1.1 Language policy types

Genesis	*Top-down* Macro-level policy developed by some governing or authoritative body or person	*Bottom-up* Micro-level or grassroots generated policy for and by the community that it impacts
Means and goals	*Overt* Overtly expressed in written or spoken policy texts	*Covert* Intentionally concealed at the macro-level (collusive) or at the micro-level (subversive)
Documentation	*Explicit* Officially documented in written or spoken policy texts	*Implicit* Occurring without or in spite of official policy texts
In law and in practice	*De jure* Policy "in law"; officially documented in writing	*De facto* Policy "in practice"; refers to both locally produced *policies* that arise without or in spite of de jure policies and local language *practices* that differ from de jure policies; de facto practices can reflect (or not) de facto policies

be developed at the "top", by some governing body – top-down language policy – while others can be developed by and for the communities they are meant to impact – bottom-up language policy. However, language policies are developed across multiple "levels" of policy creation and even a language policy typically considered bottom-up, like a policy developed *in* a school district *for* that school district, can still be top-down for somebody (like, teachers or students); thus, the terms *top-down* and *bottom-up* are *relative*, depending on who is doing the creating and who is doing the interpreting and appropriating. As well, there is overlap within and across categories; that is, a policy can be both top-down and bottom-up: top-down and covert; bottom-up and explicit; etc.

The explicit/implicit distinction refers to the official status of a policy (official vs. unofficial) and how a policy is documented – whether formulated and detailed in some written document or not. Implicit policies can be powerful nonetheless. For example, there is no explicit language policy declaring English the official language of the United States but unofficially, or implicitly, it certainly is. Schiffman (1996) equates the explicit/implicit distinction with the overt/covert distinction, describing the unofficial use of a particular language – for example, Nagamese in Northeast India – as a covert activity since the official language is English. Shohamy (2006), on the other hand, uses the term *covert* to describe a policy with hidden agendas, which are intentionally and covertly embedded by policy creators. Schiffman (2010) includes this collusive quality within his definition of "covert" but also notes that covert policies can be subversive, for example when a group or organization actively resists an overt language policy. In this way, covert language policy can refer to either bottom-up or top-down processes and organizations. However, it does seem useful to distinguish the explicit/implicit dichotomy from the overt/covert distinction and the distinguishing characteristic proposed here is intent; that is, the notion of "covert" carries with it strong connotations of something that is intentionally concealed and, therefore, a covert policy is one which is intentionally hidden or veiled (following Shohamy), not openly shown, for either collusive or subversive reasons (following Schiffman).

The *de jure* and *de facto* descriptors are used slightly differently. Literally meaning "concerning law" and "concerning fact," respectively, the terms are typically used to connote policies that are based on laws (de jure) versus what actually happens in reality or in practice (de facto). For example, racial segregation in the U.S. in the 1960's is sometimes referred to as de facto segregation since it was *not* supported by law. Concerning language policy, in Morocco, the official languages are Arabic and Tamazight (an indigenous Berber language) but, in practice (and in education), many Moroccans use French. While the notion of de jure does seem to line up with overt and explicit language policies, all of which reference the "official-ness" of a policy, an activity that is de facto is not necessarily covert or implicit or even a "policy" in the traditional sense – it is an activity that occurs in practice despite whatever the de jure policy states. This does appear to imply that whatever happens in practice is somewhat different than what is officially stated as a de jure language policy. For example, even within schools and classrooms which are officially monolingual, teachers can include the multilingualism of their students as resources for classroom practice (Skilton-Sylvester 2003; Cincotta-Segi 2011a; 3.4 in this volume). In this case, de facto refers to both the classroom policy as created by the teacher and the classroom practices, which are closely related but (here proposed as) distinct nonetheless; thus de facto refers to locally produced *policies* that differ from what is explicitly stated (in law) and local *practices* that may be in line with local de facto policies but do not reflect what is officially documented in de jure policies.

1.3 Example language policies

Language policies, especially when they have been used as an instrument of oppression, can be a very salient feature of life but even when we are not aware of them, language policies can nonetheless have a powerful influence. For example, the structure and language of this book is influenced by a number of language policies. First, it is guided by rhetorical conventions common to many academic discourse communities and, while these conventions or policies may not always be explicit, they are strictly enforced by editors and reviewers of academic publications. As well, the language itself is a product of multiple historical language planning and policy processes that have influenced the form of the English language, a few of which are reviewed here.

1.3.1 A brief history of English language policies

The history of the English language tends to be described with three historical periods – Old English, Middle English, and Modern English – and during each period, radical changes occurred. Many of these changes can be classified using the language planning frameworks developed by scholars such as Haugen (1966, 1983), Ferguson (1968), and Kloss (1968) – and subsequently integrated into an overarching framework (see Table 5.1 on pages 122–123) by Hornberger (2006) – who use the term *corpus planning* to describe those language planning "efforts related to the adequacy of the form or structure of languages/literacies" (Hornberger 2006a: 28). Examples include the introduction of new words (*lexical modernization*), the development and change of the writing system or orthography of a language (*graphization*), and the attempted purging of lexical items and grammatical forms deemed inaccurate, inappropriate, or otherwise unwanted (*purification*).

The Norman Conquest of England in 1066 engendered dramatic changes in the English language that would eventually influence Middle and Modern English. During the Norman Conquest, Norman French was implemented as the language of the state – in parliament and the courts – and was considered the superior variety, while English was marginalized and used primarily for oral communication. Heath and Mandabach (1983) describe the relationship between English and

French during this time as competitive, because it was not clear whether the language of the people or the language of the state would triumph. English made a strong comeback in official domains in 1258 when Henry III issued a proclamation that was first composed in French and then, in order to directly address the people, was issued in Old English. This is one of the oldest written documents in English and it serves as an important language policy because it officially recognized Old English in the domain of government (Ellis 1863).

Concept 1.2 Language contact

Language contact is the term used to describe the phenomenon of languages coming into contact with one another and in the field of sociolinguistics it has traditionally been used to describe the macro-linguistic contact between large numbers of speakers – whole societies or nations. The word *contact* makes it seem harmless enough but contact has often occurred because of conquest and colonization, which leads to the spread of languages of power and the concomitant destruction of less powerful languages. Newer research considers language contact across multiple contexts including (among many others) schools (Baker 2003), religion (Spolsky 2003), business (Harris and Bargiela-Chiappini 2003), and nursing care (Candlin and Candlin 2003).

When languages come into contact they invariably have some effect on each other and contact between French and English during the Norman Conquest was no different – English was forever changed. French was the *only* language used in the legal system until 1362 and it was still used in legal proceedings until 1650 when Parliament passed an act stating that English would henceforth occupy this domain. Many of the words associated with the law are still in use today: *attorney, judge, sue,* and *court,* for example (all borrowed from Anglo-French). Of the thousands of words borrowed from French, some of the most commonly used are fairly "obviously French" like *entrée* or *quiche* but others less so, like *government, jury, religion* – and even the word used to describe the governing body of England, *parliament,* is borrowed from Anglo-French.

A few centuries later, Noah Webster made his own mark on the English language when he published *A Compendious Dictionary of the English Language,* the first attempt at a representation of English spoken in the U.S., and later *An American Dictionary of the English Language.* Any astute reader of this book will immediately notice that I use a U.S. variety of English because of the spelling of words like /dəfɛns/ as "defense" (not "defence") and /rumər/ as "rumor" and not "rumour." These spelling conventions are the direct result of Webster, who preferred such spellings.

One historical piece of corpus planning that is a popular subject in both language arts classrooms in schools and introductory linguistics courses in universities is the rule that double negatives are ungrammatical (as in "He don't have nothing"). Many (e.g. Labov 1972a) note the arbitrariness of this prescriptive grammatical rule since it is *not* considered ungrammatical to use double negatives (or negative concord in linguistics) in other languages, like French and Russian, and, in fact, double negatives are prescriptively correct in many languages (as in "Il n'a rien" in French, literally translated as "He not has nothing."). As well, they were commonly used in Old, Middle, and even Modern English, at least until the eighteenth century when the notion "two negatives make an affirmative" became an oft-repeated phrase. Robert Lowth and his popular grammar book *A Short Introduction to English Grammar,* first published in 1762 (with a second edition in 1763), are often credited as the origin of this prescriptive grammatical rule (see Case 1.1 on page 15). However, in a historical analysis of English grammar, Tieken-Boon van Ostade (2010) finds many instances of the rule being articulated, both in grammar books, and in other written works *before* Lowth's publication. She argues that Lowth was simply repeating an idea that was already a popular notion among grammarians and a hallmark of popular usage at the time and that, therefore, Lowth's rule was in fact *descriptive* and not prescriptive (in the sense that he was simply formulated popular usage at the time): "By the time he adopted [the double negative rule] in his grammar, it had apparently already developed into a fixed expression. Lowth therefore had nothing to do with the disappearance of double negation" (Tieken-Boon van Ostade, 2010: 78). Tieken-Boon van Ostade argues that Murray's very popular *English Grammar* (1795), in which Lowth's double negative rule is cited, should be given much of the credit.

So, the credibility of the assertion that Lowth created this grammatical rule, based on his own idiosyncratic tastes and ideas about English syntax, is very suspect. Nevertheless, while he may not have created the rule ex nihilo, Lowth helped popularize it and increased the likelihood that it would be a permanent fixture in the English language. The use of negative concord has become a benchmark for the "standard-ness" of English varieties, since marginalized varieties such as African American Language make frequent use of double negatives.

Case 1.1 Robert Lowth's *A Short Introduction to English Grammar*

In his popular grammar book, Lowth issued a series of proclamations about the English language which helped to instantiate new grammatical rules as permanent fixtures, including: "Two negatives in English destroy one another, or are equivalent to an affirmative" (Lowth 1762: 126). Ostensibly appealing to logic and/or mathematics, the statement is actually mathematically inaccurate since two negative integers (whether in English or any other language) are not equivalent to a positive: –1 + –1 = –2 *not* +1. In fact, historically, multiple negatives were used to increase the negative force of a sentence (the more negatives you add, the more negative it is).

Lowth even criticizes Shakespeare and Chaucer for utilizing what he calls an outdated and ungrammatical form (for example, "[G]ive me not counsel; nor let no comforter delight mine ear" from *Much Ado About Nothing*) and argues that Shakespeare's language is an example of "a relique of the ancient style, abounding with negatives, which is now grown wholly obsolete" (Lowth 1763: 139).

Lowth was inspired by what he viewed as a lack of grammatical accuracy in English and, even amongst the "politest part of our nation" and in "the writings of our most approved authors" it "often offends against every part of Grammar" (Lowth 1762: iii). Propriety is a big concern for Lowth who desired a tool, long lacking in English, for judging the grammaticality of speech: "The principal design of a grammar of any language is to teach us to express ourselves with propriety in that language; and to enable us to judge of every phrase and form of construction, whether it be right or not" (Lowth 1762: x).

The history of the English language is a history of language planning and policies, the unique amalgamation of which has created the language we use today. Yet, far from being historical relics, these language policies are ubiquitous in the modern era and continue to be appropriated and enforced by prescriptive grammarians, ESL teachers, advice columnists, call center supervisors, and word processing programs (like Microsoft Word). Writing grammar books and dictionaries is top-down language planning, in the sense that it is concocted by some (sometimes self-appointed) authority, with implementation intended for the masses. For example, the *Oxford English Dictionary* has explicitly portrayed the "standard" variety of a language as the "best" variety; this can be seen in the 1933 definition of *standard*, which describes it as the term "applied to the variety of the speech of a country which, by reason of its cultural status and currency, is held to represent the best form of that speech. Standard English: that form of the English language which is spoken (with modifications individual, or local), by the generality of the cultured people of Great Britain."

However, the impact of these top-down policies relies on the beliefs and actions of many different agents across many different LPP contexts. For example, language arts teachers who choose to enforce Lowth's rule about double negatives in their classrooms appropriate that language policy for their own purposes. As well, they may justify the policy using Lowth's logic or invoke their own, perhaps noting that the use of double negatives can hinder a job hunt or a college interview. In this way the teacher has *recontextualized* (see Concept 5.14) Lowth's language policy, a process whereby texts are interpreted and appropriated in new ways depending on the agents and setting (Wodak 2000). But the teacher's actions might be, in part, influenced by the school district curriculum, or a higher education course, or supervisors, and thus, the impact of any particular language policy – even a so-called "top-down" policy – relies on the varied interpretations and appropriations across multiple contexts and layers of language planning and policy activity.

1.3.2 Indigenous languages and policy

Planned language change was a central part of the Norman Conquest – French replaced English in many domains, including the government and the courts. However, the resulting change to the English language was not "planned" per se, even if Anglo-French was forced into certain domains. On the other hand, the language planning of colonizers has often been very intentional and colonial language policies have forever changed the linguistic ecology of the world. Consider this evidence:

- The number of languages in the world has been cut in half over the past 500 years (Nettle and Romaine 2000) and of the 6500 or so languages left in the world today, linguists estimate that at least half are at risk of extinction within the next 100 years (Romaine 2006).
- Approximately 95% of those 6500 languages are spoken by less than 5% of the world's population and most of the 5% are indigenous languages and speakers (Hornberger 2008b).

Krauss (1992) categorizes languages as *moribund* (no longer being learned by children), *endangered* (are currently being learned by children but, if the present conditions continue, this will change), and *safe* (more than 100,000 speakers). He calculates:

- Of the 6500 or so languages in the world, there are currently about 600 safe languages in the world, meaning that more than 90% of the world's languages are either endangered or moribund and Krauss predicts that these will become extinct in the next century.
- The most destructive of the "safe" languages is English as it has replaced 90% of the languages it has come into contact with in what is now called the English-speaking world.
- 90% of the 250 aboriginal languages spoken in Australia are moribund and very near extinction.

It should be noted, too, that Krauss wrote this almost two decades ago and one wonders about the state of some of the languages he then reported on, such as Iowa, Mandan, and Coeur d' Alene, each at that time with 5, 6, and 20 speakers, respectively.

While these numbers are only a snapshot, they give us a sense of the intense decline of linguistic diversity around the world, much of which was engendered by colonial language policies that eradicated or endangered the languages and cultures of Indigenous peoples. Whether it was thought that acquisition of the colonial language and concomitant eradication of the indigenous languages would inspire better citizenship, better observance of Christianity, or prevent uprisings, colonial language policies around the world were consistently restrictive (Chimbutane 2011; see discussion in this volume, section 3.2). For example, in 1887, the United States Commissioner of Indian Affairs, J.D.C. Atkins, who was a strong advocate of replacing Indigenous languages with English, released a report on how to deal with U.S. Indian languages:

Quote 1.6 J.D.C. Atkins on U.S. Indigenous languages

It is a matter not only of importance but of necessity that the Indians acquire the English language as rapidly as possible...When they take upon themselves the responsibilities and privileges of citizenship their vernacular will be of no advantage. Only through the medium of the English tongue can they acquire a knowledge of the Constitution of the country and their rights and duties thereunder... It is also believed that teaching an Indian youth in his own barbarous dialect is a positive detriment to him. The first step to be taken toward civilization, toward teaching the Indians the mischief and folly of continuing in their barbarous practices, is to teach them the English language.

(cited in Prucha 2000)

Rarely are the intentions behind a language policy so clearly evident as when they are motivated by conspicuous bigotry. As Atkins argues, eradicating American Indian languages and replacing them with English is vital for a number of reasons: (1) Only through English can one comprehend the U.S. constitution and the duties of being a U.S. citizen; (2) Concomitantly, Indigenous language use prevents an understanding of what it means to be "American"; (3) In order to stamp out "barbarous practices", and become "civilized", the barbarous languages must also be blotted out and English put in their place.

That same year, the U.S. Congress passed the *General Allotment and Compulsory Education Act*, which established boarding schools for Indigenous youth designed around forced assimilation. Not only were the students made to cut their hair, wear uniforms, and attend Christian church, but the use of Indigenous languages was strictly prohibited in these schools and infractions inspired punishment. In her ethnographic account of Indigenous schooling in Rough Rock, Arizona, McCarty (2002) reports on the experiences of Navajo youth forced to attend these boarding schools in the late nineteenth and early twentieth centuries – they were notorious for their English-only curriculum, militaristic discipline, inadequate food, and manual labor systems.

Quote 1.7 Navajo youth on Indian boarding schools

Thomas James (Fort Apache School)
It was like being in Jail. There wasn't even coffee, only water. That is all we ate. The boys I came with began to feel homesick. We were starving.

Galena Dick (Chinle Boarding School)
We were forced and pressured to learn English. We had to struggle. It was confusing and difficult....Students were punished and abused for speaking their native language...[S]chool was not a place for Navajos to be Navajos.

Fred Bia (Chinle Boarding School)
If you were talking there [in the dormitory], whispering...they would sneak up on you and go and lay a big old two-by-four...This is not a ruler, this is – you know what rebars are? – and they would lay that across your back there. And [you] just roll over and just lay there and don't make a sound, but you just hold it in there until that [pain] barely goes away.

(Quoted in McCarty 2002: 42–46)

The belief that one must speak the dominant language of the state to be a good citizen of that nation (see Concept 5.2 on pages 135–136) is certainly not unique to the colonization of North America. Following World War I, the League of Nations wrested Germany's colonial hold on Cameroon, dividing it into Cameroun (French) and Cameroons (British), and French and English were forced upon Cameroonian students. Esch's (2010) ethnographic study of modern-day interaction in Cameroonian schools includes an historical analysis of language policy, including a report to the Ministry of the Colonies:

Policy text 1.1 Report to the Ministry of the Colonies regarding languages in Cameroon

La population du Cameroun n'est pas homogène et les nombreuses tribus qui la composent se servent de dialectes fort differents. Il est donc de toute nécessité de créer entre elles *un langage commun qui ne peut être évidemment que celui du peuple à qui est dévolue la souveraineté du pays.*

The population of Cameroon is not homogeneous and the numerous tribes of which it is composed use very different dialects. It is thus necessary to create between them *a common language which obviously can only be the language of the people to whom the sovereignty of the country has been devolved.*

(quoted in Esch 2010: 241)

Colonial language policies have been destructive to the world's linguistic diversity. For example, out of the more than 300 Indigenous languages that were spoken in what is now called the United States, only 175 remain, with only 20 of those still being acquired by children as a first language (McCarty 2009). However, despite the top-down efforts to eradicate Indigenous languages in the U.S. and throughout the world, there have been important grassroots or bottom-up efforts to save and revitalize them, a process Fishman (1991) refers to as *reversing language shift* (see 2.5.1). Research that focuses on bottom-up language policy and planning efforts to promote Indigenous languages in schools and society include: Navajo (McCarty 2002), Quechua and Quichua (Hornberger 1988; King 2001), Māori (May and Hill 2005), Ñähñu (Pedraza 1997), and Sámi (Hirvonen 2008). Edited volumes that examine Indigenous language policy and education include *Indigenous Literacies in the Americas* (Hornberger 1997a) and *Can Schools Save Indigenous Languages?* (Hornberger 2008a). The Project for the Study of Alternative Education in South Africa (PRAESA) (see 6.3.1) promotes the inclusion of African languages in schools and publishes on their language planning and policy work (see http://web.uct.ac.za/depts/praesa/OCCPapers.htm).

1.3.3 Oil production and language policy in Equatorial Guinea

The "discovery" of large amounts of oil off the western coast of Africa has led U.S. and European oil companies to develop relationships with African countries and their leaders in an effort to develop oil extraction and production operations. This has meant the introduction of new languages, notably English, into linguistic ecologies and the potential for both official and unofficial language policy changes. Here, I focus on Equatorial Guinea (EG) because I lived there and taught a course at the University of Equatorial Guinea in the capital city of Malabo. The discovery of sizable oil reserves off of the coast of Equatorial Guinea in 1996 engendered relationships between the Equatoguinean government and oil companies (most prominently, Exxon Mobil) and has resulted in the country being the third largest producer of oil in Africa. This has led to a dramatic increase in government revenue, with Equatorial Guinea ranking first in Gross National Income (GNI) of all African countries in 2011. However, while the governmental leaders have enjoyed a great increase in their personal wealth, it has not impacted the economic wellbeing of EG citizens, most of whom still live under the United Nations poverty threshold.

After the Portuguese explorer Fernando Po landed on EG in 1471, he led the way for Portuguese colonization until 1778 when it was ceded to Spain. Because of pressure both within and without EG, Spain granted independence to the country in 1968 and, subsequently, helped develop a draft constitution and electoral law. Shortly after Francisco Macias Nguema was elected in October 1968, he effectively dissolved the constitution, created a single-party state, and declared himself president for life. Under his rule, education ceased, the country's infrastructure and economy crumbled, and up to one third of the inhabitants were killed or went into exile (U.S. D.O.S. 2012). The current president, Teodoro Obiang Nguema Mbasogo, has held that position since 1979 when he overthrew Nguema in a bloody *coup d'état*. While not officially declaring himself "president for life" the 1991 constitution of EG grants the president extensive powers that give Obiang a tight despotic grip on the country with which he is able to repress any political opposition. EG is often cited by various human rights organizations as committing very egregious human rights abuses, notably in the infamous Black Beach Prison where Human Rights Watch and Amnesty International have reported beatings, unexplained deaths, illegal detentions, and torture. In 2011, Freedom House ranked EG as one of the ten most repressive societies in the world based on its treatment of political rights and civil liberties, a characterization of countries in which "state control over daily life is pervasive, independent organizations and political opposition are banned or suppressed, and fear of retribution for independent thought and action is ubiquitous" (Freedom House 2011: 1). Still, EG has experienced the development of infrastructure and the opening of schools under Obiang's rule.

Since finding the oil, the relationship with the U.S. government has been less chilly than in the past and, especially, relationships with U.S. and European oil companies have strengthened dramatically. Notably, U.S. passport holders have the unique privilege of entering the country without a visa for short visits. EG leaders allow for companies like Exxon Mobil to set up large gated communities or compounds for their employees with intense security systems monitored by the EG government. Entering one of these compounds is somewhat bizarre, as a visitor has the experience of exiting the capital city of Malabo and entering a U.S. suburb, complete with Sport Utility Vehicles, paved roads and driveways, air conditioning, and English.

The two dominant African groups in EG are the Fang (who are the majority at roughly 80%) and the Bubi (who are indigenous to Bioko island, home of the capital city of Malabo). Both groups have their own languages (Fang and Bubi) and there are at least two varieties of Fang – Fang-Ntumu and Fang-Okah – which are mutually unintelligible. The Fang and Bubi languages are used extensively among friends and family members but Spanish reigns as the lingua franca in schools, businesses, governmental institutions, and for interaction between the Bubi and Fang. The appearance to any outsider is that EG is Spanish-dominant and, while French and Portuguese are the other two official languages along with

Spanish, visitors would be hard pressed to find anyone speaking these languages. However, what one does increasingly find is English.

Exxon Mobil does not have an explicit language policy regarding hiring practices, at least not one that they openly publish on their website or as responses to email queries. While you can apply for a job at Mobil Equatorial Guinea in Spanish, English is the language used in the office buildings (in EG and the U.S.) which oversee the production of the oil. Thus, there is an implicit English-only policy, with Spanish perhaps being tolerated in unofficial interaction. How this plays out in daily operations or in informal conversations is unclear (and the potential subject for a study, see Example project 7.1 onpages 219–220) but one might imagine a fair amount of Spanish (or Fang or Bubi) being used among EG workers while at work. However, formal communication in employee manuals, business meetings, and advertising material is in English.

The presence of Exxon Mobil, and the implicit English-only policy, has had an effect on the rest of the country. There are at least five primates that are endemic to the island of Bioko, all of which are endangered, which has led biologists (especially from the U.S.) to come to EG. Funded by U.S.-based grants, they have created opportunities for biology students from the U.S. to study on the island in the hopes of studying the primates and saving them from extinction. Many of the Equatoguineans I met referred to this group as "monkey counters" and wondered out loud why anyone would want to go around counting monkeys. I went to EG as a visiting instructor, with the task of teaching a course to both U.S. and African students on language diversity and language learning. The idea was that the students would come together to learn about each other's languages and, subsequently, provide tutoring lessons for one another. This did not happen. While I attempted to make the course as bilingual as possible, creating bilingual PowerPoint presentations and encouraging Spanish in group work, the class quickly became English-dominant. One reason was because the African students' English was better than the U.S. students' Spanish. However, the big motivating factor was that most of the African students in this class were seeking a career with an oil company and wanted the opportunity to learn and speak English. This affected the tutoring sessions as well, which eventually became one-way tutoring sessions, in which the U.S. students gave English lessons to the Equatoguineans (much to the chagrin of some determined Spanish learners). Thus, attempts to create parity between the languages were met with resistance because, as the African students put it, their livelihood depended on English acquisition, and all other considerations were trivial by comparison.

At the University of Equatorial Guinea, English acquisition was viewed as a necessary and valuable tool for the African students to acquire economic resources and it was largely tolerated as an unthreatening and foreign presence. Phillipson's (1992) theory of linguistic imperialism (see this volume, section 2.5.2) applies here, in which core English-speaking countries (like the U.S.) enjoy unequal distribution of economic and political power over periphery countries (like EG) due to the spread of English. One might argue that only with the assistance of oil companies like Exxon Mobil could the country extract as much oil as it does, and enjoy the profits that it does, which therefore benefits the economic opportunities of EG citizens. This is true. However, the benefits for EG citizens pale in comparison to the benefits for the EG government and while this is not necessarily the fault of the oil companies, their leaders have to implicitly accept the unequal distribution of wealth in EG when they go into business with Obiang. Also, the benefits for EG citizens are outweighed by the benefits to native English speakers, especially those with connections to the oil companies, who receive preferential treatment when being hired to run EG operations.

With Spanish having strong ethnolinguistic vitality as the major lingua franca of the country and English quickly rising in importance for those seeking employment in the largest industry in the country, one wonders about the fate of Fang and Bubi. Chimbutane (2011, and 3.2 in this volume) notes the remarkable strength of African languages in Mozambique, even after centuries of colonial rule and Portuguese dominance in most governmental and educational institutions. However, the implicit English-only language policy of Exxon Mobil has undoubtedly led to increasing English use in EG and has bled over into implicit language policy in university classrooms. Further, while working for oil companies does offer Equatoguineans the opportunity for economic prosperity, the implicit English-only policy benefits some (native English speakers, foreigners) more than others (non-native English speakers, Equatoguineans).

Finally, it is not just Exxon Mobil, nor the EG government, which promote the spread of English and allow implicit English-only policies to advantage some more than others. As teachers of English, and as English-speaking scholars, we are physical manifestations of the spread of English around the world. My presence in the country, and the course I taught, in its small way helped cement English as a permanent fixture and a language of power in EG. With this in mind, I did have the students read selections from Hall and Eggington's (2000) *The Sociopolitics of English Language Teaching,* including a piece by James Tollefson entitled "Policy and ideology in the spread of English" (Tollefson 2000); yet the concerns as expressed in the book seemed distant and far removed from the economic reality faced by the African students. The oil companies favored English and, therefore, it was a natural thing to learn English. The spread of English relies on public perceptions of English language teaching and learning as natural and ideologically neutral, which reveals the extent to which linguistic imperialism relies on the hegemonic positioning of dominant social systems as natural and legitimate (see also Pan 2011, and 3.6 in this volume).

1.4 Discussion

This chapter began with the question – What is language policy? We have seen an expanding body of work characterize "language policy" in increasingly varied ways, from official documentation of language plans, to overtly political mechanisms of power, to a multi-layered process that relies on both bottom-up and top-down forces, to sociocultural phenomena that are embedded with local ideologies and in language practices. Based on a review of these definitions and conceptualizations, a new definition was offered, which led to another question – What *isn't* language policy? While the ever-expanding conceptualizations that include increasingly varied phenomena potentially open the door to new types of LPP research, I argue that without ongoing conceptual refinement, "language policy" may become so loosely defined as to encompass almost any sociolinguistic phenomena and therefore become a very general descriptor in which all language attitudes, ideologies, and practices are categorized.

This chapter also reviewed policy types, focusing on a series of dichotomies often used in the literature but less often defined, including top-down/bottom-up, overt/covert, explicit/implicit, and de jure/de facto. Some policies are created from on high, like so-called "top-down" language policies, while others are generated at the grassroots level. No matter where they begin, there will still be interpretation and appropriation. Language policies: (1) are created, interpreted, and appropriated across multiple levels or layers; (2) can be written down in the form of a de jure policy but do not have to be, especially if they are de facto or unofficial policies; and (3) may be generated by an agent or agency who has some intention or they may be unintentional.

Finally, this chapter also gave a very brief review of a (not necessarily representative) sample of a few language planning and policy initiatives; however, even in this very brief overview, we find a wide range of activities that constitute "language policy." Language policies can be official documents that declare some intention regarding language use, like Atkins' policy on American Indigenous languages. Other official policies may not be written down but are powerful nonetheless, like French as the official language of the government in Norman-controlled England. Other language policies are unofficial but still powerful, like the implicit English-only policies of Exxon Mobil in Equatorial Guinea, which facilitate the spread of English and impact the unofficial language policies of educational institutions like the University of Equatorial Guinea. Further, we have seen that these language plans and policies are created, interpreted, appropriated, and instantiated across multiple contexts and layers of activity, a theme that is examined throughout the book.

2

Theories, concepts, and frameworks: An historical overview

Chapter outline

2.1 The origin and development of early language planning scholarship
2.2 Expanding frameworks and conceptualizations in the 1970's and 80's
2.3 Critical language policy
2.4 Ethnography of language policy
2.5 Reversing language shift and linguistic imperialism
2.6 Ecology of language
2.7 Educational language policy
2.8 Discussion

The field of language policy is not lacking in theoretical robustness – conceptual frameworks abound – but the geneses of, and connections between, all of the various theories and frameworks are not always clear. Ricento (2006b: 17) argues that this theoretical fragmentation means that there is not, as yet, "some grand theory which explains patterns of language behavior...or can predict the effects of specific language policies on language behavior," and Tollefson (2013b: 25–26) argues that the wide range of conceptual frameworks "does not constitute a theory of language policy." This chapter is intended to provide a conceptual aerial map, covering the important theoretical developments that have defined the evolution of the field. I incorporate Ricento's (2000a) review of the historical developments in the field and our reprise (Johnson and Ricento 2013) of that original article, which considers newer developments since 2000. While there is perhaps no grand theory of language planning and policy, there are traditions of research within the field which proffer important concepts, frameworks, methods, and theoretical developments, and this chapter attempts to cover some of the major contributions.

2.1 The origin and development of early language planning scholarship

The field was formed in the early 1960's by language scholars interested in solving the language problems of new, developing, and/or post-colonial nations. During this era, many linguists were recruited to help develop grammars, writing systems, and dictionaries for Indigenous languages and, out of this, an interest in how best to develop the form of a language – i.e. corpus planning – grew. Considered by many to be the father of the field, Haugen introduced the term *language planning* in 1959, defining it as "the activity of preparing a normative orthography, grammar, and dictionary for the guidance of writers and speakers in a non-homogeneous speech community" (Haugen, 1959: 8). What Haugen describes there would become known as *corpus planning,* which includes activities related to the manipulation of the *forms* of a language. While many language planners and scholars were interested in developing the form(s) of languages, others became interested in how a society could best allocate *functions* and/or *uses* for particular languages, known as *status planning,* a distinction introduced by Kloss (1969). Status planning questions include: Which language should be official? Which language should be used in schools? Which language(s) should be used in the media? Rubin (1977) offers a more contemporary definition of language planning, reflecting thinking in the field that language planning is enacted by some governing body (i.e. top-down), is intentional, and impacts the language corpus (i.e. corpus planning), use (i.e. status planning), or both.

Quote 2.1 Rubin's definition of language planning

Language planning is deliberate language change, that is, changes in the systems of a language code or speaking or both that are planned by organizations established for such purposes or given a mandate to fulfill such purposes.

(Rubin 1977: 282)

After Kloss introduced the status/corpus distinction, much of the early language planning scholarship focused on theoretical frameworks to account for corpus and status planning processes and steps. One such influential theory was presented by Haugen (1966, 1983), who delineates four steps in the language planning process:

> **Concept 2.1 Haugen's language planning steps**
>
> 1. selection of a norm (i.e. selecting a language variety for a particular context)
> 2. codification – development of an explicit, usually written, form
> 3. implementation – attempt to spread the language form
> 4. elaboration – continued updating of the language variety to "meet the needs of the modern world".
>
> (Haugen 1983: 273)

Haugen identifies *selection* and *implementation* as status planning and *codification* and *elaboration* as corpus planning. Others, for example Fishman (1979: 12), have noted the close relationship between status and corpus planning: "[S]tatus planning without concomitant corpus planning runs into a blind alley. Conversely, corpus planning without status planning is a linguistic game, a technical exercise without social consequence" (see also Jaffe 2011, Quote 2.2 below). Haugen's language planning steps were proposed as both a theoretical model of language planning and a practical roadmap for those interested in actually engaging in the planning of languages. Other models and roadmaps followed (e.g. Rubin 1971) including a revised, more detailed model offered by Haugen (1983: 275), summarized here in Table 2.1.

Table 2.1 Haugen's (1983: 275) model of language planning

Form (policy planning)	**Function (language cultivation)**	
Society (status planning)	1. Selection (decision procedures) a. identification of a problem b. allocation of norms	3. Implementation (educational spread) a. correction procedures b. evaluation
Language (corpus planning)	2. Codification (standardization procedures) a. graphization b. grammatication c. lexication	4. Elaboration (functional development) a. terminological modernization b. stylistic development

Quote 2.2 The connection between corpus and status planning

[A]ll interventions that shape the uses or social functions of a particular language have implications for language form – in terms of both the frequencies with which particular forms get used, and of the value attributed to them. And, of course, status planning constitutes an ideological framework for corpus planning.

(Jaffe 2011: 208)

Much of the early language planning scholarship purported to divorce the supposedly objective science of language planning from the ideological and sociopolitical reality of language use. For example, Tauli (1974: 51) asserts that languages can be categorized objectively according to usefulness or efficiency: "The efficiency of a language can be evaluated with objective scientific, often quantitative methods...Not all languages describe things equally effectively." Inefficient languages include "ethnic languages" that Tauli describes as primitive and not constructed "methodically according to plan." Therefore, primitive ethnic languages are good candidates for language planning and for improvement in efficiency and descriptiveness, which Tauli argues is the responsibility of language planners. Such proclamations suggest a hierarchy of languages for language planning, with ethnic and/or Indigenous languages on the bottom and more carefully planned languages, like colonial languages, on the top. Similarly, if less forcefully, Kloss argues that certain languages are more suitable for national development (Kloss 1968).

Tauli's formulations were, predictably, the subject of criticism, even amongst his contemporaries (Jernudd and Das Gupta 1971). Describing a language as primitive or unstructured is an idea that conflicts with linguistic theories and findings (see Concept 2.3) and is prejudicial towards those who speak one of the "primitive" languages in question. Tauli's assertions were, admittedly, rather extreme and not necessarily representative of the field; yet, early language planning work has been criticized for a variety of reasons – because it was exclusively focused on *deliberate* language planning done by governing polities, because the work was dominated by a structuralist or positivistic epistemology, and because the frameworks ignored the sociopolitical context in which languages are planned.

Cobarrubias (1983a), for example, acknowledges the ideological nature of language planning but resists the notion of an analysis that includes an ideological dimension: "[L]anguage-status decisions are affected by ideological considerations of powerful groups and counteracting forces. However, we should not saddle the theory with ideological considerations" (Cobarrubias 1983a: 6). Haugen disagrees, arguing that any theory of language planning must "take a stand on difficult value judgements" (Haugen 1983: 276), but wonders exactly how that would work or which values to adopt – for example, which languages to cultivate, and what types of language education to favor. In other words, language planning theories should not be sullied by value judgments or political belief and must remain 'objective'. Ricento (2000a) argues that this orientation helped facilitate the continued dominance of European colonial languages because they were the languages that were invariably more suitable for high-status domains like education and technology.

2.2 Expanding frameworks and conceptualizations in the 1970's and 80's

Ricento (2000a) divides the intellectual history of the field into three stages: (1) classic language planning theory as explained above, (2) critical language policy as explained below, and (3) an intermediary stage, lasting from the early 1970's to the late 1980's. It is difficult to neatly and/or cohesively characterize the work during this era as interests became more diffuse, extending beyond the corpus/status distinction, and many language planning scholars, including those who were active in the first era, began to question the viability of earlier models of language planning. This was a time in which positivistic linguistic paradigms and structuralist concepts were increasingly being challenged across disciplines. Critical linguists and sociolinguists questioned earlier approaches that attempted to divorce linguistic data from the sociocultural context in which it was produced and these two related, yet distinct, areas of research have helped shape the field of language policy.

2.2.1 Dell Hymes' sociolinguistics

Bringing perspectives from linguistics and anthropology, and setting some theoretical and methodological foundation for modern day qualitative sociolinguistics, Dell Hymes introduced the notion of communicative competence (1972a) and the theory/method of the ethnography of speaking (1962, 1964), both of which have become vital to the field of language planning and policy. Hymes did not write about language policy specifically, but a look at the nature of the field today reveals how integral his ideas have become. Hymes was especially critical of Chomsky's (1965) distinction between linguistic competence (i.e. the tacit linguistic knowledge of fluent speakers of a language) and performance (i.e. the imperfect manifestation of competence – production and comprehension of language). Chomsky was interested in the competence of what he called an "ideal speaker-listener, in a completely homogeneous speech community, who knows its language perfectly" (Chomsky 1965: 3). Hymes countered that no such individual exists, that speech communities are not homogenous, and that sociocultural knowledge is essential to the notion of "competence". He therefore proposed that what needs to be accounted for in any adequate theory of language users and language use is a speaker's *communicative competence*, which includes the linguistic "competence" as described by Chomsky, but also sociolinguistic knowledge to interact appropriately in particular sociocultural contexts.

Quote 2.3 Sociolinguistics

It is not necessary to think of sociolinguistics as a novel discipline. If linguistics comes to accept fully the sociocultural dimensions, social science the linguistic dimensions, of their subject matters and theoretical bases, sociolinguistics will simply identify a mode of research in adjacent sectors of each...Its goal is to explain the meaning of language in human life, and not in the abstract, not in the superficial phrases one may encounter in essays and textbooks, but in the concrete, in actual human lives.

(Hymes 1972b: 41)

Hymes' proposal represented a paradigmatic shift in what a theory of language should include and, even though it failed to change the direction linguistics was heading, it did offer an alternative route (which many followed). He further proposed that the way to go about studying this was the ethnography of speaking (1962), later re-formulated as the ethnography of communication (1964). Borrowing from the ethnographic tradition within anthropology, the ethnography of communication includes long-term participant observation within a particular (speech) community, a commitment to inductive discovery, and focuses on the patterns in communicative behavior (see Saville-Troike 1996 for a helpful review). The notion of communicative competence is foundational to the field of sociolinguistics in general, and therefore, the field of language planning and policy; however, it is also directly observable in work which, for example, focuses on language policy as a sociocultural phenomenon (McCarty 2011b) or analyses of the interaction between language planning and particular ways of speaking

(Hornberger 1988; King 2001). As well, the ethnography of speaking is a forebear of ethnographic studies of language policy, including the ethnography of language policy (Hornberger and Johnson 2011; Johnson 2009).

2.2.2 Critical (socio)linguistics

> **Concept 2.2 Structuralism and post-structuralism**
>
> *Structuralist linguistics* is defined by an interest in linguistic forms and structures but not their social meaning or force. Chomsky drew a distinction between surface structure, or the performance of individual language users, and the deep structure or the language user's competence. The mind of a language user transforms deep structure elements into surface structures (i.e. speech) and thus the origin of language is the mind. One important implication of this work is that, because all humans share the same human brain, all share the same basic deep structure and, thus, all have the same capacity for language – there are no primitive, unstructured, rule-less, or deficient languages. This finding is essential for many movements important to the field of sociolinguistics including the struggle for linguistic human rights.
>
> *Post-structuralism* was an intellectual movement formed outside of linguistics but it has had a strong impact on critical linguistics, critical sociolinguistcs, and critical discourse analysis. Post-structuralist scholarship on language tends to focus on the relationship between language and power – how social structure and discourses form and inform individual behavior, including language use – and, importantly for language policy research, rejects the search for a uniform knowable authorial intention in texts (see Barthes, Quote 4.6).

Hymes was responding to the *structuralism* that had become dominant in linguistic inquiry, which placed emphasis on the structures or forms within a language and the relationship between those structures but not the social function or meaning of those structures. Kress (2001) categorizes language research that makes connections between structure and context, between language use and the sociocultural environment, into three approaches:

1. The *correlational* approach seeks to find correlations between linguistic features and sociocultural variables (such as social class). For example, in his classic study of New York City English, Labov

(1972a) showed a correlation between post-vocalic r-lessness and social class.

2. A focus on *choice* is exemplified in the work of Michael Halliday and his systemic functional linguistics (1978). For Halliday, the choices that speakers make are conditioned by their assessment of the socio-cultural environment.
3. A focus on *critique* is exemplified in critical linguistics, which views language as a way to understand and critique the social and the focus is on the relationship between language and power; or, how power motivates, and is embedded in, language use.

Inspired both by Halliday's focus on choice and neo-Marxist (e.g. Althusser 1971) theories of power, *critical linguistics* was born and Fowler *et al.* (1979) (a group which includes Kress) are typically given credit for its founding.

Quote 2.4 Critical linguistics

All linguistic (inter)action is shaped by power differences of varying kinds, and no part of linguistic action escapes its effects...Language is a means to instantiate, to realize and to give shape to (aspects of) the social...In critical linguistics the social is prior; it is a field of power; and power (and power differences) is the generative principle producing linguistic form and difference. Individuals are located in these fields of power, but the powerful carry the day, and the forms which they produce are the forms which shape the system.

(Kress 2001: 35–36)

2.2.3 Expanding frameworks in language planning and policy

The critical movement in linguistics and sociolingustics eventually influenced the field of language planning and would be explicitly incorporated into critical language policy in the 1990's, but before that there were at least three important developments: (1) the focus shifted away from "language planning" being understood solely as something imposed by governing bodies to a broader focus on activity in multiple contexts and layers of language planning and policy; (2) an increasing interest in language planning for schools, including the introduction of *acquisition planning* by Cooper (1989) to the original status/corpus distinction; and (3) increased interest in the sociopolitical and ideological nature of language planning and policy.

Kloss's book *The American Bilingual Tradition* (1977/1998), first published in 1977, is an ambitious analysis of how the U.S. has dealt with multilingualism throughout its history. Through historical-textual analysis (see 5.2 below) of a large swath of government publications, laws, legal proceedings, newspaper articles, and various historical texts, Kloss concludes that the predominant orientation toward minority language rights throughout U.S. history has been one of tolerance. Examples include the toleration of non-English languages in families, on public street signs, in churches, on radio programs, in newspapers, and in private schools. Such tolerance, Kloss argues, is built into the U.S. constitution (the first amendment, for example) and is an essential thread in the fabric of U.S. history. As he puts it, "Tolerance-oriented minority rights have been handled very generously in the United States" (Kloss 1998: 51).

Quote 2.5 Tolerance-oriented minority rights

Tolerance-oriented minority rights are the sum of those legal norms, customary laws, and measures with which the state and the public institutions dependent upon it (especially the public schools) provide for the minorities and which, if need be, protect for the minorities the right to cultivate their language in a private sphere, namely, in the family and private organizations.

(Kloss 1998: 20)

Kloss contrasts *tolerance-oriented* minority rights with *promotion-oriented* (or promotive) minority rights which "regulate how public institutions may use and cultivate the languages and cultures of the minorities...[and] promises them the recognition and use of their languages by the organs of the state" (Kloss 1998: 21). Though less common throughout U.S. history, promotion-oriented policies include government-sponsored promotion of German in Pennsylvania education, federal publications (pamphlets, posters etc.) in non-English languages, bilingual instruction in public schools, and French and German translations of Continental Congress publications in the eighteenth century (which he interprets as an official recognition of the German language by the Continental Congress).

Kloss's conclusions are appealing – indeed, one wants to believe in the power of an "American bilingual tradition" – but he tends to underestimate the impact of societal discrimination toward non-European minorities, his focus primarily being on European immigrants and languages. It should be noted that Kloss was German and perhaps his psychological and physical distance from the American experience engendered some obviously false assessments such as: "Members of national minorities are seldom directly discriminated against because of such membership" (1998: 52). However, apart from its fastidious attention to historical detail and the useful framework for policy orientations, the sheer number of official and unofficial language policies covered in the book makes it a valuable resource.

Conscious of and critical of (see Macías and Wiley 1998) these limitations, Wiley (2002) synthesizes and expands upon Kloss's original framework and introduces new categories (Table 2.2). *Expediency-oriented policies* ("policies" replace "rights" in Wiley 2002) – a sub-category of promotive policies in Kloss's framework but a separate category in Wiley (2002) – are designed to meet the needs of the government, not the minority languages, and include short-term measures that do not actively promote the maintenance and/or development of minority languages. The example par excellence is transitional bilingual education instruction, which uses students' mother tongues as a bridge to transition them into instruction in the dominant language. *Repression-oriented policies*, for which Kloss found no evidence, are designed to eradicate minority languages. Wiley classifies the curtailment of American Indian languages in federal boarding schools as *restriction-oriented policies* – which place "legal prohibitions or curtailments on the use of minority

Table 2.2 Kloss's and Wiley's policy orientations framework (adapted from Wiley 2002: 48–49)

Policy orientations	**Policy characteristics**
Promotion-oriented	The government/state/agency allocates resources to support the official use of minority languages
Expediency-oriented	A weaker version of promotion laws not intended to expand the use of minority language, but typically used for only short-term allocations
Tolerance-oriented	Characterized by the noticeable absence of state intervention in the linguistic life of the language minority community
Restrictive-oriented	Legal prohibitions or curtailments on the use of minority languages
Null policies	The significant absence of policy recognizing minority languages or language varieties
Repression-oriented	Active efforts to eradicate minority languages

languages" (Wiley 2002: 48). The distinction between restriction and repression seems to rest on whether the policy represents an active attempt to eradicate a language in toto (repression) or an attempt to quell use of the language (restriction) in official institutions and contexts. However, one might reasonably characterize the systematic decimation of Indigenous and minority languages throughout the world as relying on repression *and* restriction. Finally, Wiley (2002) includes *null policies* as a category meant to capture the absence of official policy on minority language.

Another useful proposal for classifying the orientations of language policies came from Ruiz (1984) in his influential article entitled "Orientations in language planning" in which he proposes a tripartite set of goals, or "orientations" as he calls them, of language planning *in education* (specifically). He argues that policies can take a language-as-problem, language-as-right, or language-as-resource orientation toward minority languages.

Concept 2.3 Ruiz' orientations in language planning

- A *language as problem* orientation, which treats minority languages as problematic roadblocks for majority language acquisition, is characterized by transitional policies, the goals of which are linguistic and cultural assimilation, such as early-exit transitional bilingual education.
- A *language-as-right* orientation is reflected in efforts to grant linguistic human rights around the world and may be characterized by one-way developmental bilingual education, in which minority language students learn the dominant language while maintaining their mother tongue.
- A *language-as-resource* orientation envisions linguistic diversity and multilingual education as resources for native and non-native speakers and therefore two-way additive (sometimes called two-way immersion or dual language) bilingual education, in which both native and non-native English speakers learn in both languages, epitomizes this orientation.

(Ruiz 1984)

While it could be argued that critical language policy was first formulated in Tollefson's (1991) book *Planning Language, Planning Inequality*, some of the ideas inherent in the critical approach were evident in

Ruiz' 1984 article. For example, striking a decidedly post-structuralist tone, Ruiz (1984: 2) argues that "Orientations are basic to language planning in that they delimit the ways we talk about language and language issues...they help to delimit the range of acceptable attitudes toward language, and to make certain attitudes legitimate. In short, orientations determine what is thinkable about language in society." The connection Ruiz draws between discourse and power, between language and social control, is central to critical theory (e.g. Foucault 1978) and critical discourse analysis (e.g. Fairclough 1989, 2010), and the idea that the discourse of language policies can hegemonically normalize particular ways of thinking, being, and/or educating, while concomitantly delimiting others, would become a feature of critical language policy and continues to be an important consideration within the field.

Scholars like Kloss and Ruiz developed frameworks to describe the goals and/or ideological orientations to language planning, a clear move towards a critical approach since there was the assumption that language policies *had* ideological orientations. As the title to his 1989 book *Language Planning and Social Change* suggests, Cooper, as well, was acutely interested in the sociopolitical aspect of language planning – "Language planning, concerned with the management of change, is itself an instance of social change" (Cooper 1989: 164) – and his book has proven to be an indelible part of the field. Cooper conceptualizes language planning differently from his predecessors, as activities that move upwards as well as downwards (Quote 2.6).

Quote 2.6 The scope of language planning

Microlevel, face-to-face interactional circles can both implement decisions initiated from above and initiate language planning which snowballs to the societal or governmental level. In short, I believe it an error to define language planning in terms of macrosociological activities alone.

(Cooper 1989: 38)

Cooper cites the feminist language campaign to promote more gender-neutral language as an example of micro-level language planning that snowballed to the societal level. Cooper also added *acquisition planning* to the status and corpus planning distinction, by which he meant to capture language teaching and other educational activities designed to increase the users or uses of a language. The eventual acceptance of acquisition planning as an important addition to the already established status/corpus distinction gave *educational* language policy (see Concept 2.8) an official status so to speak and, since then, it has become an integral part of the field.

Table 2.3 (Johnson 2004) attempts to integrate Ruiz', Kloss's, and Wiley's frameworks by aligning the language policy orientations with educational program types and portrays only additive bilingual education programs (those with bilingualism and biliteracy as the goal) as having a "language as right" or "language as resource" orientation. Transitional bilingual education, English as a second language (ESL) programs, as well as no program at all, take a "language as problem" orientation. Both two-way (in which minority language speakers are paired with majority language speakers) and one-way (which target minority language speakers only) additive bilingual programs are *promotion-oriented* because they involve the federal government allocating funds for minority language development. Transitional bilingual education lines up with an *expediency orientation* because such programs make short-term use of minority languages in order to transition students into all-English instruction; development and maintenance of the minority languages is not the goal. Any ESL program, whether pull-out or sheltered immersion or some other programs, are classified as *restrictive* because they do not allow for the development of minority languages. However, it should be noted that, even within an ESL program, a teacher may still incorporate the students' first languages as resources (for example, see Skilton-Sylvester 2003), ameliorating the restrictive nature of the policy orientation and perhaps better aligning it with an expediency orientation. When there are no extra-linguistic services offered in a student's education (i.e. submersion), there are no policies recognizing minority

Table 2.3 Language policy orientations in educational language policy

Policy orientation (Kloss 1977/Wiley 2002)	**Program type**	**Orientation toward minority languages (Ruiz 1984)**
Promotion	Two-way additive	resource/right
	One-way additive	right
Expediency	Transitional bilingual	problem
Restrictive	Sheltered immersion/ESL	problem
Null	Submersion (no ESL)	problem
Repression	BIA boarding schools	problem
Tolerance	depends upon local language planning and policy	

languages and this lines up with a *null orientation*. Examples such as U.S. boarding schools for Native Americans and Cameroonian schools which disallowed use of African languages are good examples of programs exhibiting a *repression orientation* because these programs actively sought to eradicate minority language use. Finally, *tolerance-oriented* policies, defined as a lack of actual policy, neither create nor close space for multilingual education and private citizens are left to their own devices. Therefore, if a community drives the formation of a bilingual program or school, a tolerance orientation may lead to local languages being used as a resource or considered a right; however, if a community seeks to eradicate the minority languages from their children's schooling, their efforts will be oriented towards language as a problem.

2.3 Critical language policy (CLP)

Critical language policy (CLP) emerged as a response to earlier language planning work and as a byproduct of the increasingly critical bent within linguistics, applied linguistics, and sociolinguistics. In this book, the terms "classic" and "early" are used to describe the original language planning scholarship but others use more evaluative terms like "technocratic"(e.g. Wiley 1999: 18) or "positivist" (e.g. Ricento 2000a: 208), which implicitly critique the assumption that one can divorce the "science" of language planning from its inherent sociopolitical and ideological implications. Tollefson (1991) distinguishes between what he calls the *neo-classical approach* – which he characterizes as claiming to be scientifically neutral and dominated by an interest in the individual – and the *historical-structural approach*, which instead focuses on the social and historical influences that give rise to language policies. Language policy is expressly political and ideological in Tollefson's (1991) conceptualization, with the underlying assumption that a language policy or plan serves the interests of dominant groups.

Quote 2.7 The historical-structural approach

[L]anguage policy is viewed as one mechanism by which the interests of dominant sociopolitical groups are maintained and the seeds of transformation are developed ...The historical-structural model presumes that plans that are successfully implemented will serve dominant class interests.

(Tollefson 1991: 32, 35)

Tollefson's (1991) historical-structural approach has since become an integral line of research, which he has further developed as critical language policy (CLP) (Concept 2.4). There is a critical element in much of the modern-day language policy scholarship, whether it is called "critical language policy" or not, and certainly the notion that language policies create social inequality among dominant and minority language users (#1 in Tollefson's definition) is a central tenet in a lot of work (e.g. Phillipson 2003; Shohamy 2006). The second part of Tollefson's definition – research that seeks to develop, or at least document, more democratic policies for minority and Indigenous languages – is evident in scholarship that examines Indigenous and minority language maintenance and education (e.g. May and Hill 2005 on Māori in New Zealand, see 6.3.3 in this volume; Hornberger 1987 and 1988 on Quechua in South America; Martin-Jones and colleagues on Welsh in Wales, see 3.1 in this volume; McCarty 2002 on Navajo in the U.S.; see also Hornberger's 1997b and 1998 reviews of many cases throughout the world).

Concept 2.4 Critical language policy (CLP)

Critical language policy (CLP):

1. eschews apolitical LPP approaches and instead "acknowledge[s] that policies often create and sustain various forms of social inequality, and that policy-makers usually promote the interests of dominant social groups";
2. seeks to develop more democratic policies that reduce inequality and promote the maintenance of minority languages; and
3. is influenced by critical theory.

(summarized from Tollefson 2006: 42)

The third part of Tollefson's definition – the influence of critical theory – is evident in research that relies on, for example, Bourdieu's (1991) theory of linguistic and cultural capital (see Pan, discussed in 3.6), Gramsci's (1992/2007) conceptualization of cultural hegemony (see Hult, discussed in 3.5), Foucault's notion of governmentality (1991, see Concept 2.5), and especially the Foucauldian (1978, 1979) sense of *discourse*. For example, Pennycook (2002, 2006) incorporates Foucault's (1991) notion of governmentality to examine how the production of language policy power is not solely in the hands of the state but, locally, within micro-level practices and discourse which operate in relation to some authoritative criteria. Pennycook's (2002, 2006) application of governmentality to LPP work proffers a technique for operationalizing the first aspect of CLP in Tollefson's framework, suggesting a method for uncovering how policies create inequality that takes the focus off of "the state as an intentional actor that seeks to impose its will on the people, and instead draws our attention to much more localized and often contradictory operations of power" (Pennycook 2006: 65). The locus of power is not just contained in the policy text alone, nor is it perpetrated solely by the will of the state, but is enacted (or, perhaps performed) in micro-level practices and discourses.

Concept 2.5 Governmentality

The notion of *governmentality* was developed by Foucault in a series of lectures in 1978 and 1979; one of these from 1978 (entitled "Governmentality") has been published and reproduced (Foucault 1991). Foucault defines 'government' not as a sovereign and singular power, but as an ensemble of multiple, interconnected practices, including government of oneself, government within social institutions and communities, as well as government of the state. Thus governmentality takes the focus off of a singular *state*-driven hegemony: "The state...does not have this unity [as portrayed by others], this individuality, this rigorous functionality, nor to speak frankly, this importance" (p. 103). Instead, the focus is on how power circulates across various contexts, within micro-level practices and discourses. Nevertheless, when a state is run well or efficiently, individuals will, in turn, "behave as they should" (p. 92), i.e., in line with the state, and, therefore, a certain amount of self-governing is relied upon. In this way, governmentality refers not merely to the governing of a state apparatus, but to the governing of individuals: "Government... [designates] the way in which the conduct of individuals or of groups might be directed: the government of children, of souls, of communities, of families, of the sick...To govern, in this sense, is to structure the possible field of action of others."

(Foucault 1982: 790)

Responding to, and taking up, Pennycook's (2002) work, I utilize this approach (Johnson, 2012) in a study of language policy power in a large U.S. school district, which looks at who is positioned as having language policy decision-making power within a school district. I argue that particular individuals are positioned as being powerful language policy arbiters (Concept 4.1), while others are positioned as mere implementers. These roles emerge across a series of speech events, which establish participation frameworks (Goffman 1979; see Concept 6.2) that privilege certain individuals while marginalizing others. I further argue that while some educators do "behave as they should" and practice a form of self-governance, others resist dominant and marginalizing discourses.

While CLP, as defined by Tollefson (2006), promotes democratic policies that champion the rights of linguistic minorities, Pennycook (2006) questions the viability of this and instead champions a post-modern approach, the goal of which is the disinvention of the categories that sculpt the discussions of language rights and language maintenance. He makes the point that arguments that favor minority language rights and mother-tongue education still remain caught within the same paradigm: "Although such arguments may be preferable to blinkered views that take monolingualism as the norm, they nevertheless remain caught within the same paradigm: They operate with a strategy of pluralization rather than a questioning of the inventions at the core of the whole discussion" (Pennycook 2006: 70).

CLP scholarship has helped illuminate ideologies enmeshed in language policies and presents a rich picture of language policy development as one aspect among many sociopolitical processes that may perpetuate social inequality, but, like the critical theories underpinning it, it has also been criticized for being too deterministic and underestimating the power of human agency (Ricento and Hornberger 1996; see also discussion in Tollefson 2013b) and not capturing the processes of language planning (see Davis 1999). Pennycook takes state-driven intentionality out and places the locus of governance within micro-level operations like, say, classroom language use, which are themselves exercises in conformity to imposed norms. Pennycook's move to the micro-level does not insert agency into language policy processes as much as it positions discourse (and therefore discoursers) as perpetuating their own subjugation since they stay trapped in positivistic worldviews. Even though Pennycook places the locus of power in the hands of local actors, they are still acting out larger power relationships over which they have little control. Further, while it may be that a disinvention of the categories – i.e. a disruption of the discourse – that construct the debate surrounding language rights and language maintenance may indeed be necessary to truly enact the necessary sea change, there is a danger in making the debate more arcane because it restricts the number of qualified participants and marginalizes everyone who hasn't been socialized into a post-modernist discourse. This does not aid the social justice agenda to which many language policy scholars are committed, which is by nature more open and egalitarian.

As well, I would argue that critical scholarship needs to take into consideration the power of its own discourse. While illuminating relations and mechanisms of power is an important task, by focusing exclusively on the subjugating power of policy, and obfuscating the agency of language policy actors, there is a danger in perpetuating a view of policy as necessarily monolithic, intentional, and fascistic – this helps reify critical conceptualizations as disempowering realities. However, it really is a question of *focus*. Tollefson (2002b) recognizes that linguistic minorities resist dominant language policies and develop alternative ideologies and, indeed, the second part of CLP's focus is the development of more democratic policies. Furthermore, critical approaches are very much compatible with other approaches that *do* focus on grassroots movements and language policy agency – like the ethnography of language policy – because both are committed to an agenda of social justice that resists dominant policy discourses that subjugate minority languages and their users. When combined, they offer an important balance between structure and agency – between a critical focus on the power of language policies and an ethnographic understanding of the agency of language policy actors, which is a balance that is very much needed in the field (see also discussion in Tollefson 2013b).

2.4 Ethnography of language policy

Ethnographic research on language planning can be traced at least as far back as the 1980's to, for example, Hornberger's (1988) ethnographic study of Quechua and bilingual education in Peru. However, the roots of the ethnography of language policy depend on how one defines "language policy." If a broad definition is accepted, with a variety of social processes, language beliefs, ideologies, and practices being "language policy", then the origins should perhaps be traced back to Hymes' work on the ethnography of speaking (1962). However, I have argued (Johnson 2009) that while there is a strong tradition of sociolinguistics research that employs ethnography to develop an insider's perspective of sociocultural and linguistic processes within communities and schools – research that has been foundational for the field of LPP – there is a difference between research on multilingualism, multilingual education, and interactional norms that proffers language policy *implications* and research that focuses squarely on language policy processes, emerges from the LPP literature, asks language policy research questions, incorporates policy text and discourse as units of analysis, and presents findings about language policy, specifically.

It is this line of research that Hornberger and Johnson (2007) had in mind when they introduced the "ethnography of language policy" as a method and theory for examining the agents, contexts, and processes across the multiple layers of language policy creation, interpretation, and appropriation. Responding to the tension between critical theoretical work that focuses on the power of language policies to disenfranchise linguistic minorities, and ethnographic and classroom-based research that emphasizes the powerful role that practitioners play in language policy processes, Hornberger and Johnson (2011) argue that the ethnography of language policy offers a way to resolve this tension by marrying a critical focus on the power of marginalizing policy (discourses) with a focus on agency, and by recognizing the power of both societal *and* local policy texts, discourses, and discoursers.

Concept 2.6 Ethnography of language policy

Ethnography of language policy can:

1. illuminate and inform various *types* of language planning – status, corpus, and acquisition – and language policy – official and unofficial, de jure and de facto, macro and micro, corpus/status/acquisition planning, national and local language policy;
2. illuminate and inform language policy *processes* – creation, interpretation, and appropriation;
3. marry a critical approach with a focus on agency, recognizing the power of both *societal* and *local* policy texts, discourses, and discoursers;
4. illuminate the links across the multiple LPP layers, from the macro to the micro, from policy to practice; and
5. open up ideological spaces that allow for egalitarian dialogue and discourses that promote social justice and sound educational practice.

(summarized from Hornberger and Johnson 2007, 2011)

There are many ethnographic studies that illuminate language policy processes. In his review, Canagarajah (2006) includes Davis's (1994) study of multilingual education in Luxembourg, his own work on classroom-level resistance to official LPP (Canagarajah 1995), Freeman's study of dual language planning at Oyster bilingual school (Freeman 1998), Jaffe's (1999) work on Corsican language policy in France, Heller's (1999) sociolinguistic ethnography of multilingualism, identity, and language politics in a multilingual school in Canada and, the earliest study he cites, Hornberger's ethnography of communication, bilingual education, and language planning in Peru (1988). To this list, I would add (see Table 2.4) Bekerman's (2005) study of a Hebrew-Arabic dual language school, McCarty's (2002) work on Navajo language maintenance and education, Ramanathan's (2005) research on English-Gujarati language policies and practices in three higher education institutions in the city of Ahmedabad, May and Hill's ethnographic work on Māori in New Zealand (Hill and May 2013), Blommaert's (2005a) account of Swahili language policy and education in Tanzania, Wedin's (2005) ethnography of multilingual education in Tanzania, Cowie's (2007) study of an accent training center in India, Hult's (2007) research on Swedish language policy, and the ethnographic studies that emerged after the anti-bilingual education initiative (Proposition 227) was passed in California, U.S. (Baltodano 2004; Stritikus 2002; Wiese 2001). As well, notable books and edited volumes have been published on reclaiming the local in language policy (Canagarajah 2005), imagining multilingual schools (García, Skutknabb-Kangas, and Torres-Guzmán 2006), schools saving Indigenous languages (Hornberger 2008a), ethnography and language policy (McCarty 2011a), and methodological and theoretical considerations in ethnography of language policy (Johnson 2013b).

Ethnographic work which is reviewed in further detail in Chapter 3 includes Martin-Jones and her colleagues' (Martin-Jones 2009; Martin-Jones, Hughes, and Williams 2009; Martin-Jones 2011) study of Welsh language policy and education (see discussion in 3.1), Cincotta-Segi's (forthcoming, 2009, 2011a, 2011b, 2011c) study of language policy and education in the Lao PDR (see 3.4), and Chimbutane's (2011) ethnography of bilingual education and language policy in Mozambique (see 3.2).

The empirical findings from ethnographies of language policy have proved an essential part of our understanding of policy processes all over the world (discussed in detail in Chapter 4), but it also has provided a theoretical and conceptual orientation that combines the macro and the micro, provides a balance between policy power and interpretative agency, and is committed to issues of social justice, particularly pertaining to the rights of Indigenous and minority language speakers. Indeed, the ethnography of language policy can both provide thick descriptions of, and *contribute to,* policy processes to validate and promote language diversity as a resource in schools and society (see Chapter 6

Table 2.4 Ethnographies of language policy

Author	Year	Context	Focus
N.H. Hornberger	1988	Peru	Spanish-Quechua bilingual education, community norms of interaction
K.A. Davis	1994	Luxembourg	Multilingual education
R. Freeman	1998	U.S.	Bilingual education and social change
A. Jaffe	1999	France	Corsica, education, ideology
M. Heller	1999	Canada	Multilingual education
A. M. Wiese	2001	U.S.	Proposition 227 and bilingual education in California
K.A. King	2001	Ecuador	Language revitalization, Quichua, educational language policy
T. Stritikus	2002	U.S.	Proposition 227 and bilingual education in California
T. L. McCarty	2002	U.S.	Navajo language policy and education
M. Baltodano	2004	U.S.	Proposition 227 and bilingual education in California
Z. Bekerman	2005	Israel	Arabic-Hebrew bilingual education
J. Blommaert	2005	Tanzania	Swahili, community norms
V. Ramanathan	2005	India	English and Gujarati language policy in higher education
A.Wedin	2005	Tanzania	Ideology, educational language policy, Swahili, English, and Rumyambo
C. Cowie	2007	India	Accent training center
D. C. Johnson	2007	U.S.	Educational language policy and practice in a U.S. school district
F. M. Hult	2007	Sweden	Educational language policy with a focus on English
M. Martin-Jones *et al.*	2009 (etc.)	Wales	Welsh educational language policy
A. Cincotta-Segi	2010	Lao PDR	Educational language policy and practice
F. Chimbutane	2011	Mozambique	Multilingual education, colonial language policy
K. Mortimer	2013	Paraguay	Educational language policy and practice
L. Valdiviezo	2013	Peruvian Andes	Bilingual intercultural education policy

on language policy engagement). Yet, ethnographers of language policy still need to interrogate their own agency in the contexts in which they study. Rampton questions whether a foreigner researching some previously unknown cultural group can ever really develop much more than "a description of conventional systems" (Rampton 2007: 591) and suggests that ethnographers should do research in institutions of which they are already a member (from the inside-out instead of the outside-in). This is one of the virtues of Chimbutane's work because, as a former teacher in the studied schools, he already has an insider's understanding and develops much more than merely a "description of conventional systems". While problems arise from being a foreigner or attempting to distance oneself from the context and participants from which the researcher is collecting data (perhaps as an attempt at objectivity), there is also a danger in being so close and "inside" that critical analyses become difficult and problematic and, therefore, findings may be influenced by unquestioned valorization. These are challenges for ethnographies of language policy going forward (see the extended discussion in 6.4).

2.5 Reversing language shift and linguistic imperialism

The promotion of Indigenous languages and concomitant resistance to the hegemony of colonial languages throughout the world has been a central movement in the field. Despite the proposed ideological neutrality of earlier language planning frameworks and linguistic concepts that supported them (*native speaker, linguistic competence,* and *diglossia* for example), the outcome of language contact between languages is never neutral or fair. This unjust outcome has motivated many scholars to resist what Skutnabb-Kangas refers to as linguistic genocide (Quote 2.9), and promote linguistic human rights.

2.5.1 Reversing language shift

For those interested in preserving linguistic diversity, the world's statistics on minority and Indigenous languages (see 1.3.2) are devastating. Yet, many have devoted entire careers and lives to Indigenous and minority language maintenance, development, and education and to what Fishman (1991) calls *reversing language shift*. This body of work is too large to review in any substantive way but a few findings are worth noting here (which are detailed further in Chapter 4). Much of this work has focused on the role that education plays in Indigenous and minority language maintenance since movements to preserve such languages often begin with community educational initiatives. Examples include the Māori-medium education movement, which has been well documented and is often cited as a success story in language revitalization (May and Hill 2005). Begun in 1982, this movement was begun by Māori community members interested in preserving the language but it has led to official recognition in New Zealand language education policy as well as the Māori Language Act of 1987 which declared Māori to be one of three official languages in New Zealand, along with English and New Zealand sign language.

Quote 2.8 Reversing language shift (RLS)

RLS constitutes that corner of the total field of status planning that is devoted to improving the sociolinguistic circumstances of languages that suffer from a negative balance of users and uses....The study of RLS represents an attempt to redress the perspectival balance and to direct attention to the fact that not only are millions upon millions of speakers of small languages on all continents convinced of the creative and continuative contributions of their languages...to their personal and collective lives, but that millions are also engaged in individual and collective efforts to assist their threatened mother tongues to reverse the language shift processes that threaten or that have engulfed them.

(Fishman 1993: 69–70)

In South America the maintenance of Indigenous languages has also been well documented (Hornberger 1988, 1997b; King 2001; López 2008). Like the New Zealand experience, efforts to preserve the descendants of Mayan and Incan languages (Quechua, Aymara, Mam, among others) have often been engendered by grassroots movements but have also received state-sponsored support in the form of widespread educational reforms. For example, the 1975 recognition of Quechua as an official language in Peru created a political opening for the Puno bilingual education project (Proyecto Experimental de Educación Bilingue-Puno/PEEB), which engendered bilingual schools in Quechua and Spanish. PEEB served as a model for other bilingual education initiatives throughout Latin America, including Bolivia's National Education Reform of 1994 which opened spaces for Indigenous language instruction in Bolivian schools. López (2008: 45) argues that "The fact that bilingual education has become part of government strategic plans and programs is without a doubt a noteworthy improvement for Latin American educational policy, which had always been based on the ethnocidal illusion of linguistic-cultural homogeneity."

An important finding from this work is that education, and especially multilingual education that promotes and develops Indigenous and minority languages is necessary but not sufficient for preserving those languages. Schools, and the surrounding community, are often the genesis of grassroots movements that help to promote language revitalization, maintenance, and development, and their efforts are absolutely essential. However, these efforts in and of themselves are not enough: "Indigenous language revitalization is subject to the vagaries of policy, politics, and power; and it is subject to the economics of the linguistic marketplace" (Hornberger 2008b: 1). Despite grassroots efforts, it is often the community members themselves who resist Indigenous language education, a finding that has been documented across contexts.

2.5.2 Linguistic imperialism

Quote 2.9 Linguistic genocide

One of the main agents in killing languages is thus the linguistic genocide which happens in formal education every time indigenous or minority children...are educated in a dominant language.

(Skutnabb-Kangas 2000a: 25)

A corollary to Indigenous language revitalization is the effort to fight the encroachment and subsequent dominance of colonial languages. Phillipson's (1992) theory of linguistic imperialism describes the process whereby the spread of colonial languages (especially English) results in linguistic hierarchization and he challenges the use of traditional terms such as "language spread" and "language death" because they obfuscate the agency involved in the subjugation of minority and Indigenous languages. One of the institutions most responsible for the subjugation of minority and Indigenous languages is school. Skutnabb-Kangas (2000a) refers to minority and Indigenous language education as a linguistic human right and describes educational programs that do not incorporate the students' home languages as engaging in linguistic genocide. The culprits, as Shohamy (2006) sees it, are teachers and principals, who internalize and implement policy ideology.

Concept 2.7 Linguicism

Linguicism, a term coined by Skutnabb-Kangas (1988), is defined as "ideologies, structures and practices which are used to legitimate, effectuate and reproduce an unequal division of power and resources (material and immaterial) between groups which are defined on the basis of language."

(Phillipson and Skutnabb-Kangas 1996: 437)

The theory of linguistic imperialism has been criticized (e.g. Davies 1996) for being too rigid in that it overgeneralizes and does not consider divergent cases that do not fit the aims of the argument, for proffering a paucity of data to support the conclusions, for delimiting human agency (especially Third World human agency), and overemphasizing the power of language: "Language is indicative, it is not causal of social divisiveness" (Davies 1996: 495). I would further argue that the term "genocide" means something very specific – the deliberate and intentional destruction of a race or culture – and what is described in Skutnabb-Kangas's definition of *linguistic genocide* opens the door to many other phenomena and processes being considered "genocide". While I am not eager to guard the discursive boundaries of the discussion, or promote prescriptivist notions of language, this is one case in which a stable definition for a term is preferable because of the historical implications and out of respect for survivors (and non-survivors) of actual genocide. However, work on linguistic imperialism has made an important contribution to how we understand the impact of colonial language spread and the hegemonic influence of language policies that promote dominant languages and marginalize Indigenous and minority languages. Concomitantly, research on Indigenous language policy and educational practice has revealed both the impact of colonial language spread and the ways in which minority and Indigenous languages can be revitalized and maintained.

Furthermore, blaming schools makes sense because they have historically been powerful institutions in which minority and Indigenous languages have been marginalized, subjugated, and eradicated. However, focusing solely on the hegemony of educational language policy obfuscates the powerful role that language policy agents (e.g. teachers) play in creative interpretation and appropriation of top-down policy and engagement with local policy processes, both of which can incorporate students' mother tongues as resources into classroom practices. I would further argue that if we are really to challenge linguistic imperialism and champion linguistic diversity in schools and society, a shift in discourse is required, both in our schools and nations and *in our universities*. That is, by focusing exclusively in our scholarship on top-down language policy as intentional, nefarious, and unjust, we help reify hegemonic policy discourses as educational realities. Instead, a critical perspective must be balanced with local understandings of how educators and community members create (local) and interpret and appropriate (macro) language policy that empowers minority languages and their users. By illuminating "success stories" other scholars and educators, working in teams, can be inspired to engage in advocacy and language policy action research (see Chapter 6).

2.6 Ecology of language

The ecology of language is a conceptualization of multilingualism, first proposed by Haugen (1972) as a means to investigate the interactions between languages and their environments. As applied to the study of language planning and policy, it serves as a guiding metaphor or heuristic that emphasizes the multiple languages and multilingualism that exist in any given language ecosystem and, therefore, the value of every language in that ecosystem. It is by nature ideologically situated in that it is concerned with the preservation of all languages. Hornberger and Hult (2008) argue that it "calls upon researchers to see relationships among speakers, their languages, and the social contexts in which LPP and language use are situated" (Hornberger and Hult 2008: 292; Hult 2010a: 9) and, thus, the ecological orientation to LPP requires breadth (an interest in a broad range of linguistic ecosystems) and depth (close attention to the details within any particular ecosystem). The concept of a linguistic ecosystem is similar to the notions of "layers" or "levels" in LPP research yet, as Hult (2010a) argues, it emphasizes how our conceptualizations of LPP layers are ultimately abstractions useful for the sake of whatever analytical lens the researcher uses.

Those who take an ecological approach to LPP emphasize a consideration of multiple languages when making language plans or policies (e.g. Kaplan and Baldauf 1997) and the value of all languages as resources within their environment (e.g. Hornberger 2002). An example might be the Council of Europe's plurilingual educational policy, which argues that all languages are valuable, everyone has a right to their own language, and plurlingual education benefits European citizens (see "Plurilingual Education in Europe" in 8.5). Phillipson and Skutnabb-Kangas (1996) contrast the "ecology-of-language paradigm" with the "diffusion-of-English paradigm" as two endpoints on a language policy continuum, the latter being characterized by a focus on capitalism, science and technology, and monolingualism, and the former being characterized by the promotion of multilingualism and linguistic human rights around the world. Hornberger (2002) similarly contrasts the "one nation-one language" ideology (Concept 5.2) with multilingual language policies in which languages are understood to: "(1) live and evolve in an eco-system along with other languages (language evolution), (2) interact with their sociopolitical, economic, and cultural environments (language environment), and (3) become endangered if there is inadequate environmental support for them vis-à-vis other languages in the eco-system (language endangerment)" (Hornberger 2002: 35–36).

While the value of the ecology of language approach in the study of language policy is well established, some question the value or appropriateness of the metaphor itself. For example, Pennycook (2004: 232) warns against the political implications of using biomorphic metaphors as they may lead to the "enumeration, objectification and biologisation of languages". Indeed, one wonders about the value of adopting terms developed in the natural sciences to argue for a particularly post-modernist and/or anti-positivistic notion of linguistic diversity and language policy. For example, Phillipson and Skutnabb-Kangas (1996) adopt the "ecology" term to describe a language policy orientation that, somewhat paradoxically, *rejects* traditional values and discourses of objectivist science. As well, while all biological species are essential to any particular biological ecosystem (reflecting the notion that all languages have value) other ecological processes do not seem to apply. If we let the ecological metaphor play out, we must consider that biological evolution ensures the survival of the fittest and any ecosystem is populated by both predators and prey and, therefore, while the metaphor suggests reasons for why we would want to save endangered languages (so as not to disrupt the equilibrium in the language ecology), portraying some languages as better suited to survive evolution, or as predators, would be not be welcome in this approach.

2.7 Educational language policy

As the field of language policy has rapidly expanded to include an increasingly diverse body of research, it has become less driven by its theoretical LPP forebears. A case in point is the expanding body of research on *educational* language policy, which tends to rely as much on anthropological, sociological, and/or educational theory and methodology as it does on socio- or applied linguistics and early language planning and policy work. Increasingly, schools are studied as sites of language policy creation, interpretation, appropriation, and instantiation and much of the theoretical and conceptual work described in this book is based on empirical work in school districts, schools, and classrooms. Yet, research on language education policy or educational language policy or language-in-education policy proffers its own set of theories, methods, and findings that have had both a theoretical impact as well as a practical impact, especially since much of this work actively supports and promotes multilingualism as a resource in schools.

A key finding in this area of research has been the agency that educators have in the interpretation and appropriation of top-down language policies. In an edited volume that focuses on this agency, García and Menken (2010) offer a helpful historical overview of the focus on educational sites as important instantiations of language planning and policy processes. They note that in Cooper's (1989) *acquisition planning*, the important role of education in societal language planning is highlighted but the role of educators in language planning and policy processes is not considered, or, as they put it, it is "undertheorized" (García and Menken 2010: 251). Building upon Cooper (1989), Kaplan and Baldauf (1997: 122) use the term *language-in-education planning* to describe what they call a "key implementation procedure [and sub-set] for language policy and planning." García and Menken use the term *language-in-education policy* to describe critical work from the past few decades that focuses on the role of schools in marginalizing minority languages and minority language users but, like its predecessors, does not consider the power of educators (e.g. Lin and Martin 2005; Tollefson 2002a).

Along with language-in-education policy, García and Menken (2010: 254) use the term *language education policy* but distinguish it by the lack of explicit attention to official language policy: "Whereas language-in-education policy is concerned with decisions only about languages and their uses in school, language education policy refers to decisions made in schools beyond those made explicitly about language itself." A notable example of language education policy is the incorporation of standardized tests because, while they do not constitute official language policies, they are a mechanism for de facto language policies and perhaps conceal a covert or hidden agenda (see Menken 2008; Shohamy 2006). Finally, they present the term *language education policies*, emphasizing the plurality of choices available to educators and the agency of educators as powerful decision-makers in language planning and policy processes. To their list, we could also add *language policy in education* and *educational language policy*, which are sometimes used interchangeably (e.g. Tollefson 2002b).

Concept 2.8 Educational language policy

This book adopts the term *educational language policy* to describe the official and unofficial policies that are created across multiple layers and institutional contexts (from national organizations to classrooms) that impact language use in classrooms and schools. Educational language policies are interpreted, appropriated, and instantiated in potentially creative and unpredictable ways that rely on the implementational and ideological spaces unique to the classroom, school, and community. Such policies can, but don't necessarily, impact language education (i.e. the teaching of languages) as they can also impact the language used in content classrooms (e.g. science, history, art). Educational language policies have historically been used to eradicate, subjugate, and marginalize minority and Indigenous languages and their users and are, therefore, instruments of power that influence access to educational and economic resources. They have also been used to develop, maintain, and promote Indigenous and minority languages, especially in additive bilingual education programs. At every level of educational language policy, and throughout the educational language policy process, there are different and potentially divergent ideologies about language and language education that are unique to the discursive processes within that level/layer/institution.

This terminological stew reflects the increasing complexity of this area of research and more and more scholars with diverse interests, many from outside of the world of applied linguistics, are taking an active role in the field. Much of this work has focused on the top-down power of educational institutions to marginalize minority languages and minority language users (e.g. Tollefson 2002a), yet others, like García and Menken (2010), focus on the power and agency of educators in the LPP process. Corson (1999) points out that top-down (policy) discourse is constantly negotiated in the ongoing production of discourse and interaction which means that practitioners can formally (in the form of policy text creation) and informally (at the classroom level) appropriate policy in creative and unpredictable ways. For example, Stritikus and Wiese (2006) note that, even after the anti-bilingual education policy

(Proposition 227) was passed in California, "[R]esistance to antibilingual initiatives has become an important part of the landscape and work of some teachers" (p. 1127). As well, both hegemonic and alternative discourses are subject to change and such change can occur in bilingual schools (see Freeman 1998; Heller 1999). For example, Freeman's (1998, 2000) ethnographic and action-oriented research on bilingual education and language planning in Philadelphia and Washington D.C. illuminates how local discourses which champion linguistic diversity and multilingual education can challenge dominant monolingual educational discourses. Although schools may be sites which reify dominant ways of educating and thus lead to social reproduction – and multilingual education alone is not enough to reverse language shift – bilingual schools can be sites of discursive emancipation that champion multilingualism and multiculturalism as resources.

2.8 Discussion

This chapter represents an attempt to cover some of the major theoretical and conceptual contributions to the field, with a focus on (1) conceptualizations that attempt to account for policy as a multi-layered phenomenon, and (2) approaches and theories that have been tested with empirical data collection. There are many other perspectives not addressed, including economic considerations in LPP (Grin 2003), political theory and language policy (Schmidt, Sr. 2006; May 2013), and legal and judicial theory and language policy (Shuibne 2013), much of which will be taken up in later chapters. However, the hope is that this chapter has laid the theoretical and conceptual foundation for the rest of the chapters, paving the way for the findings discussed in Part II and the methodological proposals covered in Part III. Still, we must return to Ricento's (2006b: 18) critique that there is no grand theory of LPP. He argues that the practice of language planning – "the development, implementation, and evalution of specific language policies" – has been under-studied in part because most sociolinguists and applied linguists are not trained in the policy sciences. While LPP is rapidly changing and studies of the practice of language planning continue to push the work forward, the field will benefit from interdisciplinary connections to other fields of "policy", including environmental policy (Shulman 2006), educational policy (Mitchell, Crowson, and Shipps 2011), and political policy (May 2001).

Part II
Findings

3
Example studies

Longitudinal Studies

3.1 Marilyn Martin-Jones
Bilingual education and literacy practices in Wales
3.2 Feliciano Chimbutane
Colonial history, language policy, and bilingual education in Mozambique
3.3 Florence Bonacina
Language policy as practice in a French induction classroom
3.4 Angela Cincotta-Segi
Language policy and bilingual education in Lao PDR

Article-Length Reports

3.5 Francis M. Hult
Language policy, linguistic ecology, and Swedish television
3.6 Lin Pan
English language education policy and ideology in China
3.7 Dafna Yitzhaki
Language attitudes, law, and Arabic language policy in Israel
3.8 Shannon Fitzsimmons-Doolan
Immigration and language ideology in the U.S.

3.9 Discussion

Part I laid the groundwork with a discussion of definitions, theories, and concepts in the field. The aim of this chapter in Part II is to explore how particular definitions, theories, concepts, and methods (Chapter 5) are put into practice in a small sample of studies from different parts of the world. The goal is to cover a range of work that utilizes a variety of theories and methods – both longitudinal projects as well as shorter studies – to study LPP processes in diverse contexts. The chapter first focuses on longitudinal studies that were either engendered by a dissertation/thesis or extended ethnographic fieldwork, the result of which is typically a book or a range of articles, while the second part reviews article-length reports. This chapter is concerned with newer scholarship in which the focus is on language policy as the *primary* object of analysis, which is a new and encouraging development in the field.

The studies in this chapter incorporate a wide range of theoretical developments (including New Literacy Studies, ecology of language, critical theory, and critical language policy) and methods (including corpus analysis, ethnography of language policy, critical discourse analysis, and conversation analysis). They examine language policy as it relates to language education, colonialism, literacy practices, television, the law, and immigration policy. The work in this chapter reflects some of the diversity of work going on in the field, as well as some of the themes and foci that circulate across studies and settings, including how language policy relates to literacy education, language revitalization, language ideologies, colonialism and colonial language policy, bilingual education, immigration, community language attitudes, the media, discourse planning, the spread of English around the world, linguistic imperialism, and language ecologies. As well, this sample of LPP work is representative of some of the methodological and theoretical themes being developed, including conceptualizations (and the study) of policy as a multi-layered phenomenon, discourse-analytic techniques, ethnography of language policy, and critical language policy. While this chapter might not offer a comprehensive review of the field, it does proffer a sense of the type of work that is at the vanguard and, therefore, where the field might be headed.

Longitudinal Studies

3.1 Marilyn Martin-Jones

Marilyn Martin-Jones and colleagues (Ivanič *et al.* 2009; Martin-Jones 2009; Martin-Jones *et al.* 2009; Martin-Jones 2011) examine how language policy and language revitalization efforts for Welsh have impacted the education of students in vocational education courses in North Wales. This ethnographic research project, entitled *Dwyieithrwydd, Iiythrennedd a dysgu mewn Addysg Bellach* (Bilingual Literacies for Learning in Further Education), focuses on the home and school literacy practices of bilingual youth in Welsh and English. One key finding that the rich ethnographic data reveal is that the literacy practices of students in bilingual vocational education are very diverse and are characterized by multiple types of engagement with electronic media, yet this diversity is not reflected in the classrooms. This work sheds light on what language revitalization and language policy efforts will need to take into account if they are to successfully adapt to new forms of literacy practices.

Quote 3.1 Ethnography and language policy

[E]thnography, combined with close analysis of everyday talk, enables us to capture the specific local ways in which language policies and new forms of language education are made and remade, by teachers and students, in the daily routines of educational life.

(Martin-Jones 2011: 232)

Context

Welsh is often cited as an example of a language that has benefited from successful language revitalization. Martin-Jones (2011) recounts the history of the Welsh language movement, begun in the 1950's when English-medium education predominated, and the resulting language policies that have helped to secure Welsh in Wales. The Welsh language movement helped mobilize grassroots demands for increased use of Welsh in many domains including education, the media, and the legal system. The parental demand for bilingual education in Welsh and English led to *Mudiad Ysgolioni Meithrin* (the Welsh Nursery Schools Movement), which in turn led to the development of bilingual primary and secondary education. Martin-Jones (2011) reports that, by 2006–2007, 30.5% of all primary schools incorporated Welsh as the sole or main medium of instruction and all students are required to study Welsh as a first or second language from ages 5 to 16.

Crucial for this expansion of Welsh and bilingual education were language policies that sought to improve the status of Welsh. The Welsh Language Act of 1993, for example, requires all public institutions to develop a language plan – which is reviewed by the Welsh Language Board (*Bwrdd yr Iaith*) – that explains how Welsh and English are treated equally. After the Welsh devolution referendum of 1997, the Welsh Assembly Government (*Cynulliad Cenedlaethol Cymru*) was created in 1999, which has been instrumental in crafting language policies that promote Welsh. For example, in 2002 the Assembly Government published a policy entitled *Dyfodol Dwyieithog* (Bilingual Future), which stated that:

> ...in a truly bilingual Wales both Welsh and English will flourish and will be treated as Equal. A bilingual Wales means a country where people can choose to live their lives through the medium of either or both languages; a country where the presence of two national languages, and other diverse languages and cultures, is a source of pride and strength for all (quoted in Martin-Jones 2011: 235).

These policies created important ideological space (see Concept 4.3) for increasing implementation of bilingual education but, as Martin-Jones (2011) points out, Welsh-medium and bilingual education has been slower to develop in the Further Education colleges, which are the main provider of vocational education for students aged 16–19. Martin-Jones and her colleagues focus on Coleg Meirion-Dwyfor, a Further Education college that *has* developed bilingual programs, which she describes as having "a distinctly Welsh ethos, and an explicit policy on the equal use of Welsh and English in written communication" (Martin-Jones 2011: 236). The focus is on the differences in student literacy practices inside and outside the school and, then, the efforts to incorporate these diverse literacy practices as resources within the classrooms.

Theory

Martin-Jones (2009) and colleagues (Ivanič *et al.* 2009; Martin-Jones *et al.* 2009) incorporate New Literacy Studies (NLS) as the main orienting theory for their project. Instead of viewing "literacy" as a set of reading and writing skills within individuals, it is viewed as a social practice that differs "across domains of social life, with different styles, genres and types of texts being used and produced in different domains, in local life worlds and in different institutional worlds" (Martin-Jones 2009: 49). This approach reveals how cultural values are associated with literacy practices in multiple languages and how young bilingual learners appropriate multiple and diverse literacies to negotiate different identities and relationships. To illuminate these evolving literacy practices, ethnography is essential for an understanding of how "reading, writing, and using texts are observable in particular, situated events...which are moulded and remoulded by social structures, institutional conventions, and relations of power" (Martin-Jones *et al.* 2009: 46).

Method

This body of work incorporates ethnographic methods and is aligned with ethnography of language policy (see 5.5) and data collection included: participant-observation in classrooms; audio-recordings of classroom talk; interviews with teachers and students; collection of teachers' literacy logs; multi-sited observation in the students' college, work, and home; and historical-textual analysis (see 5.2). Most of the interviews were conducted in Welsh, including the "diary-based interviews" (see Jones, Martin-Jones, and Bhatt 2000), for which the students kept a diary about their literacy practices and languages used over the course of two days. The students also took photographs of literacy events in their lives and they made captions for the photographs. These diary notes and photographs were the foundation for the interviews with the students and were intentionally designed to make the interviews as collaborative, dialogic, and non-threatening as possible. Martin-Jones argues that this allowed the researchers to get insights into the students' emic perspectives of the literacy practices. Following two years of ethnographic data collection, data analysis focused on building case studies of individual students (i.e. "vertical slicing") and then identifying commonalities and difference across case studies (i.e. "horizontal slicing").

Findings

Despite macro-level language policy support for Welsh, one of the key findings is the challenge the educators face in providing bilingual instruction where there is a shortage of Welsh teaching materials (see also Chimbutane 2011; 3.2 in this volume). For example, one section of an Agriculture course taught by Anwen Williams focused on water pollution on farms but the UK-wide legislation about water pollution, and the instructional films produced by the UK Environmental Agency, were all in English. Therefore, Williams had to creatively incorporate Welsh into classroom discussions about monolingual English texts; the vignette included in Martin-Jones (2011) about Williams reveals how teachers must creatively adapt their bilingual instruction to monolingual texts when bilingual texts are not available.

Many of the findings highlight the unique bilingual literacy practices in the students' lives and the teachers' eventual incorporation of those home literacy practices into the classroom. Martin-Jones and her colleagues are able to develop very descriptive case studies about individual students, full of ethnographic detail. Engagement with electronic media was common among many of the students who, for example, frequently used mobile phone texting (in Welsh and English) for communication with friends and frequently used websites (in English) for their recreational interests. Computer-mediated literacy practices were not only used for personal communication and recreation, however, as many of the agriculture students helped out with farm work at home that involved ordering farm equipment from websites, utilizing computer software, and managing electronic data systems.

The use of Welsh when interacting with new media was limited but the students relied on their bilingual resources to do things like maintain farm paperwork (e.g. registering animal births, keeping track of medicines, or applying for grants/loans), deal with customers, read magazines, send text messages, develop websites, and participate in sports. Furthermore, because there has been a decline in the viability of family-run farms in Wales, many farmers make an attempt at diversification, which can involve moving into the tourist industry (e.g. opening a bed and breakfast), expanding into the food industry (e.g. opening a food market), or taking on agri-environmental projects (e.g. growing organic foods) which are increasingly supported by Wales funding agencies. This diversification is aided by the students' bilingual literacy skills and Martin-Jones *et al.* (2009: 59) note that the students' "language and literacy resources, particularly their facility with computing and their familiarity with on-line literacies, in Welsh and in English, were being harnessed with a view to exploring and taking up opportunities for diversification of income sources." The teachers in the study were startled by the diverse range of literacy practices that the students engaged in outside of school (see Rogers 2003) and, in the second phase of the project, these literacy skills were incorporated into the classes by having students create bilingual websites, prepare bilingual wall displays for a local doctor's office, and meet with and interview a Welsh poet. These findings reveal that educational language policies and practices will have to adapt to the diverse, often computer-mediated, and often multilingual, literacy practices in which students engage. Further, this research illuminates how Welsh language policy is instantiated (or not) in classroom educational practices that must adjust to both the macro-level policy context and local literacy practices.

3.2 Feliciano Chimbutane

Feliciano Chimbutane's (2011) study of bilingual education and language policy in Mozambique is a good example of an analysis revealing how both macro- and micro-level language policy play out in bilingual education schools. He examines the historical, sociopolitical, and policy context in Mozambique, and includes a rich ethnographic description of educational practices and beliefs in a school. The educational language policies in Mozambique are representative of a larger movement in Sub-Saharan Africa to change the monolingual colonial legacy through language policy and, particularly, through bilingual education that includes the previously excluded African languages.

> **Quote 3.2 Rethinking bilingual education in post-colonial contexts**
>
> [M]y main concern in the study was to explore how different views about the purpose and value of bilingual education in Mozambique are manifested in bilingual classroom discourse practices and how these practices relate to local, institutional, and societal discourses.
>
> (Chimbutane 2011: 1)

Context

Even though African countries have gained their independence from European colonizers, the colonial legacy of a dominating European language has remained, and schooling has been a primary vehicle for supporting this dominance. Portuguese colonial rule enforced racial stratification, social and legal injustice, and a monolingual educational policy that attempted to supplant African languages with Portuguese. Unlike Britain and Germany, which tolerated African languages in schools, Portugal enforced monolingual Portuguese education in Mozambique as a tool of cultural assimilation and positioned African languages as inferior forms of speech (*dialectos*) which should be eliminated from schools. Acquisition of Portuguese was a necessary, although not sufficient, precondition for becoming an *assimilado,* a class status that ranked lower than white Europeans but higher than the large majority of indigenous Africans. In 1965, a ten-year struggle began against Portuguese colonial rule, mobilized by the Frente de Libertação de Moçambique (Frelimo) (which, notably, adopted a Portuguese name), who ultimately secured independence for Mozambique in 1975. In developing a new nation-state, Frelimo maintained Portuguese as the official language in order to (a) preserve national unity through a common lingua franca, and (b) preserve national unity by not choosing one African language over another. Somewhat ironically, Portuguese was seen as a uniting force among the revolutionaries and a vehicle to fight the Portuguese. The "one nation-one language" ideology (see Concept 5.2) is evidenced in a quote from Fernando Ganhão, a very influential Frelimo thinker:

> The decision to opt for Portuguese as the official language of the People's Republic of Mozambique was a well pondered and carefully examined political decision, aimed at achieving one objective, the preservation of national unity and the integrity of the territory. (quoted in Chimbutaine 2011: 43)

The monolingual ideology has been increasingly challenged because there has been a growing consensus, both within and outside of Mozambique, that a monolingual educational policy has failed to empower Africans and has contributed to the under-development of Sub-Saharan Africa. Furthermore, the colonial policy of supporting the dominance of Portuguese was, at least in part, ineffective since in the 2007 census 85.3% of the population of Mozambique reported speaking a Bantu language as their first language while only 10.7% claimed Portuguese as a first language. Such a context would seem to support the development of bilingual education. Chimbutane argues that the push for a bilingual educational system that institutionalizes African languages in educational contexts has been motivated by (a) the growing consensus that monolingual education in European languages has been inefficient or ineffective because such languages are second or foreign languages for the students, and (b) success stories like the Ile-Ife Project in Nigeria (1970–1978), which provided bilingual education in Yoruba and English. Nevertheless, there has been a lack of follow-up to these successful programs, and educational systems have tended to maintain the dominance of the colonial languages, leading some to postulate that language policy decisions are guided by ideology, not evidence.

It was not until 2003 that the policy that supported Portuguese as the only official language of formal education was changed but the seeds of this transformation can be found earlier, in the 1990 constitution, which promoted the use of African languages:

> The state values the national languages as a cultural and educational heritage and promotes their development and increased use as vehicles of our identity. (quoted in Chimbutane 2011)

Chimbutane describes the current political climate as *favorable* for the promotion of local languages, which has led to bilingual education experiments backed by the Ministry of Education such as the Projecto de Escolarização Bilingue em Moçambique (PEBIMO) from 1993 to1997. While there is no explicit educational language policy, Chimbutane characterizes the de facto policy as multilingual, with 16 African languages being offered as initial media of instruction even if most of these programs are transitional. Chimbutane questions the solidity of such de facto policies, however, since there is no official policy in place holding anyone accountable for the implementation of bilingual education. The focus of Chimbutane's study is on grades 4 and 5 (ages 9 to 13) in two bilingual education schools in a rural area in Mozambique. In one school Changana was used as a language of instruction alongside Portuguese while in the other it was Chope. Chimbutane chose grades 4 and 5 because these are considered the transitional grades, after which students tend to transition into an all-Portuguese instructional setting.

Theory

Chimbutane's theoretical orientation is influenced by other ethnographic and discourse-analytic work (e.g. Heller 2006; Martin-Jones 1995) that "investigates the sociolinguistic and socio-historical background against which language interactions and positionings in bilingual classrooms can be perceived and interpreted" (Chimbutane 2011: 5). This approach takes a multi-layered view of linguistic phenomena, incorporating an analysis of the connections between societal, institutional, and local discourses. The work of Bourdieu (1991) is influential as well, especially the notion that schools are key sites for the reproduction of the social order, which invest some languages with more cultural capital and which create an educational and linguistic marketplace that assigns legitimacy to some languages but not to others. Yet, Chimbutane (2011: 7) challenges the notion that such a social order will go uncontested and emphasizes the agency (see 4.1.1) of educators in interpreting and appropriating larger discourses, especially in bilingual educational contexts (see Cincotta-Segi and Bonacina, this chapter). "Speakers can opt to collude, challenge, or transform the symbolic order...the line between legitimate and illegitimate language as well as between formal and informal linguistic markets is not always and in all contexts neat and/or static."

Method

Chimbutane (2011: 1) describes his study as an "ethnographic study of discursive practices in two primary bilingual schools in Mozambique."

While the data analyzed were collected over a one-year period (2007–2008), Chimbutane had worked in both schools from 2003 to 2006, positioning him as an insider and granting him unique access to these sites. It was also important that he was knowledgeable about both African languages offered at each of the schools (alongside Portuguese) – Changana and Chope – and he notes that his ability to speak Changana was perceived as an expression of shared identity, while his ability to understand and his willingness to try to speak Chope were appreciated by the Chope community. Data collection included classroom observation, audio-recordings, note-taking, interviewing, questionnaires, and document analysis, and after he had collected the data he went back to some key participants to check its accuracy. This allowed the participants to reflect on their own educational practices; for example, the Chope speakers were surprised by how many Changana words they used in the transcripts and attempted to convince Chimbutane to translate those words back to Chope.

The analysis of the larger historical, sociopolitical, sociolinguistic and policy context in Mozambique is akin to Tollefson's (1991) historical-structural approach, even though Chimbutane does not refer to it as such. Combining this macro-analysis with ethnography and discourse analysis in the two schools allows Chimbutane to reveal how the colonial history of educational language policy plays out in the local policies and practices in the schools.

Findings

There are a number of compelling findings in Chimbutane's study. The main purpose of bilingual education, he argues, is still to help students transition into Portuguese, which still retains a good deal of social power. Nonetheless, Chimbutane challenges the notion that transitional bilingual education always leads to cultural assimilation and loss of the L1: especially in a context where pupils are surrounded by their L1 outside of school, these programs can strengthen the maintenance of low-status languages.

Chimbutane's analysis reveals that students felt at ease in the L1-medium classes and participated freely and often. This led to greatly increased oral production in the L1-medium classrooms, and these intriguing interactions are captured by Chimbutane. In turn, the community members viewed the inclusion of their L1 as official recognition of their existence, and the involvement of parents, especially when course materials were in their native language, helped build connections between the school and the community. Chimbutane argues that this led to an "increased sense of ethnolinguistic pride and identity affirmation among the communities concerned" (p. 125). In this way, bilingual education can be viewed as a tool for social and cultural transformation; as the African languages are legitimized in the classroom, they become increasingly legitimized outside of the classroom, creating the potential for a shift in societal attitudes.

Within the community of Changana and Chope speakers, Portuguese is still viewed as *the* mechanism that allows access to educational and socio-economic opportunity and participants viewed African languages as providing important ties to the community, as symbols of authenticity, but not as "marketable assets" (p. 153). Furthermore, teachers in the Portuguese classrooms strictly enforced a Portuguese-only policy, which (a) caused the students to remain silent because they did not understand much of the instruction, and (b) reflected the former colonial practice of marginalizing African languages. Thus, while the bilingual schools have helped open the door to supporting African languages, giving them visibility and increasing their ethnolinguistic vitality, old colonial language ideologies still linger. Furthermore, these schools face major challenges in any transition to Indigenous languages because there is a paucity of printed materials in Changana and Chope for the students to use and Mozambique lacks a strong cadre of educators trained to teach in bilingual classrooms.

3.3 Florence Bonacina

Florence Bonacina's analysis of a multilingual induction classroom in France is a good example of the "new wave" of LPP research that takes up both McCarty's conceptualization of language policy as "modes of human interaction, negotiation, and production mediated by relations of power" (McCarty 2011b: 8; see Quote 1.4 above) and the first part of Spolsky's tripartite definition of language policy as "language practices – the habitual pattern of selecting among the varieties that make up its linguistic repertoire" (Spolsky 2004: 5; see Quote 1.3). Bonacina is particularly interested in how language policy manifests in interaction in a multilingual classroom, which she refers to as *practiced language policies*. In this approach, language policy is not just something that is created outside of the classroom but something that is created from within, emerging in the interactional norms of the interlocutors. Her dissertation/thesis takes up Spolsky's definition but also draws on conversation analysis (CA) to examine practiced language policy in a classroom:

> **Quote 3.3 Practiced language policy**
>
> Spolsky's significant contribution is his claim that there is a policy in practices, which I propose to call a 'practiced language policy' (see also Bonacina 2008). However, this new conceptualisation of language policy remains essentially programmatic since Spolsky does not indicate how practiced language policies can be investigated. It is this methodological gap that I aim to address in this thesis. Indeed, my primary aim is to propose an approach to the investigation of practiced language policies. And my main claim is that a practiced language policy can be investigated using Conversation Analysis, a method specifically developed to describe conversational practices.
>
> (Bonacina 2010: 11)

Context

France is often considered the paradigm for having an overtly monolingual language ideology and policy. L'Académie Française is a language planning institution that prescribes linguistic norms and seeks to promote the primacy of French. Bonacina argues that France's monolingual language management is based on two principles: *National Unity* and *Equality for All*. The principle of *National Unity* reflects the one-nation one-language ideology (see Concept 5.2) and positions French as the one and only language to unify France as a nation. The *Equality for All* principle suggests that ensuring equality for all citizens requires treating all citizens the same – i.e. in French – and linguistic homogeneity is a tool to provide equal opportunity. While the *Equality for All* principle is implicitly enacted in the language policy of classroom teachers in many parts of the world (including the U.S.A.) it is explicitly supported by the French constitution and the French Constitutional Council. For example, after the Council of Europe passed the European Charter for Regional or Minority Languages, which promoted the use of minority languages in education, the French Constitutional Council forbade ratification of the charter in France, relying on article 1 of the French constitution, which states that all citizens should be treated equally. This interpretation of "equality" can be contrasted with how the U.S. Supreme Court has interpreted equal rights. In the Lau v. Nichols case (see 5.3.1), the judges decided unanimously that the same treatment of linguistic minorities (i.e. the same English instruction) was *unequal* because it delimited access to the curriculum and therefore violated the students' civil rights.

The result is a predominantly monolingual French educational language policy that, Bonacina argues, positions linguistic diversity as a problem and French as the sole vehicle for educational success. French is the official language of instruction and regional languages are allowed if they support transition into French. Notably, this language policy is directed primarily at the home languages of bilingual children, *not* French-speaking students who are acquiring a foreign language. The dominant educational model for non-native French speakers is the induction programme, which provides educational services for newly arrived immigrants for no more than twelve months. Students attend an induction classroom for part of the day and a mainstream classroom for the other part (very similar to what are called Newcomer Centers in the U.S.A.). These induction classrooms are attended by students with diverse ages, levels of French, and first languages. While the explicit objective is to allow the students "to be rapidly integrated into a successful mainstream curriculum" (French Ministry of Education, cited in Bonacina 2010: 66), there is no explicit language policy that addresses how this aim should be realized, which leaves implementational space for the teacher to use any combination of French and the students' first languages. Bonacina argues that these classrooms are still subject to the wider monolingual policy, yet the classroom in which she collected her data was very multilingual, with a teacher who allowed and sometimes promoted using the students' first languages. Bonacina conducted her study in an induction classroom at "La Plaine" primary school in the académie of the Versailles (region). The ages of the students ranged from 6 to 13 and multiple first languages were spoken, including Japanese, Spanish, Polish, Peul, English, Filipino, Cantonese, and Arabic.

Theory

Bonacina's study incorporates Spolsky's definition (see Quote 1.3) which splits language policy into three elements (language management, language beliefs or ideology, and language practices) but her focus is on the third, which she refers to as 'practiced language policy'. Bonacina also incorporates Ball's conceptualization (1993) of policy as text and policy as discourse (see Concept 4.2) but introduces a third category called "policy as practice". Even though previous LPP research *has* focused on the micro-level local agency and discourse in language policy processes, she argues that this work has only investigated language practices vis-à-vis language policy instead of looking at language practices *as* language policies, in and of themselves. She argues: "Whether LP scholars conceptualize language policy as either text or discourse or both, language practices are systematically interpreted with regard to a language policy determined *outside* interaction. This is the main difference between the first strand of research and the second strand of research in which LP is argued to exist *within* language practices" (p. 40).

Method

Bonacina views interactional norms and language policy as emerging from language practices and she uses conversation analysis (CA) to analyze the discourse data. CA practitioners have traditionally been wary of making assumptions about how the wider context – including the interlocutors' age, gender, identity, power, and institutional roles – impacts the interactional acts (although for an alternative perspective of CA which does site the analysis within an institutional framework, see Antaki 2011). "Conversation Analysts adopt instead an 'active perspective' (Seedhouse, 2004: 42) to context whereby participants are seen to talk context into being. This means that aspects of the situatedness of talk such as social structures and institutional roles are co-constructed *within* talk-in-interaction" (Bonacina 2010: 88). This emic approach to context compels the analyst to show that the interlocutors are orienting to, or referring to, particular aspects of the context in particular ways in order to include it in the analysis. This has sometimes put CA at odds with critical discourse analysis (CDA) since CDA is often criticized for making assumptions about the role that context (notably, power) plays in interactions and imposing this on the data, as opposed to letting findings emerge from the data (see the discussion in 5.6.3).

This emic perspective becomes very relevant in CA when code-switching in multilingual classrooms is being investigated. Bonacina does not analyze code-switching in a classroom as a reflection of society (e.g. Myers-Scotton 1993) or as a reflection or reaction to some language policy, but as "practical social action" (p. 111). Her CA approach to code-switching moves away from looking at the choices of language in an interaction as a reaction to or reflection of some external social factor and, instead, seeks to "to reveal the underlying procedural apparatus by which conversation participants themselves arrive at local interpretations of language choice" (Li Wei 2005: 381, quoted in Bonacina 2010: 94). Influenced by the notion that there is an overall order to conversations, including those in which code-switching occurs, Bonacina's aim is to examine the order of language alternation, and, how norms of interaction can be formulated as language policies.

Bonacina's methods of data collection included the following:

1. *Gaining access.* Bonacina describes the "trajectory of access" that eventually led to the classroom in which she collected data. She first approached representatives at the Centre Académique pour la Scolarisation des Nouveaux Arrivants et des Enfants du Voyage (or CASNAV), who introduced her to two induction teachers. However, perhaps because the teachers viewed her as someone associated with CASNAV, access became difficult, so she took a bottom-up approach and contacted teachers herself, which eventually led her to Miss Lo's class. Bonacina notes that Miss Lo's positive attitude toward the use of students' L1s might be unique among the induction teachers.
2. *Preliminary semi-participant observation.* Because of her desire to maintain a level of objectivity and 'neutral' status in the school – and not be viewed as a teacher, for example – Bonacina incorporated semi-participant observation, as opposed to (full) participant-observation, delimiting the amount of participation. This attempt to position herself as a fly on the wall (see Concept 5.7) can be contrasted with Chimbutane's insider positioning and full participant observation. However, while Bonacina does include some ethnographic methods (such as participant-observation) the ethnographically derived data are mainly included as background, to substantiate particular emic concepts, and are intentionally used cautiously and sparingly.
3. *Semi-participant observation and audio-recordings.* Conversation analysis demands careful attention to minute occurrences in talk and, therefore, presupposes quality audio-recordings. Bonacina incorporated an external microphone because it recorded sounds in all parts of the classroom and was less obtrusive and less noticeable, thus mitigating problems arising from the observer's paradox (Labov 1972b).
4. *Collecting additional information.* This included written documents such as school demography and policies, together with interviews with teachers and students, to gather information on student and teacher ideologies and beliefs. For the students, a semi-structured group interview was organized around a card game, which allowed the students to relax.
5. *Feedback.* Bonacina shared her findings with the research participants through informal oral presentations to the head-teacher and all interested teachers. Miss Lo was provided with more detailed feedback because she wanted to examine the data in order to improve her own teaching practices. Interaction with the school continued beyond

the time of data collection and Bonacina planned professional development workshops for the teachers.

> **Concept 3.1 The observer's paradox**
>
> Labov (1972b: 181) describes the challenge of collecting samples of natural speech in unnatural situations like interviews as the *observer's paradox*. "Any systematic observation of a speaker defines a formal context in which more than the minimum attention is paid to speech...The aim of linguistic research in the community must be to find out how people talk when they are not being systematically observed; yet we can only obtain this data by systematic observation."

Findings

Bonacina's findings concentrate on language alternation practices (i.e. code-switching) in the multilingual induction classroom and she focused on how the students used the multiple languages available as their communicative codes (what she calls "the mediums of classroom interaction"). Very much in contrast to the French monolingual policy within the school's mainstream classrooms, the mediums of classroom interaction in the induction classroom included French monolingual, English monolingual, Spanish monolingual, French and English bilingual, and French and Spanish bilingual. While language alternation was sometimes an accepted medium for the students, at other times it was seen as deviant; however, this deviance was often accepted (or "licensed") by the induction teacher, Miss Lo, who incorporated the students' first languages to increase their understanding of concepts (see also Skilton-Sylvester 2003).

Bonacina shows how these language alternation practices are governed by interactional norms and argues that the institutional roles of "teacher" and "pupil" are not fixed identities but emerge as "something people do" in interactional practices. Bonacina distinguishes "teacher-hood" – which is associated with teaching activities like assessing, correcting, and controlling the floor and can be performed by students, as well as the teacher – from the institutionally prescribed role of "teacher". The norms governing the language choice and alternation practices include:

- *When someone is 'doing being the teacher of language X', that language is adopted as the medium of classroom interaction.* Whether it's Miss Lo or a student, if they position themselves as the teacher of a language, that language is adopted as the medium of interaction.

- *When no-one is 'doing being a language teacher' and there is a shared preferred language, that language is adopted as the medium of classroom interaction.* For example, when the students teach each other about class concepts, they will adopt the language they share if there is a shared preferred language other than French.
- *When no-one is 'doing being the language teacher' and there is no shared preferred language, the language common to all speakers (namely French) is adopted as the medium.* This norm expresses the implicit de facto language policy in the classroom, which not surprisingly promotes French as the lingua franca.
- *When there is a problem, language alternation may be licensed by way of attending to it.* This occurs, for example, when a student cannot think of the correct term (or *mot juste*) in French and the teacher licenses the use of their L1 to make the concept clear. In this way, alternation between French and the students' L1s is not only allowed by the teacher but incorporated as a teaching tool to ensure understanding by the students.

Bonacina's study reveals how norms of interaction – or practiced language policies – emerge in the course of classroom interaction and she argues that this is done without direct intervention from some outside language policy. While she acknowledges that influence can come from outside language policies, "The practiced language policy is likely to have the strongest influence on speakers' language choice and alternation acts" (p. 253). This finding is reminiscent of E. Johnson's (2013a: 58) notion of *instantiation,* which he describes as "the way a policy is enacted and the ways in which languages are used as a result. Regardless of what a policy states, the instantiation of that policy is apparent through the patterns of language use that emerge based on a broader set of social, political, and cultural influences." The work of both Johnson and Bonacina is representative of LPP research that focuses on the emergence of language policy in language use and the interactional norms that govern that use.

3.4 Angela Cincotta-Segi

Angela Cincotta-Segi's work (Cincotta-Segi forthcoming; 2009; 2011a; 2011b; 2011c) on language policy and education in the Lao People's Democratic Republic (Lao PDR) contributes to a growing body of research (Johnson 2010b; Jaffe 2011) showing that the impacts of a language policy cannot necessarily be predicted based solely on the language of that policy or the perceived intentions of its authors. While the Lao PDR has an explicitly pro-monolingual educational language policy that supports only the Lao language, multilingualism is incorporated to varying degrees by teachers in Lao classrooms (see Bonacina, 3.3 above). Cincotta-Segi's data reveal the agency of teachers as policymakers (see also Menken and García 2010), even within an ostensibly restrictive policy context.

Quote 3.4 Teacher agency

[T]he policy of L2 medium of instruction in a context where students often do not speak that language upon entering school can lead teachers to devise their own classroom approaches which may or may not adhere to the official policy. These approaches are based on teachers' own understandings and preferences around language use in the classroom and the wider community, the perceived needs of their students, and the expression of teachers' identities in relation to those students...Furthermore, the language choices each teacher makes are not necessarily those which seem most predictable or those which are expected by policy makers in that context.

(Cincotta-Segi 2011a: 206–207)

Context

The Lao PDR is a country of roughly six million people, which has experienced about 800 years of political domination by the ethnic Lao group. The official language of the government, media, and education is Lao, which also has the highest number of native speakers. Still, the government recognizes 48 other languages even though Cincotta-Segi (forthcoming) suggests that there could be anywhere between 84 and 200 other languages. Cincotta-Segi describes the dominance of Lao language and culture, a discourse reproduced by the government, as a project of "Lao-isation" (Cincotta-Segi forthcoming), which is promoted through educational language policy. The Lao PDR is classified as one of the "least developed" in Southeast Asia by the United Nations Development Program and most of Laos has not undergone industrialization. About 80% of the population subsists on farming, the basic literacy rate is about 45%, and around 40% of households do not have electricity. The country is mountainous with many villages populated by ethnic and linguistic minorities who experience both a physical, cultural, and linguistic separation from urban areas. Cincotta-Segi reports that, while all of the curriculum and teaching materials are in Lao, almost 45% of the children do not speak Lao as their first language.

Cincotta-Segi reveals how Lao educational policy conflates educational, political, and cultural goals and promotes Lao language and culture as of central importance. She argues that Lao educational policy positions the Lao language and culture as crucial to political and moral unity and ignores non-Lao cultures and languages. For example, all female students are required to wear the Lao traditional skirt (*sinh*). The vehicle for transmission of this cultural teaching is the Lao language and no other languages are recognized as having legitimate use in schools. Nevertheless, Cincotta-Segi's interviews with officials within the Ministry of Education reveal that there is some openness to allowing minority languages as transitional tools for helping students acquire Lao.

Cincotta-Segi collected data in seven primary school classrooms in Nalae District, Luang Nam Tha Province, in Northwestern Laos. Most of the people in this area are ethnic Kmhmu, a Mon-Khmer group unrelated to the ethnic Lao, who speak Kmhmu language. The other main ethnic group is Tai-Lue who speak a language that is distinct but closely related to Lao. She focused on three classrooms as case studies, two of which were taught by ethnic Tai-Lue and one by an ethnic Kmhmu. All of the teachers spoke both Kmhmu and Lao. Upon entering the primary school, most of the students spoke little or no Lao.

Theory

In a similar manner to Bonacina, and also influenced by Ball (2006) (see Concept 4.2), Cincotta-Segi conceptualizes language policy as a multi-layered phenomenon that includes policy as text and discourse, but, following Lo Bianco (2008), she adds policy as performance (similar to Bonacina's "policy as practice"). She is interested in investigating policy at multiple levels: "as issued by its producers; as implemented (or not) by social actors engaged in the relevant activities, including policy makers themselves and those closer to the ground; and as lived by those whom it affects" (Cincotta-Segi 2009: 69). Thus, she examines the varying language policy texts, the public talk around and interpretations of those texts, and then how these texts impact (or do not) language education and use in Lao classrooms.

Method

Cincotta-Segi incorporates critical discourse analysis (see 5.6.1) to analyze language policy texts (policy as text) and classroom language use (policy as performance) but incorporates ethnography of language policy (see 5.5) and historical-textual investigation (see 5.2) to provide a more sophisticated understanding of the social context. Before entering the research sites, Cincotta-Segi had worked in Lao schools as an educational consultant, and this initial experience helped her develop an emic perspective concerning which language policy texts were most pertinent. She not only developed relationships with the schools but also with officials in the Ministry of Education (MoE). Accordingly, the language policy texts to be analyzed were selected on the basis of (1) whether they were referred to by actors, including Ministry officials, Lao and foreign development workers, and foreign consultants, and (2) "my professional experience of their primacy in the context of language and education in Laos (through working under the MoE)" (Cincotta-Segi 2009: 29). She used CDA to analyze the selection of policy texts but acknowledges a common criticism that CDA privileges the analyst's reading of the texts (see 5.6.3) and, accordingly, considered the producer's and consumer's readings as well. Further, the particular linguistic features which are analyzed emerged from a close reading of the data rather than being determined *a priori* and then imposed on the texts. An essential aspect of the analysis of policy in her work is Cincotta-Segi's interviews with MoE officials on how they themselves interpret the policies as both producers and consumers.

The analysis of policy texts and discourse was combined with ethnographic fieldwork in seven classrooms, which led to an eventual focus on three of them as case studies. These data included classroom observation, video-recordings of classroom interaction, and teacher interviews. Cincotta-Segi developed a coded transcript for each video-recorded lesson, which included the speaker, transcript, language, act, interaction type, and participants. The notion of "act" as used here is similar to the speech act, developed by Searle (1969), and the "interaction types" were classified as 'content', 'management', 'interpersonal' and 'metalinguistic'. An example is shown below (Cincotta-Segi 2009: 38). Lao language is written in normal text, Kmhmu is in bold, and words or phrases which could be either Lao or Lao words borrowed into Kmhmu are underlined:

Sample transcript from Cincotta-Segi showing language, actions, interactions and participants (2009: 38)

Sp.	Transcript	Lge	Act	Interact.	Pts
T	Lεo tit ta:m **go meh (?) ti.**	K	Inst	Mgt	3:cl
	Yeeng (?) hnaay, ci lav ca' g'me'?		Inst		
	Ee. Tit ta:m **yo'.**		Rt		
	Meh me' pe khao chai **le maan,**		Inst		
	aan ge gi pe bwan lɨ lav ca' g'me'.		Inst		

(*continued*)

Continued

Sp.	Transcript	Lge	Act	Interact.	Pts
T	[reading aloud] [loud] Tha:o Yangli:	L	R al	Cont	3:cl
	[quiet; fast] **Ge gi meh tha:o Yangli ci lav**, tɛ va leuang (?)	K	Fr		
	[loud; slow] Mɨ: sao ni:, na:i khu: oe:rn na:ng mai khɨn lao bot thɔ:n. La:o kɔ: vao dai, hi:an dai di.	L			
	Lɛ sama:t tɔ:p khamtha:m dai i:k duay.Tɔ: cha:k nan, khu: kɔ: oe:n sɨ: khɔ:i. Khɔ:i tɨ:n nyup ba:t nɨng, hua chai khɔ:ng khɔ:i ten tɨp ta:p tɨp ta:p		R al		

T = teacher; K = Kmhmu; L = Lao; Inst = instruction; Rt = repeat; R al = read aloud; Fr = frame; Mgt = management; Cont = content; 3:cl = third grade, whole class

Findings

While scholars like Ball (2006) reject the quest for authorial intentions behind policy, I argue that "it is still useful to analyze how the creators themselves interpret the intentions of a policy because their beliefs help form the discourse within and without the policy text and help contextualize its interpretation" (Johnson 2009: 147). Policy texts and discourses are not necessarily an intentional reification of homogenous ideologies; instead, what are often multi-authored texts emerge from heterogeneous intentions and ideologies and may be interpreted and appropriated in varying ways, a process often characterized by a tension between the power of policies as mechanisms of hegemony and the power of individuals as creative agents. However, this tension is sometimes portrayed as something that exists between macro-language policy creators (i.e. the state) and micro-language policy creators and appropriators (i.e. educators). Within Lao language policy text and discourse, there is a tension between recognizing the value of multiethnicity and positioning Lao cultural predominance as desirable and inevitable. Yet, Cincotta-Segi argues that this tension does not suggest a dichotomous relationship between the de jure intentions of the State and the de facto appropriation by the community. Instead, "differing and conflicting agendas in language policy are not only the result of disparities between the aims of different stakeholders, but of disparity in the aims of the State itself" (Cincotta-Segi 2009: 320). This important finding is a direct result of her relationship, and her interviews, with MoE officials and serves as a reminder that our assumptions about the goals or intentions of macro-language policy creators need to be evidenced with data collection within those contexts and among those participants. What is often presented in the LPP literature as some homogenous and intentional document is instead revealed in her study as a heterogeneous mix of ideologies about language, culture, and education.

The question then becomes: How is such heterogeneity interpreted and appropriated by educators? MoE officials assume that official Lao-dominated discourses will be reproduced by teachers, especially given the lack of materials and curricula in anything but Lao language; however, Cincotta-Segi (2009: 321) finds that: "This research has demonstrated for the first time in the Lao context that while teachers do reproduce the official discourses through particular classroom language practices, this reproduction is never total and in some cases is eclipsed by strong adaptations and contestations." Saisana, for example, was one of the participating teachers in the study who did seem to reproduce the dominance of Lao language and culture through her almost exclusive use of Lao in classroom interaction, but still allowed rampant use of Kmhmu by the students (which contradicts both the local and national language policy) and accepted the use of the mother tongue in the classroom and community as natural. In this way, her *policy as performance* contradicted official policy texts and discourses. Furthermore, another teacher (Ceng) only minimally used Lao in classroom interaction, which was conducted mostly in Kmhmu, even for Lao language lessons.

Cincotta-Segi's research reveals the importance of considering the multiple intentions and ideologies that engender policy text and discourse, as well as the multiple, unpredictable, and agentive forms of interpretation and appropriation unique to a particular context. The unique combination of a critical focus on the power of language policy as a mechanism of hegemony (through CDA) with an understanding of the power of language policy agents (through ethnography) is a balance needed in the field (see Johnson 2011a).

Article-Length Reports

3.5 Francis M. Hult

In his article, "Swedish television as a mechanism for language planning and policy" (Hult 2010b), Hult analyzes the role that television plays in the positioning of languages within the linguistic ecology of Sweden. Hult's work has been central in developing an ecological orientation to LPP (see 2.6), referred to as *the ecology of language policy* (Hornberger and Hult 2008; Hult 2010a). In this approach, language planning and policy processes are seen as existing within, and contributing to, social and linguistic ecosystems. The media play a crucial role within language ecologies by promoting some languages, ignoring others, and thus propagating ideologies and discourses about language.

Hult's research primarily focuses on Sweden (Hult 2003, 2004, 2005, 2010a, 2010b, 2012) and, here, he sets his sights on the programming of Sveriges Television (SVT), the public service television company of Sweden. He draws upon a unique mix of documents as data – Swedish laws and language policies, government bills, broadcast licenses, and public service reports from SVT – to reveal how the Swedish government explicitly incorporates SVT as an instrument for language planning. For example, in a government-issued broadcast license for SVT (entitled *sändningstillstånd*), Hult finds the declaration that "SVT has a special relationship for the Swedish language and its status in society" (cited in Hult 2010b: 163), thus cementing its role as an instrument of maintaining the status of Swedish. The broadcast license does consider minority languages: "SVT shall consider the interests of linguistic and ethnic minorities...The minority languages Sámi, Finnish, Meänkieli, and Romani Chib shall hold a prominent position" (cited in Hult 2010b: 164). While this statement does seem to reflect a positive attitude toward minority languages, Hult argues that they are still relegated to a marginal position with respect to Swedish and are "linked more narrowly to the interests of their speakers rather than framed more broadly as part and parcel of Swedish society and culture" (Hult 2010b: 164).

Because SVT must produce a public service report, in which programming details are published, Hult is able to determine exactly how much broadcasting time is devoted to the various languages that SVT purports to support. Of the four minority languages mentioned as receiving a "prominent position", an average of only 1.2% of the broadcast hours were devoted to these languages over the period 2001 through 2008 (with a notable 0.003% devoted to Meänkieli). Other minority languages get short shrift as well and Hult finds that the largest group of foreign-born individuals in Sweden, a group comprising people from Asia, Africa, Central and South America, represents 6.3% of all Swedes, yet receives only 1.2% of broadcast hours in their first language. On the other hand, while not mentioned specifically in the broadcast license, English-medium programming made up 13.6% of total broadcast hours, reflecting the strong position of English in Sweden. Hult argues that this is not surprising given the amount of programming available from English-medium countries, especially the U.S., yet the amount of English programming reflects a disproportionate amount of attention to English since only 0.5% of Swedes were English-dominant in 2008.

> **Quote 3.5 Discourse planning**
>
> While language status refers to the functional position of a certain language in relation to other languages within a particular social environment, discourse planning refers to the discursive construction of specific language regimes through, for example, the ways in which languages are represented in public discourse and language problems are defined.
>
> (Hult 2010b: 160–161, building on Lo Bianco 2005)

Hult argues that this hierarchy, with Swedish at the top, followed closely by English, and minority languages at the bottom, reflects a similar value hierarchy in Swedish society, with minority languages only minimally visible on the airwaves. In his analysis, Hult reveals the explicit involvement of SVT in status planning since it actively participates in the functional positioning of language, but he also shows how SVT's programming plays a role in discourse planning "by projecting through the television screen a way of understanding multilingualism that (re)produces the current linguistic order of Sweden" (Hult 2010b: 172). SVT reproduces discourses about multilingualism, and the relative value of minority languages, and thus engages in implicit discourse planning that impacts the Swedish ecology of language planning and policy.

3.6 Lin Pan

Lin Pan's research on Chinese foreign language education policies (FLEP) is timely, as many countries around the world increasingly adopt English language acquisition policies and programs, and theoretically pertinent to the field – as it presents a challenge to Phillipson's notion of linguistic imperialism (see 2.5). Pan's analysis focuses on how language ideologies (see Concept 4.5) concerning English manifest in FLEP which, in turn, position the teaching and acquisition of English as an ideologically neutral endeavor that is a benefit to both the Chinese state and Chinese citizens. Her analysis relies on critical scholarship – notably Bourdieu (1991) and Gramsci (1971) – both of whom emphasize the hidden or invisible power invested in ideologies, which hegemonically portray dominant ideas and social systems as natural and legitimate. Pan contends that language policies are a product of state ideologies and FLEP reflects the Chinese government's attitudes towards English.

Pan's analysis relies on policy documents produced by the Chinese government but also includes historical analysis of social movements and direct quotes from policy authors, which importantly demonstrate intertextual links between the written and spoken texts. For example, in the document entitled *English Curriculum Requirements at Compulsory Education Stage*, the importance of English is declared in the following manner:

> The informatization of social life and economic globalization have increased the importance of English. As one of the most important carriers of information, English has become the most widely used language in various sectors of human life (quoted in Pan 2011: 249).

Pan compares this to a quote from a Ministry of Education official who says, "As a result of [FLEP] informatization and globalization, learning and mastering a foreign language has become a basic requirement of all citizens of the twenty-first century" (Pan 2011: 249). While the Minister might simply be reflecting (and not generating) the ideas expressed in the language policy text above, Pan's analysis reveals intertextual links ("informatization", "globalization") between spoken and written language policy texts, both of which were engendered within the Ministry of Education.

Pan also draws connections between the increasing prevalence of English in Chinese language policy and its historical rise in Chinese society. In tracing the history of this language ideology (which she describes as establishing a "historicity of ideology"), Pan argues that the desire for economic development, modernization, and globalization gave rise to educational reforms which elevated the status of English and English language learning. In the document entitled *English Curriculum Requirements at Senior High Education Stage* (pp. 1–2), we find:

> English courses can help improve the nation's quality, help promote the country's opening up and international exchange and help improve the overall power of the nation. (quoted in Pan 2011: 252)

Pan argues that by promoting English language acquisition as indispensable for both individual and societal development, the state is practicing ideological hegemony, instantiated in FLEP, which portrays the powerful position of English in Chinese society as something natural and legitimate, as opposed to something that has been socially engineered (in part) through language policy. Access to English education is not equitable and those who attend schools in economically developed areas will be more likely to get a better education in English and, in turn, "will have better chances and opportunities than others to become central in national modernization" (Pan 2011: 259). Furthermore, as Pan argues (Quote 3.6), the notion that English necessarily facilitates social and economic success is a fallacy anyway.

Quote 3.6 English and ideological hegemony

[T]he assumption that English is a tool for getting ahead in social life and that teaching English is empty of ideological content is exactly an exemplification of ideological hegemony. And requiring individuals to learn English for education and jobs and for social development often helps to sustain existing power relationships. The belief that learning English will help people gain advantages is therefore at the centre of the ideology of Chinese FLEP. And the individuals, the product of power, accept English as a neutral tool and misrecognize the state's cultural governance as legitimate for their own benefit.

(Pan 2011: 253)

Some might read what is happening in China and FLEP as an example of the linguistic imperialism of English, through which "the 'Centre' (English speaking countries) imposes its own cultural, political, and economic power and values upon the 'Periphery'" (Pan 2011: 255). However, Pan argues that the spread of English in China is not a one-way process but is characterized by "two-way absorption", aided from within by the Chinese state's active embrace and promotion of English language acquisition through FLEP. Furthermore, Pan argues that FLEP, and English language education in particular, are portrayed as tools for spreading and cultivating *Chinese* patriotism and culture. Thus, Pan contends that the ideological hegemony of English comes both from without and within the Chinese state, whose governance is strengthened by the acquisition of English by its citizens.

3.7 Dafna Yitzhaki

Both Hebrew and Arabic are official languages in Israel. Referred to as the Israel Arab minority or (in Yitzhakis's terms) Arab Palestinian citizens, this group represents one-fifth of the population of Israel, and they predominantly speak Palestinian Arabic Vernacular as their first language. Still, while some laws enforce the use of Arabic in official contexts – e.g. media, ballot slips, and security instructions – other laws and policies give clear precedence to Hebrew; for example, the Citizenship Law of 1952 states that "a certain knowledge of the Hebrew language" is necessary for Israeli citizenship (cited in Yitzhaki 2010: 337). Therefore, as Yitzhaki argues, the position of Arabic in Israel is, in reality, marginal and its equal status according to Israeli law is only theoretical (see also the discussion in Spolsky and Shohamy 1999). There have been attempts to elevate the status of Arabic, notably in Hebrew/Arabic bilingual schools, but these attempts have faced major challenges. For example, based on ethnographic research in a bilingual school, Bekerman (2005) finds that despite local support and institutional legitimation (from the Israeli Center for Bilingual Education), the school was largely unable to overcome the macro-level segregationist and monolingual policies and could not sustain symmetry between Arabic and Hebrew.

In this paper, Yitzhaki (2010) examines the attitudes toward Arabic and Arabic language policy in Israel, asking the following questions:

1. What are the main notions that best characterize the desired role of Arabic in Israel?
2. Which policies are viewed as legitimate and which are delegitimized and on what grounds?

To answer these questions, she conducted a "macrolevel empirical study" of the attitudes towards the public role of Arabic held by public figures and members of the linguistic groups. She analyzed data collected in four focus groups consisting of Arabic- and Hebrew-speaking university and college students, in which Yitzhaki focused on the use of Arabic in government services, schools, the Israeli parliament, and on public television. All sessions were digitally recorded and fully transcribed. In her analysis of the data, Yitzhaki incorporates grounded theory (Glaser 1978), which she describes as "an analysis style in which a limited number of theoretical principles ('core categories') evolve out of a longer list of concepts during the systematic process of data assessment" (Yitzhaki 2010: 340). She coded the data along "lines of argumentation" that characterized participants' positions and attitudes.

Two constructs were eventually decided upon, which organize the analysis – *indigenousness* and *functionality* – which were continually referenced when the participants made their arguments for or against pro-Arabic language policies. Prior to the establishment of the state in 1948, Arab Palestinian citizens were already a native population in what would become known as modern-day Israel. Because of this, there is a growing tendency to characterize this group as an *indigenous* or homeland minority, especially when comparing Arab Palestinians to 'newer' and non-indigenous immigrants, like Russians. Some participants in the focus groups, both Jews and Arabs, argued that Arabic should receive preferential treatment in Israeli language policy because the Arabic speakers had been in Israel longer, and newer immigrants should be expected to acquire Hebrew, especially considering that many of these immigrants are Jewish. On the other hand, some of the Jewish participants argued that because of the longstanding presence in Israel, Arabs had a distinct advantage in learning Hebrew and, therefore, immigrant languages are the ones that need support. Finally, some of the Jewish participants argued that distinguishing between different types of immigrants is unimportant since all need to acquire Hebrew, the majority language. For example, one participant said:

> In my opinion it doesn't matter what kind of minority you are, there is a majority language, so deal with it. The state cannot adapt itself to a thousand little languages that have emerged. (Yitzhaki 2010: 344)

In analyzing how *functionality* is referenced by her participants, Yitzhaki makes a distinction between functional and symbolic justifications for language policies (Quote 3.7), the former being directed towards concrete benefits like having access to information in one's language, and the latter being focused on non-concrete benefits like fostering solidarity with a particular ethnic group or a nation as a whole.

Quote 3.7 Functional vs. symbolic justifications for language policies

Functional justifications for language policies are directed toward the functional interests of a linguistic group. That is, they are concerned with concrete and immediate benefits, such as having access to

> information, ensuring that language is not an obstacle to fulfilling everyday-life tasks, or that language does not create a threat to one's personal safety...*Symbolic interests* are concerned with non-concrete benefits. That is, the use of a language is perceived as a way to achieve goals with symbolic and identity elements. This definition is two-fold: 1. The symbolic nature of language policies may strengthen one's feeling of belonging to a distinct ethnic group...they concern one's 'core marker' of cultural identity. 2. 'Symbolic' and 'identity' elements also involve one's ability to identify with and feel part of the general societal framework to which one belongs ('the state').
>
> (italics mine, Yitzhaki 2010: 347–348)

Most of the participants agreed with the functional argument – that access to linguistic services in Arabic was justified in theory – but for many of the Jewish participants such arguments were irrelevant because it was perceived that Arabs speak Hebrew quite well and they can still get Arabic-language information from outside sources (for example, news shows on public television). Regardless of their ability to use Hebrew, both Jews and Arabs referred to symbolic justifications for pro-Arabic language policies, because Arabic is an essential part of Arab Israeli identity *and* such policies are representative of how integral the Arab population is in Israeli society. In this way, some argued that the symbolic argument outweighed the functional argument, as exemplified in the following quote from a Jewish participant:

> It is more a matter of Arabs' rights to have their share in the dominant culture, the Israeli culture. The practical issue of having access to information is not really relevant here. (Yitzhaki 2010: 349)

However, other Jewish participants rejected the notion that language policies should be developed for symbolic reasons, because such policies are a financial burden to the state.

Finally, there was disagreement about the use of language in the Knesset (Israeli legislature). While some Arabs felt that use of Arabic in the Knesset would symbolize the legitimacy of the Arabs' existence as a meaningful political body, some Jews felt that Hebrew should remain the (only) lingua franca because the Knesset represents the state, and the state is Hebrew-dominant. Yitzhaki argues that, "When the minority's symbolic interests clash with those of the majority, the latter take precedence...[T]he minority's right to function properly without their language being an obstacle is not a completely stable right that is valid in all contexts and under all circumstances [like the Knesset]" (Yitzhaki 2010: 352).

In summary, Yitzhaki argues that most majority group members rejected the indigenous justification for Arabic being granted equal status to Hebrew and instead preferred the dominance of Hebrew. As well, while this indigenous argument has entered the Israeli political discourse, most of the Arabic speakers in Yitzhaki's study use it sparingly and typically only when arguing that Arabic should receive preference over newer immigrant languages, like Russian. Furthermore, most majority group members accept the functional justification for pro-Arabic language policies rather than the symbolic justification and most participants see little value in recognizing and fostering an Arab identity through policy. However, even the functional justifications are questioned by Jewish participants, since Arabs are viewed as having a good command of Hebrew and easy access to Arabic-language media. Within all of the focus groups, there was little evidence that multilingualism is viewed as a resource or that mother tongues are viewed as rights.

Yitzhaki ends with two proposals for moving the policy discourse forward: (1) The assertion that Arabs are proficient in Hebrew needs to be challenged because it is not always true. Some Arabs (younger, urban) have more access to Hebrew than others and proficiency varies; and (2) While official policy seeks to normalize the presence of Arabic in Israeli society, it is still viewed as marginal by Arabs and Jews. Therefore, the argument that symbolic goals, and not just functional goals, for language policy are justifiable needs to be further developed and promoted.

3.8 Shannon Fitzsimmons-Doolan

The notion that language policies are influenced by language ideologies or, in even stronger terms, language policies are an instantiation of language ideologies, is a prominent sentiment within the field. Similarly, some argue that language policies are rarely only about language and are motivated by the desire to control immigrant groups or immigration. In other words, the enactment of monolingual language policies is influenced by, or a reflection of, negative attitudes towards immigration, immigrants, and their languages. In her review of this argument, Fitzsimmons-Doolan (2009) distinguishes between two competing narratives about U.S. language policy. *Pluralists* not only favor multilingual language policy but tend to characterize monolingual language policies as being a reflection of negative attitudes towards immigrants (e.g. Schmidt Sr. 2002). Some further argue that monolingual language policies are not just a reflection of anti-immigrant ideology but a means for controlling immigrant groups and their languages (e.g. Shohamy 2006). *Assimilationists*, on the other hand, view monolingualism and monolingual language policy as helping to create national unity and prevent the fracturing that would result from multilingualism. As Fitzsimmons-Doolan (2009) points out, both assimilationists and pluralists link language policy to immigration; yet, she argues, little empirical research has been done to test this link.

For this study, Fitzsimmons-Doolan (2009) used corpus linguistics to examine whether there is overlap in public discourse about language policy and public discourse about immigration, as reflected in newspaper articles (see also Fitzsimmons-Doolan 2013). Corpus-based research uses computer software (in this case Wordsmith Tools) to analyze large bodies of naturally occurring texts. Common techniques of analysis include *concordancing* – the extraction of all examples of a word or words – and *collocating* – the examination of the word(s) that tend to co-occur with other word(s). For this study, Fitzsimmons-Doolan used keyword analysis, which identifies the words in a text that indicate what it is about or, as she describes it, the *aboutness* of a corpus. Keywords, as she argues (2009: 383), are emblematic of the corpus and "should reveal what interlocutors are talking about and ideological beliefs underlying the discourse." Fitzsimmons-Doolan (2009: 382) identifies the advantages of corpus-based techniques, including:

1. the speed of analysis which enables researchers to examine far larger bodies of text than they could by hand;
2. the accuracy and consistency of analysis, in that issues associated with human raters of text such as inter- and intra-reliability are moot; and
3. the depth of analysis such as the ability to apply additional and specialized analysis such as part of speech taggers to the corpus.

The U.S. state of Arizona, and the newspaper discourse therein, is ripe for such a study because the public debate about immigration and language policy is very robust. A series of English-focused language policies have been passed in Arizona including the (2000) Proposition 203, which restricted access to bilingual education and promoted English as the medium of instruction for ELLs; and the (2006)

Proposition 103, which made English the official language of the state. As well, Arizona is often at the forefront of national debates about immigration and immigration policy and these debates are often acrimonious. Because one might reasonably assume that these two policy movements – anti-immigration and anti-multilingualism – are related, Fitzsimmons-Doolan (2009) analyzed whether there is overlap in keywords in a corpus that included newspaper articles on Official English and educational language policies and another that included newspaper articles on immigration. She chose newspapers in both Tucson and Phoenix because, as she characterizes them, the former is a traditionally politically liberal city while the latter is much more conservative. This created four corpora, representing newspaper articles about language policy and immigration in the two cities: (1) Tucson language policies, (2) Tucson immigration, (3) Phoenix language policies, and (4) Phoenix immigration. A fifth corpus was collected from the *San Jose Journal* for comparing the keywords found because "a word identified as a keyword in the topic-based corpus [i.e. the corpus of interest] can be said to play a special role in that corpus because it is significantly more frequent in the topic-based corpus than in the reference corpus" (Fitzsimmons-Doolan 2009: 387).

Results revealed that, of the top 20 keywords in each of the corpora, only six words (6%) overlapped and none of those words were especially related to policy – *Tucson, Arizona, to, law/s, Napolitano*, and *federal*. This finding challenges the argument that there is a link in public discourse about language policy and public discourse about immigration, as reflected in newspapers. Fitzsimmons-Doolan (2009) argues that there is little evidence to suggest that these corpora share *aboutness*. She further examined collocations of the keywords, finding that across all of the corpora the word *Spanish* was often preceded by a quantifier (like *more, no*, and *only*) and limiting verbs (like *banning, prohibit*, and *refrain*) while *English* collocated with *language*. While neither *immigrants* nor *immigration* were keywords in the corpora, when they did occur (which was rarely), they collocated with *illegal*. Thus, while she did not find shared aboutness in the immigration and language policy corpora, a look at the collocations of non-keywords did reveal biases against Spanish, the naturalization of English as a/the *language*, and negative sentiments about immigrants and immigration.

Fitzsimmons-Doolan finds that public discourse in newspaper articles about immigration does not overlap, or does not share aboutness, with public discourse in newspaper articles about language policy. However, the limitations of this work (as Fitzsimmons-Doolan herself notes) is that this is all *public* discourse in *newspapers* and doesn't consider interaction that takes place in communities and classrooms or actual policies concerning language and immigration. In other words, while corpus linguistics can compare the bodies of texts, and reveal connections and disconnects between the corpora, Fitzsimmons-Doolan (2009) doesn't show that there is no connection between language policies and immigration policy; only that there is no connection between the two *in newspaper articles*. It still could be the case that circulating ideologies about immigration influence the creation of language policy and circulating ideologies about language influence the creation of immigration policy. Still, Fitzsimmons-Doolan's (2009) findings are intriguing, especially since media discourse (see section 5.4) is often considered to play an important role in social change and political policy. Further, her work raises important questions about making assumptions concerning connections between immigration, ideology, and language policy without empirical data that provide evidence for those connections.

3.9 Discussion

This small group of studies does not cover the depth and breadth of the field but it does give a sense of the kind of variety that exists in LPP research, with very diverse methods, theories, and contexts being represented. Looking at commonalities across the studies, we see that all of the longitudinal studies rely on ethnographic data collection to some extent (even if Bonacina's work is only "partial" ethnography) which, as Martin-Jones argues (2011), allows the researcher to examine how macro-level language policies interact with local educational practices and the making and re-making of local language policy. In a discussion of the ethnography of language policy (section 5.5) Hornberger and Johnson (2011) further argue that ethnography of language policy facilitates examination of the multiple layers of policy creation, interpretation, and appropriation and balances a critical focus on the power of policies with an ethnographic focus on the agency of individuals to manipulate policy in creative and unpredictable ways. The tension in the field between structure and agency and between critical conceptualizations of the power of policy and ethnographic foci on language policy agency is captured in many of these studies, especially by Cincotta-Segi, who combines a critical analysis of Lao-ization with an ethnographic understanding of how teachers respond to language policies which, as she argues, cannot be easily predicted based on the language of outside language policies.

Most of these studies address the theme of this book – making connections between policy and practice – and a major challenge for the field: How do we make connections between macro-level language policy texts and discourses and the multiple layers of activity – creation, interpretation, appropriation – that ultimately lead to the instantiation (or lack thereof) of policy into practice? As well, how do micro-level language policy discourses, texts, and practices appropriate, reject, alter, manipulate, and/or ignore the macro-level policy texts and discourses? This 'perennial challenge' (Hult 2010a) in the field is articulated by Ricento (2000a: 208) in this way: "Why do individuals opt to use (or cease to use) particular languages and varieties for specified functions in different domains, and how do those choices influence and how are they influenced by institutional language policy decision-making (local to national and supranational)?" In some of the cases (Bonacina, Cincotta-Segi) the decisions by the individuals (in this case, teachers) regarding language use are *not* influenced by national language policies, at least not solely. This represents a general finding in the field that even within restrictively monolingual policy contexts, educators make creative and agentive choices, which may or may not reflect macro-level policy texts and discourses and may in fact explicitly *reject* them (see 4.1.1). In other cases (Chimbutane, Yitzhaki), the beliefs and practices of individuals fall in line with dominant (policy) discourses about language and, notably, align with imperialistic and marginalizing notions of what counts as a "good" or "useful" language in a society or school.

But this leads to another question: Why? Why do some individuals exercise agency while others do not? In which contexts is this more likely to occur? And, how can we as researchers and educators interact with the policy process to promote an agenda of social justice, which fights for the rights of language minorities and views multilingualism as a resource for everyone? (An answer to this question will be attempted in Chapter 6.) Further, while many of these studies make policy–practice connections, the ways in which they do it – the particular methods – are not always clearly spelled out. This speaks to another major challenge going forward: What research methods are most effective for establishing connections between macro- and micro-level policy activity? How do we know when there is a connection and what kind of data are necessary to justify that there is, in fact, a connection? (An answer to this question will be attempted in Chapter 5.)

The notion that language policies have an important relationship with language ideologies is a well-established and accepted tenet in the field. However, this brief review of LPP studies reveals that we need to be clearer about the nature of that relationship; we need substantive methods for drawing connections between particular language ideologies and particular language policies, especially when research like Fitzsimmons-Doolan's (2009) suggests that we cannot make *a priori* assumptions about relationships between ideology, immigration, and policy. My criticism of establishing cause-effect, linear relationships between language ideologies inherent in the belief systems of members of the state or other macro-level policy creators and the "ideas" in a language policy document is laid out in sections 4.5.1 and 4.5.2. In summary, my contention is that language policy documents are rarely the result of homogenous ideological orientations which are intentionally inserted into policy language. Furthermore, claims about the intentions behind a policy require an insider understanding of the ideologies and intentions of the policy authors, something that is not usually provided. Instead, these (hidden) ideologies, (retrievable) intentions, and their direct relationship to the "ideas" expressed in language policy language, are uncovered by the analyst through a close reading of language policy documents. The analyst's interpretations of the texts are presented as the sole possible reading, obfuscating the potentially multiple intentions that made the text and multiple perspectives that will go into interpreting the text.

Finally, this brief review of some exemplary case studies reveals the variety of definitions that circulate and the expanding notion of what "language policy" is. Building upon Spolsky (2004), Bonacina equates language practices and language policy – they are one and the same and need not be seen as distinct – but she also equates this practiced language policy with Hymes' (1972b) notion of interactional norms. This presents some conceptual challenges. First, what is the advantage of introducing a new name for an already existing concept (i.e. interactional norms)? What is the advantage in calling these "policies" when we already call them "interactional norms"?

Second, new interactional norms may emerge within language practices but others are still outside of language practices in the sense that they precede and guide a variety of practices within and across multiple sociolinguistic contexts; in other words, they are not necessarily hyper-local. Furthermore, while it's clear that language practices can reflect, illuminate, instantiate, appropriate, and create new language policies, is every language practice, in and of itself, a policy? By including "practices" or "interactional norms" within our definition of language policy, what conceptual, theoretical, or methodological advantage does this afford us in language policy research? If all language practices, or interactional norms, are language policies, can every study of language practices or sociolinguistic norms now be re-positioned as a study of language policy? Opening the discursive boundaries about what is considered "language policy" is intriguing, exciting, and should provide for healthy debate going forward. While these new definitions may well represent the "new wave" of LPP research (Hult 2012: 235) or, as McCarty, Collins, and Hopson (2011: 338) call them, "New Language Policy Studies", there are still some conceptual and logical challenges that need to be sorted out. Also, it should be noted that a similar argument can be found in 'older' research like Schiffman (1996) and Ricento and Hornberger (1996: 417): "We suggest that, because human society is constituted of, by, and through language, all acts and actions mediated by language are opportunities for the implicit (or explicit) expression of language policies."

4 Findings

Chapter outline

4.1 Appropriation vs. implementation
4.2 Language policies as instruments of power
4.3 Language policies as instruments of empowerment
4.4 The multiple layers of policy text, discourse, and practice
4.5 The nature of language policy text and discourse
4.6 Conclusion

The previous chapter reviewed eight studies that incorporate innovative methods and theories, offer intriguing findings, and suggest new directions for the field. This chapter builds on the findings from those studies, and many others, to proffer a list of twelve general findings that have been evidenced by multiple studies. While the field of language policy is theoretically rich, empirical data collection on language policy creation, interpretation, appropriation, and instantiation has, historically, not matched the theoretical and conceptual robustness. In part, this is a natural result of the inchoate nature of the field. Recently, however, there have been an increasing number of micro-level studies that examine the impact of macro-level language policy texts and discourses on schools and communities, the development of local language policies and practices, and the interaction between the two. Hult (2012: 235) characterizes this as the "new wave" of LPP research, which "aims not at comprehensive sociological inquiry but at representing specific ways in which language policies are socially and discursively situated, thereby documenting instances of how LPP takes shape in texts and practice." This chapter synthesizes the findings from this line of research (as well as the old wave) and presents twelve findings. It will attempt to address the following questions:

- How are language policies created, interpreted, appropriated, and instantiated around the world?
- What impact do language policies have in schools and communities?
- How can language policies open as well as close spaces for multilingual education and language diversity in schools, workplaces, and other organizations?
- What is the nature of language policy text and discourse?
- How do language policies structure educational and economic opportunity and what role do language policy agents play in this process?

4.1 Appropriation vs. implementation

Traditional policy research looks at implementation from a technocratic perspective, conceptualizing policy as a top-down process and foregrounding the intentions of policymakers. However, this approach does not tell us much about bottom-up policy formation, it assumes the intentions of the policymakers are knowable, and renders powerless those who are meant to put the policy into action since they are portrayed simply as "implementers" of a policy over which they have no control. Responding to technocratic approaches that strip away agency, Levinson and Sutton (2001) introduced the term *appropriation* to emphasize the important role that multiple actors across multiple contexts play in the policy process.

Quote 4.1 Appropriation vs. implementation

We believe the now conventional distinction between policy formation and implementation as distinct phases of a policy 'process' implicitly ratifies a top-down perspective, unnecessarily divides what is in fact a recursive dynamic, and inappropriately widens the gulf between everyday practice and government action...[W]e prefer to analyze policy in terms of how people appropriate its meanings. Appropriation, of course, highlights the way creative agents 'take in' elements of policy, thereby incorporating these discursive and institutional resources into their own schemes of interest, motivation, and action. Appropriation is a kind of taking of policy and making it one's own.

(Levinson and Sutton 2001: 2–3; see also Levinson, Sutton, and Winstead 2009)

While Levinson and Sutton's theory of policy has been applied by LPP scholars, their focus is not on language policy, but general educational policy. A similar argument made by Ricento and Hornberger (1996) applies more directly to *language* policy. In what has become a very influential article in a *TESOL Quarterly* special issue on language planning and policy, they introduced the metaphor of an onion to evoke the multiple layers through which language policy develops and argued that LPP research has not successfully accounted for activity in all layers. They emphasize the language policy power of the teacher, which is exercised through pedagogical decisions – for example at one moment a teacher may choose to incorporate a student's L1, thus creating a space in which L1s are used as resources (Bonacina, section 3.3 in this volume; Skilton-Sylvester 2003); conversely, the teacher may choose not to, thus closing potential spaces. Teachers are, therefore, not just policy implementers but policy *makers* (see Menken and García 2010; Cincotta-Segi, section 3.4 in this volume). Expanding upon this onion concept a decade later, Hornberger and Johnson (2007) argue that the choices of educators may well be constrained by language policies, which tend to set boundaries on what is allowed and/or what is considered "normal", but the line of power does not flow linearly from the pen of the policy's signer to the choices of the teacher. The negotiation at each institutional level creates the opportunity for reinterpretations and policy manipulation. Local educators are not helplessly caught in the ebb and flow of shifting ideologies in language policies – they help develop, maintain, and change that flow.

Quote 4.2 Language policy "layers"

We suggest that LPP is a multilayered construct, wherein essential LPP components – agents, levels, and processes of LPP – permeate and interact with each other in multiple and complex ways as they enact various types, approaches, and goals of LPP...We suggest that, because human society is constituted of, by, and through language, all acts and actions mediated by language are opportunities for the implicit (or explicit) expression of language policies...

We place the classroom practitioner at the heart of language policy (at the center of the onion). In the [English language teaching] literature, the practitioner is often an afterthought who implements what "experts" in the government, board of education, or central school administration have already decided. The practitioner often

> needs to be "educated," "studied," "cajoled," "tolerated," even "replaced" by better prepared (even more pliant) teachers. In contrast, we claim that educational and social change and institutional transformation, especially in decentralized societies, often begin with the grass roots.
>
> (Ricento and Hornberger 1996: 419–420, 417)

4.1.1 Finding #1: Language policy agents have power

What evidence do we have for this assertion? Critical scholarship has shown that educational institutions can facilitate the marginalization of minority languages and their users through implementation of hegemonic language policy (Tollefson 2013a). Shohamy argues that top-down language policies are mechanisms that implement the hegemonic intentions of those in authority, a process that is facilitated by educators (Quote 4.3). However, other research focuses on how educators *resist* top-down language policy or interpret and appropriate it in unexpected and creative ways. For example, in ethnographic portraits of classrooms in the U.S. state of California, post-Proposition 227 (an anti-bilingual education law), the power of teachers is evident. Baltodano (2004) finds that the formerly pro-bilingual education parents in her study began to internalize the English-only ideology in Proposition 227, thus succumbing to its hegemonic influence. Valdez (2001) and Stritikus (2002), on the other hand, discuss the agentive role that teachers played in implementation, sometimes sculpting the English-only focus of Proposition 227 to meet the needs of their classrooms. Stritikus (2002: 74) argues that teachers are not simply "conductors" of policy implementation; the teachers in his study shaped how Proposition 227 was experienced: "The complete experience of Proposition 227 implementation was created through dynamic interactions between what the district and schools decided about Proposition 227 and the teachers' actions vis-à-vis those decisions." Even within the same English-only school, the "individual qualities of the teachers (and their ideological orientations toward Proposition 227) influenced how they dealt with their students' L1." This research reveals that, even within an explicitly anti-bilingual education policy, like Proposition 227, teachers still have agency in language policy interpretation and appropriation.

Menken and García (2010) include a number of case studies illuminating the power of educators as policymakers in very diverse contexts (France, Peru, South Africa, China, Lebanon, Israel, Ethiopia, Chile, and the U.S.). For example, since 1957 India has had as its national educational language policy the "three-language formula," which promotes use of a mother tongue, Hindi, and/or English in all schools. Yet, as Mohanty, Panda and Pal (2010) report, the implementation of this policy at the local level, filtered as it is through the states, has been quite heterogeneous and English has ascended up this tripartite linguistic hierarchy to a position of privilege across India, replacing both minority languages *and* Hindi. Still, even within official English-medium schools, teachers actively incorporate the students' mother tongues into their educational practices (see Chimbutane 2011, discussed in 3.2; Bonacina 2010, discussed in 3.3) and because classroom interaction often incorporates the (multiple) students' languages, not only are the teachers making policy, but the students are too.

Quote 4.3 Are teachers simply cogs in the language policy wheel?

Teachers are not uncritical bystanders passively acquiescent of the state practice; in their own ways, they resist and contest the state policy or rather, in the Indian context, its absence and injustice by default. It is quite clear that the agency of the teachers in the classrooms makes them the final arbiter of the language education policy and its implementation.

(Mohanty *et al.* 2010: 228)

The language policy literature has tended to dichotomize policy "creation" and "implementation", ignoring the agentive role that "implementers" play in policy appropriation. Educator interpretation of macro-policy is, I would argue, an act of creation since it has influence over what a policy does. We should certainly recognize the ability of language policies to define the limits of what is educationally normal and/or possible – and the ability of schools and teachers to internalize hegemonic ideologies and restrict the educational and social possibilities of students – and language policy research should investigate this (see Ball's policy as discourse perspective, Concept 4.2). Still, even within ostensibly restrictive language policies, local educators and language planners can take advantage of *implementational spaces* in macro-level language policy and *ideological spaces* (see Concept 4.3) in schools and communities, both of which can open educational and social possibilities for language learners and challenge disempowering educational discourses and language ideologies. Language policy research should investigate this as well.

4.1.2 Finding #2: Language policy power is differentially allocated among *arbiters* and *implementers*

Both Mohanty *et al.* (2010) and Menken (2008) use the term *arbiter* to characterize the power of teachers as the ultimate decision-makers in how a policy is implemented. E. Johnson (2012) and D.C. Johnson (2013a) expand on this notion and describe all individuals with potentially powerful influence on the language policy process as *language policy arbiters* (Concept 4.1). While LPP is a multi-layered process, and teachers may be the ultimate arbiters in classroom implementation of policy, language policy power is differentially allocated across, and within, institutions, contexts, and layers of language policy activity. I argue that language policy power is determined by who gets positioned as an arbiter and who gets positioned as a mere implementer of policy, and this positioning can emerge across a series of speech events and situations in a community of educators who oversee educational language policy and practice in a U.S. school district. I incorporate Goffman's (1979) concept of *footing*, which refers to the participants' alignment or positions in an interaction. The relative footing of participants in an interaction characterizes the *participation framework* (Concept 6.2) which is engendered by the *participation status* of each of the participants. I argue that non-traditional participation frameworks – in which teachers and administrators engage in egalitarian decision-making and language policy action-research projects (see Chapter 6) – can alter traditional hierarchical decision-making structures and lead to the positioning of teachers as language policy arbiters, not just in policy implementation and classroom teaching, but in *creation* of bottom-up policy and *interpretation* and *appropriation* of top-down policy. On the other hand, when school district administrators, who are typically invested with more language policy power, rely on hierarchical participation frameworks that position teachers as lacking the expertise to make language policy decisions, teacher agency is stripped (yet resistance becomes more probable).

Concept 4.1 Language policy arbiter

A *language policy arbiter* wields a disproportionate amount of power in how a policy gets created, interpreted, appropriated, or instantiated relative to other individuals in the same context. Their position within an institution or community is not predictable and they may exist throughout the various language policy layers and levels of institutional authority. They act as a filter through which a policy must pass. The language policy agents rely on policy texts (either restrictive or promotive) and policy discourses (which hegemonically sculpt what is perceived as normal, acceptable, or doable).

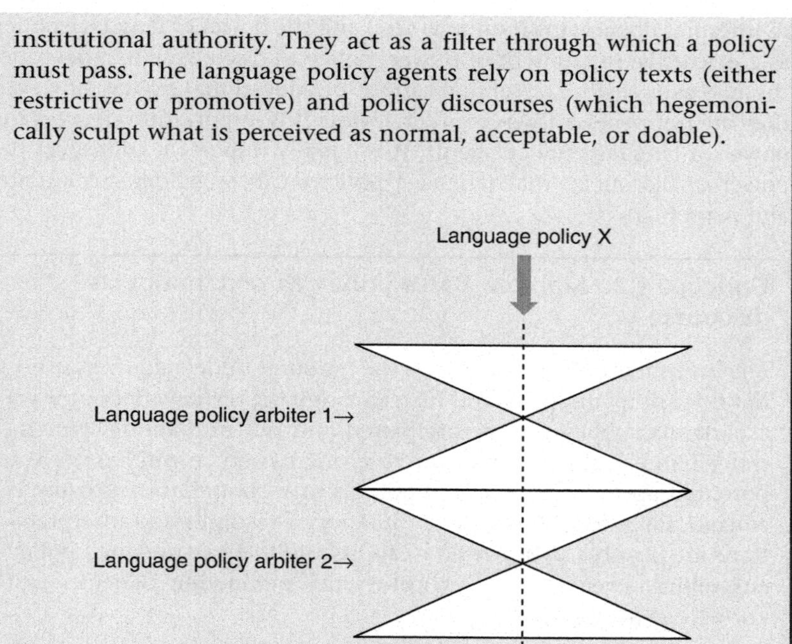

4.2 Language policies as instruments of power

Despite the agency of policy appropriators, the power of language policies to set discursive boundaries on what is considered educationally normal or feasible cannot be ignored. Indeed, current work on language policy can be characterized by a tension between structure and agency; between critical theoretical work that focuses on the power invested in language policy to disenfranchise linguistic minorities (e.g. Tollefson 2013a; Yitzhaki, in section 3.7) and ethnographic and action-oriented research that emphasizes the powerful role that educators play in language policy processes (e.g. Menken and García 2010; Cincotta-Segi, in section 3.4). Capturing this tension, Ball (1993) offers two conceptualizations of policy – policy as *text* and policy as *discourse* – which articulate both the power of language policy agents to creatively interpret and re-interpret documents (policy as text) and the power of language policy as a discursive instrument of power (policy as discourse). Ball describes the two as *opposing* conceptualizations of educational policy; however, they are not necessarily in conflict – while it is important to respect the power of language policy agents, it is equally important to respect the power of discourses that language policies can engender, instantiate, and perpetuate.

Concept 4.2 Stephen Ball's policy as text/policy as discourse

A *policy as text* orientation rejects the quest for understanding authorial intentions in policy and instead emphasizes the variety of ways a particular policy text is interpreted and put into action. On the other hand, Ball's *policy as discourse* orientation re-emphasizes the potential power of educational policies to set boundaries on what is educationally feasible. While a plurality of readings and interpretations are possible, "[W]e need to appreciate the way in which policy ensembles...exercise power through the production of truth and knowledge as discourses."

(Ball 1993: 23)

4.2.1 Finding #3: Governing bodies use language policies for control

In Chapter 1, the impact of colonial language policies on Indigenous languages and Indigenous peoples was discussed, revealing that national language policies can and do restrict particular languages and marginalize their users within, and outside of, educational contexts (see also Chimbutane 2011, discussed in section 3.2). Tollefson (2002c) analyzes another example, recounting how Yugoslav language policy was used for political purposes by the Serbian Nationalists, led by Slobodan Milošević. Before the Yugoslav wars, which splintered the country into separate nations (Slovenia, Croatia, Kosovo, Montenegro, Federation of Bosnia and Herzegovina, Serbia, Macedonia, and the Republic of Srpska), the former Yugoslavia enacted policies between 1953 and 1980 that were increasingly accommodating to the linguistic diversity in the country. National language policy helped ensure language use and maintenance for a wide range of languages, including Serbian, Croatian, Macedonian, Slovene, Hungarian, and Albanian. However, during the 1980's and under the leadership of Milošević, the Serbian Nationalist movement sought to centralize Serbian control over all political policy – including language policy and education – and foreground Serbian language, literature, and history. Within this sociopolitical context, criticism and dissent became illegal and in 1988 four Slovene journalists were accused of treason for publishing articles about military corruption. While the journalists were all Slovene speakers and their rights to be tried in their own language were guaranteed under the constitution, the trial was instead conducted solely in Serbo-Croatian. As Tollefson (2002c) notes, this trial marked the end of a pluralistic Yugoslav language policy and signaled the increasing ostracism of non-Serbian languages and non-Serbs, and the eventual civil war.

4.3 Language policies as instruments of empowerment

Critical approaches foreground the power of macro-level language policies to marginalize minority languages and minority languages users while ethnographic and discourse-analytic research in schools and communities focuses on the communicative norms, multilingual classroom practices, and either the agency (or lack thereof) of individuals to resist marginalizing macro-level policy texts and discourses. However, a third focus is also possible: the power of both macro-level and micro-level language policies to *promote* and *protect* minority and Indigenous languages. From the 1954 UNESCO declaration in support of mother-tongue education to the 1994 official language policy of Ethiopia, which allows every language in the country to be a medium of instruction, language policies can be powerful champions of linguistic diversity.

4.3.1 Finding #4: National multilingual language policies *can* and *do* open spaces for multilingual education and minority languages

Hornberger has long argued (and shown) that national language policies that value multilingualism as a resource can create political openings for bilingual education which, in turn, can promote Indigenous and minority language education and use (Hornberger 2006a, 2009). She has documented the creation, interpretation, and appropriation of two such policies in South America: The Puno bilingual education project (PEEB) in Peru and Bolivia's National Education Reform of 1994, both of which incorporate Indigenous languages and Indigenous language education into official policy text and discourse. On the other side of the globe, the Māori Language Act of 1987 in New Zealand declared Māori as one of New Zealand's official languages and has supported the Māori-medium education movement (see May and Hill 2005). These national multilingual language policies open what Hornberger (2002) refers to as *ideological space* (see Concept 4.3) for multilingual education, which educators can use to create *implementational space* for bilingual educational programs that incorporate minority and Indigenous languages as resources.

Concept 4.3 Implementational and ideological spaces in language policy

Hornberger (2002) introduced the *implementational and ideological space* concepts in an article published in the first issue of *Language Policy*. Implementational and ideological spaces can be formed by multilingual language policies and/or arise when localized educational practices and practitioners take advantage of spaces in policy to enact multilingual education. Multilingual language policies that promote multilingualism as a resource, like Bolivia's National Education Reform of 1994, open *ideological space* for multilingualism and bilingual education but this space is, in a sense, only a potential space, because language educators and language users must take advantage of this space by implementing multilingual educational practices. In other words, these opened ideological spaces "carve out" *implementational spaces* at classroom and community levels which language educators and users, in turn, must "fill up" with multilingual educational practices. Such ideological spaces need the support of local educators and language users but they can also be strengthened by other language policies. For example, the 1974 Lau v. Nichols Supreme Court decision (see section 5.3.1) opened ideological space for bilingual education in the United States but it took the Lau Remedies and the Bilingual Education Act of 1968 to create the *implementational space* for bilingual education. Other language policies, like the U.S. No Child Left Behind Act (NCLB) of 2002, *close* ideological space for multilingualism but, just as educators must fill up the implementational spaces created by multilingual language policies, educators can also take advantage of local implementational spaces for incorporating minority languages as resources even though the ideological space created by the macro-level language policy is restrictively monolingual (for an example, see Johnson 2010a). In turn, these local implementational spaces carved out for multilingual educational practices can "serve as wedges to pry open ideological ones" (Hornberger 2005b: 606).

4.3.2 Finding #5: Local multilingual language policies *can* and *do* open spaces for multilingual education and minority languages

By local language policy, I do not mean local linguistic culture (see Quote 1.2) or de facto language practices (see Concept 1.2) that emerge with or without official policy support, both of which can also open spaces for multilingualism. Instead, we are here talking about explicit and official policies that are developed *by* local communities *for* local communities. For example, working alongside school district teachers, principals, and administrators, Rebecca Freeman's (1998, 2000; see also section 6.3.2) ethnographic and action-oriented research on bilingual education and language policy in Philadelphia and Washington D.C. has revealed how local language planning and policy can help sustain multilingual education in schools. Her ongoing thesis is that schools are discursively constructed and, although schools may be sites that reify hegemonic and marginalizing discourses and thus lead to social reproduction, *bilingual* schools can also be sites in which dominant discourses are resisted, local alternative discourses are created, and the seeds of social change are developed. Based on their ethnographic research, Johnson and Freeman (2010) argue that educators who are committed to fostering linguistic diversity and bilingual education can create local spaces for preserving the linguistic diversity within a school district and these efforts can be supported by district-wide language policy. They propose that teams of educators and researchers who understand the local context, federal and state policy, and the body of language education research, can develop educational language policy and programs that promote multilingualism; and, this can even be done within the confines of a national language policy that does *not* actively support multilingualism or bilingual education.

4.4 The multiple layers of policy text, discourse, and practice

Implicit in the discussion in this chapter thus far is the idea that there are macro-level or top-down language policies on the one hand, and micro-level or bottom-up (or grassroots or local) language policies on the other (see Concept 6.6). Conceptualizations and theories of macro-level language planning and policy have grown increasingly complex, exemplified by the range of critical approaches found in Tollefson (2013a) for example. At the same time, ethnographic and other qualitative research that focuses on multilingual practices in communities and schools has tended to portray local classroom practices or ideologies as "policy" (e.g. McCarty 2011a; Bonacina, section 3.3). A major tenet of this book is that both perspectives are essential and only by combining them can we fully understand the relationship between the multiple (and multiply layered) official and unofficial language policies and linguistic practices as they occur in schools and communities. Of central concern is how the macro-level policy texts and discourses relate to micro-level policy texts, discourses, and practices and how they may, or may not, enter into a dialectic (and dialogic) relationship.

Educational policy in general (Bowe and Ball 1992; Ball 2006) and educational language policy in particular (Ricento and Hornberger 1996) are generally conceptualized and researched as multi-layered phenomena and processes. Researchers talk about these "levels" in different ways – borrowing terms used in economics and sociology (macro and micro) or incorporating terms generated within the field (top-down and bottom-up) – but there is general agreement that an understanding of the multiple levels is necessary to fully understand how policy works. In the LPP field, many different conceptualizations have been proffered. A metaphor that has gained a lot of traction in the field is Ricento and Hornberger's (1996) LPP onion (see Quote 4.2), which is meant to depict the multiple layers through which a particular policy moves. The goal of the researcher, as Hornberger and Johnson (2007) put it in a re-examination and application of the onion metaphor, is to slice through the onion to illuminate the various layers. Hult (2010a) describes this as the "perennial challenge" for the field.

Example projects that take on this challenge are discussed at length in Chapter 3 and Chapter 6 and, as mentioned in Chapter 2, Hornberger and Johnson (2007) proposed the ethnography of language policy as a method for making connections between policy and practice. Various discourse-analytic techniques have been proposed including nexus analysis (Hult 2010), communicative speech chains (Mortimer 2013), and intertextuality/interdiscursivity (Johnson 2011a), to track the connections between the multiple layers of policy text and discourse. An edited book by Hult and Johnson (2013) reviews the major methodological approaches to LPP, many of which address the challenge of analyzing the multiple layers of LPP. This work is ongoing and growing both in number (as more researchers enter the fray) and depth (as the theory and method become stronger and more rigorous).

Inherent in Spolsky's (2004) definition (see Quote 1.3) of language policy is a multi-layered conceptualization. Spolsky (2004) distinguishes between three components of what he calls the language policy of a speech community: "(1) Language practices – the habitual pattern of selecting among the varieties that make up its linguistic repertoire; (2) its language beliefs or ideology – the beliefs about language and language use; and (3) any specific efforts to modify or influence that practice by any kind of language intervention, planning, or management" (Spolsky 2004: 5, numbering mine). Based on her analysis of a multilingual classroom in France, Bonacina (see 3.3) characterizes language practices as *practiced language policies* (Quote 3.3), which are not something created outside of the classroom but something that is created from within, emerging in the interaction between students and teachers

I characterize (Johnson 2009) the multiple layers of LPP in terms of processes – *creation, interpretation,* and *appropriation* – which can occur at every level of policymaking. For example, while upper-level policymakers, say at the national level of educational administration, are typically positioned as the "creators" of policy, school districts, schools, and even classrooms can create their own explicit and implicit language policies. Thus, creation, interpretation, and appropriation of policy are all processes that can occur across multiple contexts and levels of institutional authority. To this tripartite definition, E. Johnson (2012) adds *instantiation* to describe the language use that is the result of the other processes. He argues that while the notion of appropriation illustrates the way language policies are "put into action" (i.e., defined and applied by agents across subsequent levels), it is equally important to call attention to the significance of the way language policies are eventually *instantiated.*

Quote 4.4 Language policy instantiation

Although *appropriation* describes the way language policies are 'put into action' (i.e. defined and applied by agents across subsequent levels), it is also necessary to point out the significance of the way language policies are eventually *instantiated*. Instantiation, in this sense, occurs at the interface between the way a policy is enacted and the ways in which languages are used as a result. Regardless of what a policy states, the instantiation of that policy is apparent through the patterns of language use that emerge based on a broader set of social, political, and cultural influences within a given context.

> In other words, the product of how language policies are appropriated on the ground level (e.g. in the classroom) can be determined through the actual instances of language use by individuals within a given policy context.
>
> (E. Johnson 2012: 58)

4.4.1 Finding #6: Top-down and bottom-up are relative

Policies are created at multiple levels and in multiple contexts (national, state, city, community, school, family etc. etc.) and are then interpreted and appropriated by multiple language policy agents across multiple layers of policy activity. Top-down/bottom-up language policy distinctions – typically depicted as the relationship between state-authored policy and the community affected by language policy – fail to capture the multiple levels of context which influence language policy decisions and ignore how policy-making power can be differentially allocated within the "community". Further, dichotomizing conceptualizations of top-down and bottom-up language policy that delimit the various layers through which policy develops, and dichotomize divisions between policy "creation" and "implementation", obfuscate the varied and unpredictable ways that language policy agents interact with the policy process. Because of the multi-layered nature of language policy processes, the determination about whether a particular policy is top-down or bottom-up depends upon who is doing the creating and implementing and in which layer. For example, for a state department of education official, a federal educational policy will of course be top-down but a school district policy will be bottom-up; however, for a teacher within that district, that same school district policy will be a top-down policy. What is the "top" and what is the "bottom" are relative.

4.4.2 Finding #7: Macro multilingual language policies are not necessarily enough

National language policies that promote multilingualism and linguistic pluralism might not be able to overcome either dominant societal discourses or local beliefs and practices that favor particular (especially colonial) languages, monolingual education, or prescriptive and outdated language instruction (Bekerman 2005; de los Heros 2009; McKay and Chick 2001). As Hornberger has demonstrated in her ongoing work in South America, multilingual national language policies do not necessarily translate into multilingual classroom practices – for many reasons, including the gap between policy creation and implementation, the ephemeral and ever-changing nature of policy, and, especially, the language attitudes of the communities themselves (Hornberger 1998). Indeed, enforcement of a national multilingual policy is difficult when local attitudes do not reflect the intent of the policy. This may happen because minority or Indigenous language users (1) are suspicious of the motives of the policy (i.e., Why are they encouraging *our* language and not *their* language? Is it to keep us subjugated?); (2) want their children to acquire the more powerful and dominant language; and/or (3) do not see a need for their mother tongue in the modern world.

Quote 4.5 The limitations of multilingual language policy

[L]anguage policies with a language-as-resource orientation can and do have an impact on...revitalization of endangered indigenous languages. Of course, this is not to say that protecting indigenous languages is simply a matter of declaring a language policy to that effect. There is ample evidence to the contrary.

(Hornberger 1998: 444)

We have observed this phenomenon in the U.S. state of Washington as well. Washington State language policy text and discourse is explicitly in favor of bilingual education, and particularly supports dual language education, but bilingual education policy and practice is contentious at the *local* level. Because of local language ideologies, idiosyncratic beliefs about language education research, or a focus on test scores, some educators and community-members actively promote English-only monolingual approaches, even in school districts that already incorporate bilingual education pedagogy. Therefore, when bilingual education programs fail to gather momentum, stall, or give out, it is often because of local discursive practices that challenge the dominant policy discourse in the state, which promotes additive bilingual education for all students.

4.4.3 Finding #8: Local multilingual language policies are not necessarily enough either

Evidence for this finding is found in Bekerman's (2005) ethnographic research on an Arabic-Hebrew bilingual school in Israel. Despite local commitment to bilingual education, some societal language ideologies were too much for one school to overcome. The sociopolitical context in Israel is marked by Jewish-Palestinian conflict and the concomitant domination of Hebrew and marginalization of Arabic. Within what Bekerman describes as a very monolingual context, the teachers of the dual-language school were highly motivated and committed to developmental bilingual/bicultural education, and parents (described as "liberal") were encouraged by the school's underlying philosophy of peace as well as the sound educational practice of bilingual education. Yet, despite local support and institutional legitimation (from the Israeli Center for Bilingual Education), the school was largely unable to overcome the macro-level segregationist and monolingual policies and could not sustain symmetry between Arabic and Hebrew. Bekerman believes the larger sociopolitical system, in which Arabic carries little symbolic power, is to blame (see also Yitzhaki, discussed in section 3.7).

Bekerman's research is especially interesting in light of a 2010 Israeli government program ("Ya Salam") that attempts to make Arabic language and cultural classes compulsory in public schools. Orna Simchon, an Israeli minister, is quoted as saying: "The aim is to turn the language into a cultural bridge – a means of communication. It is extremely important that every child come to know the language and the culture and thus communicate, hold conversations, and be tolerant in this country" (Greenberg 2010).

4.4.4 Finding #9: Meso-level language policies matter

We have observed this in the United States, where language policy at the state level determines how a federal policy ends up being enacted in schools. For example, while Title III of the No Child Left Behind Act appeared to diminish the opportunities for schools and school districts to grow bilingual education programs (see Wiley and Wright 2004), we have observed the opposite in Washington State – an increase in the number of bilingual education programs since the passage of NCLB. In fact, since the 2004–2005 school year, the number of students enrolled in bilingual education programs has more than doubled. On the other hand, bilingual education programs in a state like Arizona have struggled. We attribute this to different state-level language policies: In Arizona, the passage of Proposition 203 (an anti-bilingual education initiative) has made starting and preserving bilingual education programs increasingly challenging; however, Washington state-level language policy text and discourse officially promotes bilingualism and bilingual education and supports school district efforts to start programs. These initiatives are funded both by state-level legislation (Transitional Bilingual Instructional Act, see Policy text 7.1 in this volume) *and* Title

III. Therefore, we argue that state-level language policies, in this case, determine how federal language policy will be implemented at the school district level.

4.5 The nature of language policy text and discourse

The texts and discourses propagated by language policy are unique and deserve the increasingly close scrutiny they are receiving. Because a lot of language policy analysis is, essentially, discourse analysis, it behooves the field to continue to develop this mode of analyzing language policy. For this line of research, the object of analysis is *policy discourse*, formed as it is by *policy texts* which are, reciprocally, a part and product of the discourse.

Concept 4.4 Policy text and policy discourse

Policy texts are written and spoken products of policy discourse. They include all written texts and transcripts of spoken texts pertinent to the creation, interpretation, appropriation, and instantiation of policy, including (to name a few): official language policies, unofficial web-based documents, congressional/parliamentary debates, political speeches and commercials, interview excerpts, and language policy meetings. Policy texts help engender, and are engendered by, *policy discourses*, which have a dialogic relationship with social, political, and cultural practices and habits. Language policy discourses are invested with language ideologies and they tend to normalize and naturalize particular ways of speaking, behaving, and educating. Policy discourses constrain what may seem possible and hegemonically obfuscate alternatives and thus they shape, and are shaped by, relations of power. Policy discourses can both reflect or challenge dominant, popular, and otherwise marginalizing notions and myths about language and language education. Policy discourses are multiply-layered and a dominant discourse at one level of policy may not dominate in another.

4.5.1 Finding #10: National language policies are not necessarily ideologically consistent

Cobarrubias (1983b) and Ruiz (1984) offered the earliest models for examining the ideological orientations in language planning but, especially since Tollefson's (1991) critique that early research portrayed language planning as an ideologically neutral act, critical analyses have sought to uncover the explicit and implicit language ideologies that shape language planning and policy processes and documents. Of the various definitions of "language ideology" (see Concept 4.5), particular attention is paid to how language policies instantiate popular (commonsense) ideas about language, language learning, and language users that advantage dominant ethnolinguistic groups. These commonsense ideologies of language are often at odds with the research and may simply reflect language myths, which are nevertheless ubiquitous (e.g. Lippi-Green 1997; McGroarty 2006, 2011; Pan, discussed in 3.6).

Concept 4.5 Language ideology

Definitions for *language ideology* vary widely and Woolard and Schieffelin (1994) note that a fundamental distinction lies between those definitions that take a neutral and those that take a critical stance on ideology – the former tending to describe "all cultural systems of representation," the latter tending to embed "strategies for maintaining social power" into the definition (Woolard and Shiefflein 1994: 57–58). Woolard (1992: 235) offers a definition which encompasses both stances: "[C]ultural conceptions not only of language and language variation, but of the nature and purpose of communication, and of communicative behavior as an enactment of a collective order." This definition builds on Rumsey (1990: 346), who defines language ideology as "shared bodies of commonsense notions about the nature of language in the world." Language ideologies position certain linguistic features and language varieties as more natural or normal, especially those varieties popularly believed to be "best" according to prescriptive grammatical norms. In this way, language ideologies can be hegemonic in the sense that, while analysts describe them as "ideologies", their adherents see them as the natural order of things. An example is a Standard Language Ideology, which Lippi-Green defines as "a bias toward an abstracted, idealized, homogenous spoken language, which is imposed and maintained by dominant bloc institutions and which names as its model the written language, but which is drawn primarily from the spoken language of the upper middle class" (Lippi-Green 1997: 64).

Scholarship in this area has demonstrated links between language ideologies and language policy; however, other research (Johnson 2010b; Jaffe 2011) has illuminated challenges in identifying monolithic language ideologies in language policy documents. In any analysis of a federal or national policy that was developed through political legislation and debate, one must contend with the cacophony of beliefs and ideas, often at odds with each other that, nonetheless, led to the creation of a *single* language policy text. As I have argued (Johnson 2009, 2010b) about the development of the No Child Left Behind policy (NCLB) in the United States, supporters of that policy were often completely at odds concerning language learning yet they all supported the policy anyway. Both supporters of bilingual education, and those adamantly against it, voted in favor of NCLB. In the end there were a variety of interpretations from those same policymakers – to wit, even the creators of a policy may not necessarily agree on its intent and thus a single policy text may be filled with divergent, even contradictory, ideologies. Jaffe (2011) has demonstrated this in her research on Corsican in France by revealing what she calls a persistent tension between two broad models of Corsican/French bilingualism: (1) a model that emphasizes balanced bilingualism or "equivalent monolingual-like competencies in two languages," and (2) a model that does not stress the purity of the linguistic codes and validates a range of (potentially imbalanced) types and levels of linguistic competencies. Jaffe argues that both models are simultaneously present in the 2005 Corsican Regional Assembly plan for the development of Corsican bilingual education.

Finally, it is one thing to argue that some language policy language reflects a particular language ideology but it is another to claim that a language policy is the *product* of particular language ideologies, because this suggests a cause–effect relationship that must be evidenced. For this line of argument, it is not enough to show that a particular ideology is inherent or implicit in policy language; one must show how and why particular policy authors intentionally put it there. This type of analysis requires an intimate and insider's knowledge of the beliefs and practices of the policy authors, which leads to the next finding...

4.5.2 Finding #11: Policy intentions are especially difficult to ascertain

Like ideology, the motivations or intentions of a policy are of primary interest within the field (e.g. Ager 2001). For example, Shohamy argues that language policies are manifestations of the intentions of their creators and "are used implicitly and covertly to create de facto language policies...it is via these different mechanisms that ideology is meant to affect practice" (Shohamy 2006: 57). This assertion is implicit in critical analyses that portray language policies as mechanisms of power *intended* to subjugate or marginalize minorities and minority languages.

Certainly, this is often the case. For example, Wiley and Wright (2004) have traced the connections between Nativist and anti-immigrant ideology in the United States and restrictive language policies. Likewise, as was shown in Chapter 1, when conspicuous bigotry is the motive, the intentions of a language policy are sometimes easy to ascertain.

Still, the problem of analyzing intentionality in discourse is notoriously problematic (Shuy 2001) because we can never really know what someone truly meant in a particular utterance because we do not know the mind of the speaker. The challenge of identifying policy intentions is compounded by the very nature of policy: It is difficult enough to analyze the intentions in a single-authored text but language policies often have multiple authors whose intentions vary and conflict. The larger the body of individuals that creates a policy, the increasing likelihood of generic-ness of the policy language, and the decreasing likelihood of uncovering clear intentions. Furthermore, focusing on monolithic polity intentions anthropomorphizes an inorganic and potentially ideologically inconsistent document and obscures interpretive agency. Policies are not necessarily clear or closed or complete – their meanings change and shift as do their interpretations – and analyses of intentions ignores contextual slippages and localized contestation which can arise from ambiguities, contradictions, and omissions in policy language. It is because of this, that many policy scholars have suggested abandoning the search for authorial intentions (reflecting post-structuralist thought, see Quote 4.6) (e.g. Ball 2006; Bowe and Ball 1992) and instead focusing on interpretation and appropriation, both of which reveal a part of the policy process that cannot be predicted by the policy document(s) alone.

Quote 4.6 Authorial intentions

We know now that a text is not a line of words releasing a single 'theological' meaning (the 'message' of the Author-God) but a multi-dimensional space in which a variety of writings, none of them original, blend and clash...The reader is the space on which all the quotations that make up a writing are inscribed...a text's unity lies not in its origin but in its destination.

(Barthes 1967)

I am not in favor of abandoning the search for policy intentions because the sociopolitical and socioeconomic impact of language policies is more immediate and heavy than the texts to which Barthes is referring. I agree that authorial intentions are usually unknowable but there is a danger with applying post-structuralist theory about texts to the analysis of educational and language policies, which can, in a very real way (regardless of the intentions) affect educational and economic opportunity. Still, such analysis must be supported with evidence. One way to approach this problem is to study the development of a policy – the discourse and discoursers responsible for its genesis – and the creators' own interpretations of the intentions of a policy whose beliefs help form the discourse within and without the policy document(s) and help inform its interpretation. For example, Schissel (2009) interrogates the intentions behind the creation of the 1968 U.S. Bilingual Education Act (BEA) through an analysis of the narrative self-constructions of the bill's co-author and sponsor, Senator Ralph Yarborough. Utilizing data found in the congressional record, Schissel illuminates autobiographical stories delivered by Yarborough about his childhood, travels, and career, in which he positions himself as someone who has experience with, but is not an expert in, language learning. This finding is something of a paradox, as Schissel argues, since the senator focused on his lack of expertise concerning language learning and teaching yet sponsored a major educational language policy *anyway*.

Quote 4.7 Including the voices of policymakers

[P]olicy makers are often quoted, paraphrased or summarized to determine legislative intent...In addition, the voices of policy makers are also often characterized as a powerful, yet undefined group... However, within this large body of research, policy makers' discursive practices in congressional hearings are rarely studied exclusively or examined as a unit of analysis. This omission may contribute to a misrepresentation of policy makers as a homogeneous group rather than as agentive individuals.

(Schissel 2009: 82–83)

Like Schissel, I also utilize (Johnson 2007, 2009, 2010a, 2010b) the congressional record to track the development of the policy that followed the BEA, Title III of the No Child Left Behind Act, and analyze the arguments made by the lawmakers, which reveal that some were committed to abolishing bilingual education while others were committed to promoting and growing the number of bilingual education programs. When it was eventually passed, both congressional proponents and opponents of bilingual education celebrated NCLB as a victory and George W. Bush's first Secretary of Education (Rod Paige) – who was not a creator of NCLB but was arguably its arbiter of implementation – had been a vocal supporter of local choice regarding program options, including bilingual education. This legislative tug-of-war is reflected in ambiguous passages in what was eventually passed as law (Policy text 4.1).

Policy text 4.1 Title III of the U.S. No Child Left Behind Act

The purposes of [Title III] are to...provide State agencies and local agencies with the flexibility to implement language instruction educational programs, based on scientifically-based research on teaching limited English proficient children, that the agencies believe to be the most effective for teaching English. (Title III, Part A, Sec. 3102 (9))

The policy language within NCLB presents some interpretive dilemmas (or opportunities, depending on how you look at it). For example, this text simultaneously insists on local flexibility while placing at least one, and perhaps two, restrictions on local choice: any program must be based on scientifically-based research, and the agencies must *believe* in the effectiveness of their chosen program. The structure of this sentence creates some ambiguity around the word "believe" – is this a reference to beliefs about programs or scientifically based research? That is, we might assume that the passage is referring to beliefs about educational programs; however, "believe" could also refer to beliefs about the research. Faced with such questions, I conducted interviews with administrators in the U.S. Department of Education and the Pennsylvania Department of Education (cp Cincotta-Segi, in section 3.4). Both of them adamantly supported local flexibility with regard to local educational program decision-making, insisting that they "stayed out of it", and both suggested that chosen programs needed to be "supported by research" – but neither had definitive answers for what made good "scientifically-based research" nor what such research might support. While the language of NCLB, in general, and Title III in particular, certainly suggests a shift in focus towards English-focused monolingual approaches and away from additive bilingual education, even this cursory glance reveals the challenge of analyzing definitive and monolithic intentions, especially when policy documents are the primary or sole source of data.

4.5.3 Finding #12: Language policy language constitutes its own genre

Policy writing is its own genre, a characteristic of which is the constant intertextual borrowing of previous policy wording. From policy to policy, old to new, the language of the texts layer with the old language remaining completely intact, changed, or erased and this old language may or may not carry its original meaning. It can be difficult enough to pinpoint the semantic intentions of a single-authored text and an ongoing debate continues amongst literary scholars about whether the authors' intentions matter at all in light of the multitude of interpretations (Barthes 1967). If one interprets William Faulkner's *The Sound and the Fury* in a particular way, does it matter what he meant? While *The Sound and the Fury* is dense, chronologically confusing, and a challenge for any reader, policy texts like Title III of NCLB present their own unique challenges. Not only is old policy language – potentially carrying or discarding old meanings – interspersed with the newly penned, but policies are often multi-authored *and* the different authors may interpret the meaning of their creation in different ways.

Language policies, by nature, rely on intertextual connections to a diversity of past and present language policy texts and discourses, the resulting policy statements drawing upon a unique blend of genres which can create ambiguity. Language policies can be ideologically cacophonous and heterogeneous (containing varying and sometimes contradictory stylistic and semantic values). As mentioned, this cacophony of voices and ideologies has encouraged some policy analysts (Ball 2006) to wonder whether it is worthwhile even to search for intentions rather than focus on interpretation. Furthermore, policy language is often created from compromise, when created by legislatures for example, a necessary component of the policy process when a large body of individuals is crafting the policy document(s). Policy language is therefore used which satisfies everyone partially and no one completely but receives the support of a majority of its creators nonetheless.

4.6 Conclusion

This chapter presents twelve findings from the field with illustrative examples from around the world. As empirical findings have increasingly complemented the theoretical rigor in the field of language policy, our knowledge of how language policies are created, interpreted, appropriated, and instantiated has grown enormously. Yet, some important questions are not answered in this chapter, particularly the creation and impact of official and unofficial language policies in less- studied contexts, like businesses, families, and health care organizations, for example. Further, the primary focus of this chapter is the multiple levels of policy text and discourse, not the norms of interaction or language practices that some argue constitute language policies, in and of themselves. Part III will focus on research methods in language policy research and propose a series of methodological innovations along with some sample research projects.

Part III
Researching Language Policy

Compared to other disciplines, even other areas within applied linguistics, LPP is a field without much methodological guidance. There are no singular methods (yet) with pithy titles and descriptions and, therefore, LPP analysts typically rely on other disciplines (anthropology, social psychology, linguistics, sociology, political science, economics, etc.) to inform how they'll study language policy. Researchers must sift through a *lot* of LPP scholarship to determine what methods, if any, can be applied to new research projects, yet research reports in articles and books do not often have specific "methods" sections, as is customary in other disciplines. Therefore, the researcher must piece together various frameworks and theories and some methodological invention may be required. This is both a challenge and an opportunity. While a trickle of publications are coming out that specifically address LPP methodology (McCarty 2011a; Hult and Johnson 2013), this inchoate area is still being formed and new LPP work can play an integral role. Furthermore, LPP is not a field populated by scholars who jealously guard their research projects, contexts, participants, etc. There is *plenty* of work to be done. There are entire countries about which little or nothing has been published. Even in contexts where a lot of work has already been done (for example, the United States, where I work), there are still *plenty* of policies, plans, and contexts which have received little or no treatment.

Part III is intended as a methodological guide for possible research projects. It is not a step-by-step manual because there are no surefire methods that will work in every context. The methods chosen will depend on the specific opportunities and constraints unique to the context(s) under investigation. However, Part III will attempt to provide an overview of the variety of LPP methods in existence, offer many examples that illuminate these methods, and finally make suggestions for example research projects. Chapter 5 reviews some of the LPP research methods and approaches that are prominent in the field and proposes new directions. Chapter 6 considers how the researcher can *become* a connection between research and practice by engaging in educational language policy advocacy and action research. Finally, Chapter 7 proposes new directions for research and suggests doable research projects.

5
Research approaches and methods

Chapter outline

5.1 Early language planning work
5.2 Historical-textual analysis
5.3 Political theory and the law
5.4 Media discourse and LPP
5.5 Ethnography of language policy
5.6 Discourse analysis
5.7 Discussion

Chapter 5 is intended to lay the groundwork for what follows in Part III by reviewing the types of research methods and approaches employed in LPP and some of the key terms and concepts that inform this work. The term *approaches* is used because not all of the areas covered in this chapter include specific methodological guidance; however they do suggest a way to *approach* LPP. Along the way, I propose some new methodological concepts that may help engender ideas for research projects. For alternative accounts of the methods and approaches covered in this chapter, as well as guidelines for other LPP research methods, consult the edited volume on LPP research methods by Hult and Johnson (2013).

5.1 Early language planning work

Early language planning work focused on reports of language planning processes in national polities, which relied on empirical observation or historical research. In some ways, early language planning work was

Table 5.1 Hornberger's integrative framework for language policy and planning goals

Approaches	***Policy Planning*** *(on form)*	***Cultivation Planning*** *(on function)*
Types		
Status Planning (about uses of language)	**Officialization** **Nationalization** **Standardization of status** **Proscription**	**Revival** **Maintenance** **Spread** **Interlingual Communication – international, intranational**
Acquisition Planning (about users of language)	**Group** **Education/School** **Literary** **Religious** **Mass media** **Work** - SELECTION Language's formal role in society *Extra-linguistic aims*	**Reacquisition** **Maintenance** **Shift** **Foreign language/second language/literacy** - IMPLEMENTATION Language's functional role in society *Extra-linguistic aims*

Corpus Planning (about language)	**Standardization of corpus** **Auxiliary code** **Graphization** - - - - - - - - - - CODIFICATION Language's form *Linguistic Aims*	**Modernization** (new functions) **Lexical** **Stylistic** **Renovation** (new forms-old functions) **Purification** **Reform** **Stylistic simplification** **Terminology unification** - - - - - - - - - - ELABORATION Language's functions *Semi-Linguistic Aims*

Notes:

(1) LPP Types are in plain typeface, Approaches in *italics*, Goals in **bold.** (2) The six cells of goals are demarcated by double lines. Haugen's (1983) four-fold matrix is indicated by shading, and interpretive comments on those four quadrants are placed below the dashed lines. (3) Additional interpretive comments are enclosed in parentheses throughout. (4) The figure incorporates the work of Cooper 1989, Ferguson 1968, Haugen 1983, Hornberger 1994, Kloss 1968, Nahir 1984, Neustupny 1974, Rabin 1971, and Stewart 1968.

From Hornberger, N. H. (2006a). Frameworks and models in language policy and planning. In T. Ricento (ed.), *An Introduction to Language Policy: Theory and Method* (pp. 24–41). Malden, MA: Blackwell. Reprinted by permission from Taylor & Francis Ltd.

something that linguists *did,* and only later, in the sharing of experiences and then establishing frameworks and models, did it become something that linguists *studied*. Written reports tended to provide theoretical observations, accounts of specific language planning projects, analyses of strategies for implementing language planning, and historical investigations of particular language planning contexts and communities. Examples can be found in collections such as *Language Problems of Developing Nations* (Fishman *et. al.* 1968), *Can Language be Planned?* (Rubin and Jernudd 1971), *Language Planning Processes* (Rubin *et al.* 1977) and *Progress in Language Planning* (Cobarrubias and Fishman 1983). These volumes make for excellent compendia for much of the language planning work that preceded their publication.

Hornberger (2006a) reviews and synthesizes much of this early work into one integrative framework (Table 5.1). While this is not a method per se, it is useful for highlighting the foci of early language planning studies and, perhaps, inspiring new scholars and providing direction for research projects. There are two main axes for the framework: the first covers the LPP types (status, acquisition, and corpus planning) and the second distinguishes between *policy* and *cultivation* planning approaches. Hornberger (2006a: 28) characterizes these two approaches as follows: The policy approach attends to "matters of society and nation, at the macroscopic level, emphasizing the distribution of languages/literacies, and [is] mainly concerned with standard language...while the cultivation approach, seen as attending to matters of language/literacy, at the microscopic level, emphasizing ways of speaking/writing and their distribution, [is] mainly concerned with literary language."

5.2 Historical-textual analysis

Much of the data collection for LPP studies involves combing through historical documents and official and unofficial language policy texts or tracing the history of a policy or policies in a particular context. This type of analysis tends to be "macro" in the sense that the focus is on large-scale sociopolitical forces, historical movements, and policy documents created at national, supra-national, and other macro levels. These studies have less to say about how language policy is interpreted and appropriated in particular contexts but they have been essential for documenting the historical impact of language policies and the ideological and discursive context for such policies around the world. Some form of historical-textual analysis is needed in any study of language policy. As data, these studies have typically drawn on newspapers, governmental decrees, publications by political organizations and movements, historical documents, media publications, and political publications.

The International Research Project on Language Planning Projects (IRPLPP), established in 1966, was carried out by Das Gupta, Fishman, Jernudd, and Rubin, and engendered the book *Can Language be Planned?* (Rubin and Jernudd 1971). Fishman (1977: 33) describes the project as more comparative and substantive, rather than methodological and theoretical: "As the first major study of its kind it was formulated more as a demonstration of the feasibility of studying language planning processes comparatively and empirically than as an attempt to test or advance specific hypotheses." Still, these studies offer guidance on how to conduct large-scale studies of national language planning. While much of the data of this early language planning research was obtained through historical-textual analysis, Fishman *et al.* (1971) also suggest conducting surveys and interviews with both policy creators and policy targets as alternative methods of data collection. Data collection for this project was organized around four major subdivisions of language planning (partially lining up with the "goals" in Hornberger's framework in Table 5.1), i.e. policy formulation, codification, elaboration, and implementation (Table 5.2).

Tollefson's (1991) historical structural approach (see 2.3) similarly relies on historical-textual analysis, in which the focus is the social and historical influences that give rise to language policies, but incorporates critical theory (e.g. Giddens 1971) to uncover the "historical and structural pressures that lead to particular language policies and plans and that constrain individual choice" (p. 31). Tollefson examines government documents, historical and social forces, and media discourse and

Case 5.1 Das Gupta – Religion and Indian language policy

Das Gupta (1971) analyzes the complicated history of Indian religion, politics, and language before and after partition. While some leaders pushed for political ties between Urdu and Muslims and Hindi and Hindus, many others resisted these connections, especially non-Urdu speaking Muslims, non-Hindi speaking Hindus, and secularists. Das Gupta notes that language loyalties and interests in India have been fluid and elastic, morphing to fit the needs of political agendas.

Table 5.2 Research outline for comparative studies of language planning (Fishman *et al.* 1971)

Process	Data
Policy formulation – "deals with the decisions of formally constituted organizations with respect to either: (1) the functional allocation of codes within a speech community or (2) the characteristics of one or more codes within the code matrix (linguistic repertoire) of such a community" (p. 293).	Government reports and documents, organizational reports and archival materials, newspaper and journal accounts, and interviews with members of the decision-making bodies
Codification – "deals with the normalization (standardization) of regional, social, class, or other variation in usage via the preparation of recommended (or 'official') grammars, dictionaries, orthographic guides, etc." (p. 295)	Organized around the products (dictionaries etc.) of the agencies and processes, which can be obtained via official records of their activities and the processes, which can be obtained via interviews with participants
Elaboration – "deals with the need for intertranslatability with one or more functionally diversified languages by such means as the preparation of recommended (or "official") word lists, in particular, the substantive, professional, or technical fields" (p. 295).	Organized around the products (word lists etc.) of the agencies and processes, which can be obtained via official records of their activities and the processes, which can be obtained via interviews with participants
Implementation – "refers to all efforts to gain the acceptance of the policies and 'products' of language planning, including grammars, spellers, word lists, and school curricula for the implementation of language-policy decisions" (p. 299).	Surveys among target populations to determine impact of language planning and unstructured discussions with participants to obtain spoken and written language data

text to trace the ideologies embedded within language policies around the world (e.g. Iran, China, Philippines, Britain) and how language planning may create and sustain inequality. Spolsky (2004), as well, examines a wide variety of language plans and policies from around the world, generally relying on historical and governmental texts, policies, and practices, showing, for example, how French agencies and policies (including l'Académie Française) have vigorously promoted the (ideological) primacy of French on nationalist and ideological grounds.

Other historical-textual studies examine the history of one particular policy, or type of policy in one particular context. For example,

Wiley and Wright (2004) offer a detailed analysis of the connection between English-only and Nativist (Concept 5.1) ideology and the history of U.S. educational language policy. They rely on historical analysis, census data, official federal and state policy documents, legal decisions, as well as on the actions and language of political organizations/movements (e.g. The U.S. English-only movement). Wiese and Garcia (2001) trace the ideological ebb and flow of the U.S. Bilingual Education Act, from its founding and throughout each authorization, and use the texts of each re-authorization, state-level policy language, legal decisions, and texts produced by particular groups influential in the process.

Concept 5.1 Nativism

Nativism refers to anti-immigration sentiment expressed through xenophobia and a preoccupation with assimilation. In *Strangers in the Land*, Higham (1955) reviews nativism in the U.S. and defines it as "an intense opposition to an internal minority on the grounds of its foreign (i.e. "un-American") connections...[T]he nativists' most characteristic complaint runs against the loyalty of some foreign (or allegedly foreign group). Seeing or suspecting a fear of assimilation, he fears disloyalty. Occasionally the charge of disloyalty may stand forth naked and unadorned, but usually it is colored and focused by a persistent conception about what is un-American" (Higham 1955: 4–5). Higham argues that nativism has had a prominent influence on U.S. immigration and naturalization policies and that xenophobia, anti-Catholicism, and racism have helped shape the literacy policies in immigration and naturalization. Language is a tool for promoting a fear of the other and fomenting the belief that an internal minority threatens the unity of the country.

Nativism persists to this day. The first African-American president of the U.S., Barack Obama, is frequently portrayed as un-American by political opponents, a charge that is accompanied by ongoing questions about his birthplace (his father was from Kenya) and the authenticity of his birth certificate showing that he was born in Hawai'i. The year 2012 also saw a renewed nativism in Greece, where a growing anti-immigration movement has motivated anti-immigrant mobs to attack perceived immigrants, engendered clashes between these mobs and police, and supported the election of politicians affiliated with the right-wing Golden Dawn party, which is founded on extreme antipathy toward all immigrants.

What one will not typically find in the written products of historical-textual LPP studies, in general, is a methods section and, therefore, characterizing the methods used is somewhat challenging. Perhaps because it is a burgeoning field, it is largely left to the analysts' discretion to determine how the body of spoken and written texts under consideration is analyzed. Two limitations of the historical-textual approach should be noted: (1) The responsibility for interpreting the texts is largely left to the researcher, who may proffer idiosyncratic interpretations or find evidence within the texts that simply confirms *a priori* assumptions, and, (2) They say little about how language policies are interpreted and appropriated at the local level, processes which may or may not reflect the language policy texts and/or interpretation by the LPP scholars. More recent historical-textual analyses have tended to rely more on explicit discourse-analytic methods (5.6), reflecting the larger trend of increasingly diverse methods in LPP studies.

5.3 Political theory and the law

Debates about immigration, citizenship, and education are often related to debates about language (although see Fitzsimmons Doolan discussed in 3.8 for an alternative perspective) and sometimes directly address how politics and the law should handle linguistic diversity in a given polity. Language (policy) is often a central part of political agendas and many scholars examine the relationship between political movements/organizations and LPP. This work tends to focus on how political and legal bodies create language policies, how language ideologies are appropriated in the process, and the political and legal impact of policies (whether intended as *language* policies or not). Those who look at language policy from a political science or legal perspective make use of a wide variety of historical documents as data: history texts, legal decisions, census data, legislative histories of a bill or law (e.g. the U.S. congressional record, which has the full text of congressional debate), official language policies, and the publications of political entities either in print or online. There is no singular "method" for this type of research as much as a collection of methods, unique to the scholar engaging in them; however, a more robust integration of historiography (Iggers 1997) might provide clearer accounts of how the historical documents are being mined.

Case 5.2 Leibowitz – English language requirements in the U.S.

Leibowitz sees language as a weapon for other nonlinguistic targets and English language requirements as a "palatable disguise for racist action" (1984: 59). He helps elucidate the U.S. 1952 Naturalization Act which added a literacy requirement – reading and writing in English – to the already established speaking requirement for citizenship, and argues that this "codified" many courts' decisions that knowledge of English was necessary to prove attachment to the constitution (which was, in turn, necessary for citizenship). Leibowitz also documents the evolution of the English literacy requirement for voting, a language policy designed to prevent African Americans from voting. He argues that immigration, voting, and naturalization laws, imbued with racist motivation, have been enacted throughout U.S. history as a means of social control.

5.3.1 Judicial decisions and the courts

Legal decisions have had substantial impact on language policy and an understanding of LPP processes often is impossible without a clear picture of how they relate to the law. Educational language policy in the United States, for example, must be understood against the backdrop of the 1974 Lau v. Nichols Supreme Court decision, which determined that the *same* instruction for English language learners (as for native English speakers) was in fact *unequal* instruction because a lack of English proficiency denied these students access to the content of the instruction and, in effect, equal educational opportunity. The Supreme Court found that the lack of educational accommodations to the plaintiffs (in this case Chinese students) violated their civil rights. Lau v. Nichols has greatly impacted language policy throughout the U.S. (for a full discussion see Hornberger 2005b) yet, while it tends to be recognized in state-level language policy, it is sometimes ignored at the local level (see Case 5.3).

Case 5.3 The impact of Lau v. Nichols in Washington schools

One of the key features of the Lau v. Nichols decision is language declaring that the same instruction for ELLs as native English speakers is in fact unequal instruction: "[T]here is no equality of treatment merely by providing students with the same facilities, textbooks, teachers, and curriculum; for students who do not understand English are effectively foreclosed from any meaningful education." The court decided that, by failing to provide English language instruction to the Chinese students (represented by Lau), the San Francisco school system had discriminated against these students by denying them "meaningful opportunity" and thus were found to have violated the Civil Rights Act of 1964. The Lau decision changed the language policy landscape in the U.S. For example, while the official educational language policy of Washington State, the Transitional Bilingual Instruction Act (TBIA) of 1979, does not mention Lau specifically, it does contain some intertextual connections: "[C]lasses which are taught in English are inadequate to meet the needs of [ELLs]...Pursuant to the policy of this state to insure *equal educational opportunity* to every child in this state, it is the purpose of this act to provide for the implementation of bilingual education programs" (emphasis mine, c 95 § 1). The primary arbiter for this policy is the state department of education (Office of Superintendent of Public instruction or OSPI), which uses the money from the legislature for the Transitional Bilingual Instructional Program (TBIP). In unofficial publications and professional development materials, OSPI frequently cites Lau v. Nichols as a rationale for providing accommodations for ELLs. However, in practice, TBIP funding is often used for brief professional development workshops for content-area teachers who do not, subsequently, implement those (or any) strategies to accommodate ELLs. Thus, in many schools across Washington, especially in districts with historically lower numbers of ELLs and therefore no specific bilingual education or ESL programs in place, ELLs are effectively submerged with no accommodation whatsoever. In effect, these schools violate Lau v. Nichols.

European Union language policies, as well as the European Convention on Human Rights, tend to conflate language rights with minority rights and language discrimination with minority discrimination. For example, article 14 of the European Convention on Human Rights defines the prohibition of discrimination: "The enjoyment of the rights and freedoms set forth in this Convention shall be secured without discrimination on any ground such as sex, race, colour, language, religion, political or other opinion, national or social origin, association with a national minority, property, birth or other status" (section 1, article 14).

Sometimes, the *lack* of a legal decision can have an impact on language policy as well. In Israel, for example, where three languages (Hebrew, English, and Arabic) are considered official, there is a clear hierarchy of Hebrew first, English second, and Arabic last (see Yitzhaki, discussed in 3.7). Spolsky and Shohamy (1999) point out that if public signs are bilingual they always include Hebrew but tend to be Hebrew/English rather than Hebrew/Arabic. They note a series of court cases concerning the rights or requirements of integrating Arabic into public signage and, while the Israeli Supreme Court has tended to allow or, at least, not disallow the incorporation of Arabic into public signs, they have, nonetheless, avoided ruling on the official status of the Arabic language. It is not just *how* language diversity is dealt with in politics and the courts that is a question for language policy scholars but *which* languages are allowed in political domains and the courts. For example, in the Council of Ministers at the European Union, ministers can use any of the 11 official EU languages, and thus the policy is officially multilingual. Also, any EU citizen arrested is entitled to have the charges translated into a language they can understand and to have access to an interpreter (a translator) while in court.

Case 5.4 English and Filipino in Philippine educational language policy

Article XIV, section 6 of the 1987 Philippine Constitution states: "The national language of the Philippines is Filipino...the Government shall...sustain the use of Filipino as a medium of official communication and as language of instruction in educational systems." This constitutional declaration was accompanied by a 1987 bilingual education policy that promoted English and Filipino in schools. Concerned about the decline of English in Philippine schools, in 2003 President Gloria Macapagal-Arroyo issued Executive Order 210, which stated that "English shall be used as the medium of instruction for Mathematics and Science from at least the third grade level...primary medium of instruction in all public and private institutions of learning in the secondary level...It is the objective...to make [students] better prepared for the job opportunities emerging in the new, technology-driven sectors." Executive order 210 was challenged on the grounds that it was unconstitutional in the Wika Ng Kultura v. Macapagal Arroyo & Ermita, 2006 court case. While that case was dismissed, the debate over the role of Filipino and English in Philippine educational language policy is ongoing. English has an increasingly prominent role in other Asian legal systems and educational language policy as well (see Powell 2009 and Pan, discussed above in 3.6).

5.3.2 Language policy and political identity

Schmid (2001) analyzes the rise of the English-only climate in the U.S. and, like Leibowitz (Case 5.2), concludes that language policies are used to restrict immigrants with particular ethnolinguistic backgrounds from entering the country and/or becoming citizens. She compares the current flag bearer of the English-only movement, an organization called U.S. English, with the Americanization movement of the early twentieth century. Like the Nativists (Concept 5.1) of that era, current proponents of English-only legislation use the same arguments regarding new and old immigrants, claiming that while older immigrants learned English and assimilated, "newer" immigrants (notably Hispanics) do not. In fact, however, both old and new immigrants eventually transition into English, a durable phenomenon and finding (see Tse 2001).

Kymlicka and Patten (2003a) review the debates around language rights and language policy from a political theory perspective. After the fall of communism in Eastern Europe, for example, many observers expected the spread of liberal democracy and not the outbreak of ethnic conflicts that occurred, often along linguistic lines. Monolingual language policies were often the first laws enacted by the new countries and linguistic minorities felt threatened in these contexts – with good reason, as can be seen in Tollefson's examination of language policy in the former Yugoslavia (Tollefson 2002c; see also this volume 4.2.1). Kymlicka and Patten (2003a) further argue that immigration into Western countries has traditionally entailed language shift – as the immigrants arrive, they learn the language of the new country and, by the third generation, the ancestral language is typically lost. However, the rise of multiculturalism has engendered a new idea that immigrants do not have to abandon their ancestral languages in order to effectively integrate into the new country. Many countries have officially recognized this linguistic diversity by instituting multilingual language policies, including, for example, Switzerland, where the official languages are French, German, and Italian, with Romansch added as a national language. This multiculturalism has, in turn, given rise to proposals for stronger state policies that compel language shift (for example in the

U.S. and Western Europe) as well as proposals for official monolingual policies (for example, in France, where an amendment to the French constitution declared French to be the official language of the republic in 1992). Other countries, like Japan, have no official language. May (2001) argues that a political challenge for minority languages is that majority languages have traditionally been seen as vehicles of modernity and minority languages as carriers of culture and tradition. A good overview of the central concepts and models pertinent to these debates can be found in the edited volume by Kymlicka and Patten (2003b).

5.3.3 National identity, citizenship, and language

Studies of the relationship between language policy and politics and/or the law have focused upon issues such as immigration, citizenship, and naturalization and have tracked the development of immigration and naturalization language policies. Piller (2001) reviews the research on national identity, citizenship, and language. While many national projects have been driven by the ideology of one language, one nation (e.g. Standard French in France), Piller points out that "nations may be built on other unifying myths [e.g. common origin, culture, values, heritage, economic aspirations etc.] than the one of a common language" (Piller 2001: 261) and multilingualism, not a single unifying language, may also be heralded as a unifying force; for example, in the forging of a "European Union identity" (García 1997). Piller reviews the language requirements for citizenship across many countries and argues that in countries without such requirements, other ideologies make such language policies dispensable; for example, the dominant myth of common origin in Israel (see Yitzhaki, in 3.7 above) or the promotion of an official ideology of multiculturalism in Sweden (see Hult, in 3.5 above). Other countries, like Australia, do require English language ability in the test for citizenship (because the test is in English) although the level of English necessary to pass the test is described as "basic" in both the Australian Citizenship Act of 2007 (subsection 21(2)) and on the Australian Department of Immigration and Citizenship website (http://www.citizenship.gov.au/learn/cit_test/about_test/).

Case 5.5 Language testing and German citizenship

Piller (2001) argues that language testing can be used to weed out potential citizens who are positioned as undesirable and points to Germany, where the recent addition of a language requirement for citizenship emerged out of debates between the Conservative Party (who wanted the time-honored requirement of a common origin, i.e. German ethnicity, to remain) and the Labor Party (who argued that German residence alone was sufficient). The compromise became that, while ethnic Germans are granted automatic citizenship, non-ethnic Germans can only be naturalized if they pass a German language test. Piller reports that the testing requirements and German language expectations are extremely inconsistent throughout Germany, in part because the naturalization officers who conduct the interviews are given no language training nor provided with clear guidelines for what counts as passing the test; thus, the criteria for passing are arbitrary. Piller's findings are based on observations of language testing for German citizenship and interviews with both test-takers and test-givers.

The English language requirement for citizenship in the United States is about a century older than the German policy but similarly arose out of debates about who is qualified to be, or desirable as, a U.S. citizen. President Theodore Roosevelt established the Federal Immigration Commission or "The Dillingham Commission" who studied immigration in the U.S. Their conclusions, based on bogus "statistics" that the new immigrants were less intelligent and were not assimilating, nonetheless influenced the enactment of the 1906 Naturalization Act, which made the ability to speak English a requirement for citizenship. In a written report, the Dillingham Commission argued, "If he does not know our language he does in effect remain a foreigner...no man is a desirable citizen of the United States who does not know the English language" (cited in Leibowitz, 1984: 34; see also the review in McKay and Weinstein-Shr, 1993). The 1906 law drew upon circulating assimilationist ideologies prevalent at the time, including the idea that the English language helped bind the nation and was thus a prerequisite for citizenship and the idea that an understanding of English was necessary for the understanding of American principles.

Case 5.6 Nativism and language policy in Cameroon

In her study of educational and colonial language policy in Cameroon, Esch reveals how French was imposed upon Cameroonians under the guise that it was a unifying common language and the only one capable of expressing abstract concepts. She uncovers this French language policy published in 1885:

> There is a real abyss between the indigenous dialects and the French language. They express feelings, tendencies, ways of thinking which are deeply different to such an extent that it is impossible to pass from one to the other. The indigenous dialects are not able to express the beneficial ideas which we want to see developed. Their particular genius, like the mentality of the primitive individual, is opposed by its very nature to ideas of progress. The most fervent partisans of teaching via the medium of the local dialects have realized that it is impossible to spread the learnings of the modern civilisation by means of a primitive language. (quoted in, and translated by, Esch 2010: 242)

Mertz (1982) argues that a Whorfian folk theory of language – according to which the understanding of concepts considered essential for American citizenship are only expressible in English – pervades many of the judges' decisions in U.S. case law, and we see the same phenomenon in Cameroon as well. Not only is English or French necessary for expressing and understanding "civilized" concepts but the knowledge of foreign languages might have adverse effects, according to this folk theory. Mertz argues that judges' decisions established precedents beginning in 1897 that helped perpetuate the belief that American political concepts were entwined with the English language. In a decision handed down from the Supreme Court of Wyoming, the court ruled that reading a translated version of the state constitution in Finnish did not allow someone to vote: "[C]ivil liberty as it exists in the States America being unknown to the subjects of a despotic government, they could in the very nature of things, have no word or phrase in their language to describe or define it" (Supreme Court of Wyoming 1897:153, quoted in Mertz 1982: 4)

Concept 5.2 One nation–one language ideology

Political ideas, campaigns, and movements sometimes utilize language attitudes and language policy as a means to further political agendas. One example of this is the *one nation–one language ideology*, to which many politicians have appealed in order to make their case for decreased use of minority languages, the dissolution of multiculturalism, or both. Skutnabb-Kangas (2000b) refers to this monolingual reductionism (or "naivety or stupidity" as she puts it), as an ideology that rationalizes linguistic homogenization and supports the mythical homogenous nation-state – "a state with one nation and one language which probably does not exist anywhere in the world" (Skutnabb-Kangas 2000b: 238). Whether a myth or not, the ideology remains to this day, as is shown in the recent quotation below from UK Prime Minister David Cameron. Another oft-cited example comes from former U.S. President Theodore Roosevelt.

- Theodore Roosevelt (1917, cited in Crawford 1992: 85): "We must have but one flag. We must also have but one language. That must be the language of the Declaration of Independence...We cannot tolerate any attempt to oppose or supplant the language and culture that has come down to us from the builders of the Republic with the language and culture of any European country. The greatness of this nation depends on the swift assimilation of the aliens she welcomes to her shores."
- In a speech on the failings of multiculturalism, David Cameron (Munich in February 2011) argues: "We have allowed the weakening of our collective identity. Under the doctrine of state multiculturalism, we have encouraged different cultures to live separate lives, apart from each other and away from the mainstream... [E]ach of us in our own countries, I believe, must be unambiguous and hard-nosed about this defence of our liberty. There are practical things we can do...That includes making sure that immigrants speak the language of their new home and ensuring that people are educated in the elements of a common culture and curriculum."

Cameron seems to operationalize what Roosevelt merely hints at – one nation must have a collective unitary identity and culture, and a single language that binds the citizens. Cameron suggests that multilingualism carries immigrants away from the mainstream, fractures a collective UK identity, and somehow endangers liberty. Instead, "we" must protect our liberty by defending against multiculturalism. One might reasonably ask who the "we" is in this statement and who is being referred to with the phrase "different cultures" – what is the "common" or default culture to which he refers? What about those UK citizens who are multicultural and/or multilingual? Their identity does not seem to be reflected when Cameron mentions a "collective identity" and, thus, this statement marginalizes a wide array of different citizens of the UK.

5.3.4 Constitutional and statutory interpretation

Because language policy research involves a great deal of analysis of texts, the field could greatly benefit from the philosophies, principles, and schools of thought that guide statutory and constitutional interpretation. Statutory interpretation refers to how the courts interpret and apply statutory law (law created by legislative bodies). There are, of course, different schools of thought. *Textualism* is "guided by the text, not by intentions or ideals external to it, and by the original meaning of the text, not by its evolving meaning over time" (Gutmann 1997: viii). Textualists do not accept that there is a genuine collective intent behind a piece of legislation and instead the only thing that has the force of law is the text; therefore, strict textualists argue that the legislative history of a law – e.g. the committee reports that preceded its passage – should not be consulted or considered in statutory law. On the other hand, those in the *legal process* school argue that "statutory language rarely has a single, plain meaning" (Imwinkelried 2006: 36) and extrinsic materials – including the legislative history – should be consulted and may even trump the plain meaning of the language of the law. While there are different approaches, a fundamental principle that connects the different methods of statutory interpretation is that words are imperfect symbols to communicate intent – they are ambiguous and change in meaning over time. Both perspectives can inform language policy research and it is important to realize that there is rarely, if ever, a monolithic collective intent behind a language policy developed by a legislative body (like Title III of the U.S. No Child Left Behind Act). Further, while the language of the policy tends to have the effect of law, at least as it is interpreted by constituents, examining the legislative history helps illuminate the origins and varied intentions that helped develop the policy (for an example, see Schissel, discussed above in 4.5.2).

Like statutory interpretation, there are different schools of thought regarding constitutional interpretation – but two dominate in the U.S. *Originalists* argue that the goal of constitutional interpretation is to *attempt to* determine the original intent of the authors, even if those intentions are ultimately unknowable. *Pragmatists*, on the other hand, view a constitution as a living document, the meaning of which is dynamic and changes over time. This division is similar to a division in policy theory between those who try to determine the goals or intent of a policy (see Ager 2001) and those who argue that such an analysis is futile (because we can never really know what the intentions were) and instead focus on the interpretation and appropriation of a policy (see Ball 2006). To analogize, we could say that those who seek original intentions are language policy originalists while those who reject such endeavors are language policy pragmatists. Yet, it is important to note that constitutional originalists accept that uncovering the intentions behind a constitution is extremely difficult, or even impossible. The conservative Supreme Court justice in the United State, Justice Antonin Scalia, acknowledges this problem but counters that "It's not always easy to figure out what the provision meant when it was adopted...I do not say [originalism] is perfect. I just say it's better than anything else" (quoted in Gram 2004). This is an important point for language policy methodology – it may be difficult, or even impossible, to uncover the intentions of a policy. Like the writers of a constitution, the authors of a language policy are multiple, and so are their intentions; the same policy can have conflicting meanings, reflecting the conflict between the authors (for detailed discussion, see 4.5.2). A multiplicity of intertextual and interdiscursive connections to present and past texts, discourses, and discoursers, can create heterogeneity and ambiguity.

Concept 5.3 Language policy originalism vs. pragmatism

Mirroring constitutional interpretation theory, I propose *language policy originalism* as the principle of policy interpretation that seeks to uncover the original authorial intentions of a language policy, even if such intentions are ultimately unknowable. *Language policy pragmatism*, on the other hand, questions the feasibility of such endeavors and argues that intentions can be multiple, in conflict, and dynamic. While originalists try to uncover authorial intentions through historical-textual analyses, pragmatists tend to focus on the interpretation, appropriation, and recontextualization of a language policy in local contexts, usually through ethnography or other qualitative research methods.

Both positions have merit. Pragmatist criticisms of the quest for authorial intentions are well founded but this does not mean that we should abandon the hunt altogether, just that we should be very careful to provide evidence for such claims. We can also take heed of the pragmatist position by recognizing that a language policy's meaning may change over time, and, importantly, across different contexts. The meaning of a policy in one setting may be different than the meaning in another, whatever the intentions were originally. The language ideologies, beliefs, attitudes, and discourses circulating in a particular context will impact how a language policy is interpreted, appropriated, and recontextualized for that context, and this unique meaning, the *recontextualized meaning,* is worthy of analysis as well (see Concept 5.14).

Originalist language policy research is benefited by careful analysis of historical and legal documents, policy texts, and other data that may help support arguments for original intent including: interviews with policymakers; audio-recordings of committees engaged in crafting a bill or policy; audio-recordings or written documents of debate among lawmakers or policymakers; and political publications from individuals, groups, and institutions engaged in policymaking. Pragmatist language policy analysis requires participant-observation and/or interviews with language policy agents in a community or school (district) who interpret and appropriate language policy. Ethnography can be used to analyze how contextual factors influence the recontextualization of a language policy (Johnson 2011a).

Case 5.7 Applying the doctrine of last antecedent

There are numerous principles that govern statutory interpretation (see a review in May, 2006) but one which can create some trouble for language policy analysis is the doctrine of the last antecedent, which states that "qualifying words, phrases, or clauses apply to the words or phrase immediately preceding" (May 2006: 3). With this in mind, consider the following statutory law text, which is an excerpt from the U.S. Title III of NCLB:

> The purposes of [Title III] are to...provide State agencies and local agencies with the flexibility to implement language instructional educational programs, based on scientifically-based research on teaching limited English proficient children, that the agencies believe to be the most effective for teaching English. (Title III, Part A, Sec. 3102 (9))

Common sense might dictate that the "beliefs" being referred to in the clause "that the agencies believe..." are about language instructional educational programs. However, if we follow the doctrine of the last antecedent strictly, we must interpret this passage as stipulating that state and local agencies must implement language instructional educational programs based on their beliefs about "scientifically-based research," not beliefs about the best instructional programs. This seemingly odd interpretation may not reflect the spirit of the policy's plain language, but, at the very least, it highlights the ambiguity of this policy text. (see 4.5.2 and 7.4 for further discussion).

5.4 Media discourse and LPP

The media play a central role in social and cultural change (Fairclough 1995a), it is of paramount significance in circulating cultural meaning, and it is deeply embedded in daily life (Talbot 2007). Uniting media discourse studies is the assumption that the media plays a crucial role in our social life and is central in creating commonsense notions because of its ability to speak for the masses and/or speak from a supposed neutral stance. Thus, the media can both reflect and engender ideologies about language and language users that, in turn, encourage particular perceptions of the world as common sense – as "just the way things are", as *natural* – which, in turn, proliferate dominant and potentially marginalizing discourses. Its power to do this is, in part, due to its ability to claim neutrality or objectivity and, as a consequence, validity.

Quote 5.1 Why study the media?

We study the media...because of an assumption that television, newspapers, texting and the other widely available communication forms play an important role in mediating society to itself. We assume that the shared world of a culture – what its members think is real, interesting, beautiful, moral and all the other meanings they attach to the world – is partly constructed by each member and partly by institutions such as newspapers or radio stations, and prevailing ideas.

(Matheson 2005: 1)

In media discourse, a single article or television report is not as significant as the cumulative effect of presenting information in a particular way over and over. Herman and Chomsky (1988) use the phrase "manufacturing consent" to describe how the media cumulatively promote mainstream interpretations of events and topics which do not necessarily correspond with "the facts" at hand. For example, Rickford (1999) describes how the media would eschew linguists' reports (including his own) about Ebonics during the Oakland School Board (OSB) debate in the United States in favor of more mainstream or entertaining voices which did not necessarily understand the linguistic characteristics (or "the facts") of African American English (AAE). After the OSB "recognized" in 1996 that many of their students spoke AAE as their primary language, Rickford notes how the debate that followed was mostly controlled by those who were not linguists and knew relatively little about the linguistics of AAE. The media, he argues, created the impression of, or manufactured, a consensus about AAE that reflected mainstream interpretations and not linguistic findings (see 6.5.1.4 for further discussion).

According to Fairclough (1992), the mass media are imbued with hidden power because whole populations are exposed to relatively homogeneous output which does not include the type of negotiation found in face to face interaction. Media discourse is hegemonic if it normalizes dominant or mainstream ways of thinking (and obfuscates alternative accounts) while concomitantly positioning the journalist as a neutral narrator (Fairclough 1992). Yet, Fairclough also asserts that even though the conversation is one-sided, there can be discursive negotiation between the media reader/listener and the "ideal subject" for whom the broadcast or article is written. In other words, a real-life reader might not identify with the assumptions or conclusions the ideal subject (or consumer of media) was meant to take away. Furthermore, I would argue, mainstream media can challenge dominant and popular ideas about language and disseminate non-mainstream ideas; and alternative media, some of which are widely heard (e.g. satellite radio stations), read (e.g. alternative weekly periodicals), and seen (e.g. social networking services), often promote *non*-mainstream ideas.

Case 5.8 Commonsense, yet incorrect, notions about language in the media

The 2002 "English for the Children" campaign in Massachusetts, U.S. succeeded in getting an anti-bilingual education proposition in the voting booth, which was subsequently passed. The campaign was instigated by Ron Unz, who has been responsible for similar campaigns in other U.S. states, and he was aided by some influential academics, including Rosalie Porter and Christine Rossell who have published books and articles on the topic (Porter 1990; Rossell and Baker 1996); organizations mobilized to fight bilingual education (The Institute for Research in English Acquisition and Development); and the Massachusetts governor, Mitt Romney, who campaigned on the issue. Voters overwhelmingly (about 68%) voted "yes" to Question 2 which ostensibly replaced bilingual programs with "Structured English Immersion" programs.

However, after its passage the *Boston Globe* reported on growing skepticism about the success of the change. In an article entitled "English immersion is slow going" Vaishnav (2003) writes:

> When voters considered Question 2 last year, the proposition seemed simple: Immerse non-English-speaking students in the language so they could soak it up, rather than place them in bilingual education. The latter approach eased them into English over a period of months or years by teaching them in their native tongues. (Vaishnav 2003)

While this article by Vaishnav is, overall, skeptical of the "success" of "Structured English Immersion", Vaishnav makes common and false assumptions about language learning, tossing them out as simple, matter-of-fact propositions. First, there is the widespread myth (for others, see Table 6.3) that students "soak up" another language with ease as long as they are immersed in classrooms that use only that language, a very popular idea that nonetheless receives little empirical support (see Marinova-Todd, Marshall, and Snow 2000). Second, "bilingual education" is defined strictly as a transitional program which uses the students' native languages "over a period of months or years" to transition them into English. Vaishnav makes no mention of additive bilingual programs, which have as their goals native language maintenance, and thus restricts the definition of bilingual education to *transitional* bilingual education.

Concept 5.4 Probability sampling in newspaper articles

Combing through databases for newspaper articles about a topic can be extremely time-consuming and reading all those articles is well-nigh impossible. However, by using *probability sampling* one should theoretically not have to read every article about a particular topic.

Probability sampling is a method that allows the researcher to make generalizations about an entire population by obtaining information only from a sample of that population. This is how political surveys and polling data are collected. Of course, because only a subset of the population is being targeted, there will always be sampling error, which is heavily impacted by the sample size. To reduce the impact of sampling error, a bigger sample must be collected. To calculate the size of a sample, the following formula is used (Dillman *et al.* 2009: 56):

$$Ns = \frac{(Np)(p)(1-p)}{(Np-1)\left(\frac{B}{C}\right)^2 + (p)(1-p)}$$

Ns = sample size needed
Np = the size of the entire population from which the sample is drawn
p = the proportion of the population expected to choose one of the two response categories
B = margin of error (.03 = ±3%); represents one half of the width of the interval within which the sampler wants the estimate to fall. In other words, if .03 is used in the calculation, the sampler can say that the estimate will be within ±3 percentage points.
C = Z score associated with the confidence level (1.96 corresponds to the 95% level). The Z score indicates statistical confidence. So, if one uses 1.96 in the calculation, they can be sure that their sample will accurately reflect the larger population (within 3 percentage points) 95 times out of 100.

So, if the population to be sampled were 800, the equation would look like this:

$$Ns = \frac{(800)(.5)(1-.5)}{(800-1)\left(\frac{.03}{1.96}\right)^2 + (.5)(1-.5)}$$

$$Ns = 458$$

Therefore, for a population of 800, a sample of 458 will ensure that the estimate will be within ±3 percentage points 95% of the time. Interestingly, the larger the general population, the smaller the proportion needed for the sample. For example, using the same numbers for a population of 25,000 yields a sample size of 1,024. For 2 million, only 1,067 are needed. An important caveat needs to be addressed, however. As the p score indicates (.5), this formula is designed for yes/no questions (indicating the expectation that 50% will say yes and 50% will say no). So, this formula only works for simple questions like "How many articles published in Rwanda over the past five years are in favor of officialization of English and how many are against?" Probability sampling will not yield more nuanced interpretations.

5.5 Ethnography of language policy

The theoretical and conceptual orientation of the ethnography of language policy, and multiple findings based on this work, are discussed in some detail in Chapter 2 but here the focus is on method. While it is impossible to provide a complete overview of ethnographic research methods, a few key features will be covered, especially as they relate to LPP. More complete guides to ethnographic research include Hammersly and Atkinson (1995), Agar (1983/1996), Madison (2012), and Blommaert and Jie (2010) and valuable resources for ethnographic work in LPP include McCarty (2011a, 2013) and Johnson (2013b).

5.5.1 Definitions, benefits, and challenges

The word *ethnography* is a combination of ethnos (culture) and graphy (writing/representation of) and, thus, ethnography is by definition the study and description of human culture. This research approach has traditionally been employed by anthropologists who seek to develop an insider's perspective of a particular culture; that is, an understanding of a culture from the inside out, through the participants' eyes (as much as possible). Agar (1983) emphasizes two key features of ethnographic research: (1) an understanding of how participants interpret the events in their lives and (2) the search for patterns which involves "a rich collection of different kinds of information and sentiment and relations among them" (Agar, 1983: 194). Agar emphasizes that ethnographers find "stuff" (human behavior, interaction, events, etc.) they don't understand but are intrigued by, and try to make sense of it through the participants' eyes (Agar, personal communication, 27 February 2004). In order to develop this insider's perspective, the researcher needs to spend an extended period of time (often years) with the research participants, engaging in multiple types of data collection, including participant observation (see Method 7.3 on page 247), insider accounts (Method 7.1, on page 241), and document collection.

Concept 5.4 Defining "ethnography"

There is considerable disagreement about what *ethnography* truly is. Hammersley and Atkinson (1995: 1) take what they call a liberal approach: "[Ethnography] refer[s] primarily to a particular set of methods. In its most characteristic form it involves the ethnographer participating, overtly and covertly, in people's daily lives for an extended period of time, watching what happens, listening to what is said, asking questions – in fact, collecting whatever data are available to throw light on the issues that are the focus of the research." Synthesizing Harris's (1968: 16) writings on anthropological theory (who at one point simply defines ethnography as "the description of culture," Creswell (1998: 18) offers the following definition: "An ethnography is a description and interpretation of a cultural or social group or system. The researcher examines the group's observable and learned patterns of behavior, customs, and ways of life."

The focus on participant interpretation, patterns, and processes makes ethnography particularly useful for studying how research participants interpret, appropriate, and instantiate language policy. Still, using ethnography as a means to study language policy is nontraditional for at least two reasons. First, the object of study is not a culture or a people but a policy (although Creswell's use of "system" might include a policy system). However, in ethnographically based studies of language policy, the goal is not an insider's account of a policy per se, but an account of how the human agents engage with LPP processes. The language policy texts mean very little without the human agents who act as interpretive conduits between the language policy levels or what Ricento and Hornberger (1996) metaphorically refer to as layers in the LPP onion (see Quote 4.2). Second, the foundation of ethnography is typically long-term participant-observation in a particular site or community, but often there is no one "site" in which a language policy is created nor one "community" in which a language policy is penned. Therefore, ethnography of language policy is preferably multi-sited even if there is debate about whether or not a multi-sited approach counts as true ethnography (Levinson and Sutton 2001; Walford 2002). On the one hand, attempting to ethnographically collect data from multiple sites weakens the researcher's ability to provide a thick description in any one site. On the other hand, the multi-layered and multi-sited nature of policy necessitates multi-sited research. This challenge has prompted some (e.g. Johnson and Freeman 2010; Levinson, Sutton, and Winstead 2007) to suggest that single researchers are not ideal candidates for multi-sited ethnographic studies of policy and, instead, multiple researchers can collaborate to expand the policy field of vision.

Concept 5.6 Geertz's *thick description* and Sarangi's *thick participation*

Geertz argues that what defines ethnography is *thick description*. While a thin description would simply describe some event, a thick decription provides "a stratified hierarchy of meaningful structures" (Geertz 1973: 7). Thick description is an ongoing interpretive process, based on prolonged engagement, which contextualizes events in such a way that an outsider can understand them. About the task for the ethnographer, Geertz writes: "What the ethnographer is in fact faced with – except when (as, of course, he must do) he is pursuing the more automatized routines of data collection – is a multiplicity of complex conceptual structures, many of them superimposed upon or knotted into one another, which are at once strange, irregular, and inexplicit, and which he must contrive somehow first to grasp and then to render" (Geertz 1973: 10). Rendering these complex conceptual structures, i.e. the layers of context and meaning of a particular behavior, activity, event, etc., relies on thick description.

Sarangi proposes a participatory and collaborative method of research and argues that thick description relies on *thick participation* by the researcher, "which constitutes a form of socialization in order to achieve a threshold for interpretive understanding" (Sarangi 2007: 573). Thick participation depends upon cooperation between researchers and the communities with which they are involved and is necessary for research relevancy.

Another challenge is that of timing. Walford (2002: 23) asks: "When policy moves fast, how long can ethnography take?" Because of the need for extended engagement, and perhaps enculturation, ethnography is not always particularly well-suited for policy research. The ethnographer may need to move from site to site, causing discontinuous engagement characterized by heightened periods of intense data collection followed by brief lulls. Walford characterizes this type of work as "compressed ethnography" which, he says, may be better suited for ethnographies of policy.

Finally, the insider-outsider dichotomy is a dubious distinction and is better described as a multi-dimensional continuum since no outside researcher is ever truly an insider; nor is an outside researcher every truly an outsider – as soon as they enter the research context, they have influenced it in some way. Further, the goal is not an objective description of a culture but (1) a critical understanding of how imbalances of power hegemonically perpetuate and normalize linguistic and cultural hierarchies that lead to deficit approaches and (2) challenging such practices for social justice. The positionality of the researcher needs to be interrogated, particularly because this work often involves marginalized populations. A solution to this epistemological tension is taken up in Chapter 6.

Concept 5.7 Critiquing ethnography

Traditionally, *ethnography* has been affiliated with cultural anthropologists who seek to understand people and cultures alien to themselves, an orientation to "the other" reflected in the title of Michael Agar's book *The Professional Stranger* (1983/1996). Yet, Rampton (2007: 591) questions whether a foreigner researching some previously unknown cultural group can ever really develop much more than "a description of conventional systems" which may be reductive. Instead, he cites developments in linguistic ethnography in the UK, which have been built upon ethnographic research from the inside-out instead of the outside-in; that is, analyses of organizations and institutions of which the researcher is already a member (for an example, see Chimbutane discussed above in 3.2).

Other criticisms of ethnography emerge because of epistemological concerns. For example, Roman (1993) analyzes the influence of positivistic conceptions of science on what she calls naturalistic ethnography, which present the researcher with two options: subjectivism – or "going native" – and objectivism – or "being a fly on the wall". By going native, researchers attempt to blend in with the group under study as much as possible by adopting similar modes of dress, language use, and other norms. This can lead to the problem of voyeurism and uncritical valorization of the research subjects' experiences. Being a fly on the wall, on the other hand, means the researcher attempts to be an unobtrusive observer and writes in neutral and objective language about their study. This can lead to, what Roman calls, "intellectual tourism" as well as uncritical acceptance of unequal power relations and dominating relations among the research subjects. Neither approach, Roman argues, adequately analyzes power relations that mediate fieldwork: "I do argue that ethnographers' failure to challenge the discourse of naturalism may reify and mystify the knowledge required to understand and transform unequal power relations between researchers and research subjects...[R]arely do such accounts explicitly locate researchers within analyses of the larger material conditions and power relations that produce such dualisms" (Roman 1993: 282).

Fishman (1994: 96–97) warns against the sanctification of ethnography in language planning research and does not believe ethnography to be particularly "anti-hegemonic": The sanctification of ethnography and the "corresponding devilisation of other methods, smacks of Stalinism" and LPP research methods should be chosen based on "technically substantive rather than on trendy salvational grounds." Fishman (1994: 97) concludes by saying that language planning students, practitioners, researchers, and theoreticians are "co-responsible and must 'pull their weight' in creating a better sociocultural reality for all those whose lives are touched by the efforts that language planning encompasses."

While they may not be the saviors of LPP research, ethnographic studies of language policy have been useful for illuminating community attitudes about language education and policy, language planning processes, classroom practice as it relates to language planning and policy, and multiple layers of policy texts, discourses, and practices (see a review in Chapter 2). Not only does a thick description of "the intersection of meanings of policy decision-makers, teachers, community members, and others within a particular social setting" (Davis 1999: 72) emerge, but an ethnographic approach can illuminate how localized language policy and planning and classroom pedagogy interact with top-down policies and how a local educational policy can be, in Corson's words, a "powerful discursive text" (Corson 1999: 25). From these studies, we derive an idea of the variety of ways a policy is interpreted and appropriated.

Concept 5.8 Ethnography of speaking → ethnography of communication

While Hornberger and Johnson (2007; see Johnson 2007) coined the term, *ethnography of language policy* can perhaps be traced to Hymes' *ethnography of speaking* (1962) which has, at least, served as an inspiration to ethnographies of speaking/communication that have examined language policy. Re-articulated as the ethnography of communication, Hymes (1964) envisioned a method that examines communicative habits within a speech community. Saville-Troike (1996) defines the ethnography of communication as a field that "focuses on the patterning of communicative behavior as it constitutes one of the systems of culture, as it functions within the holistic context of culture, and as it relates to patterns in other cultural systems" (Saville-Troike 1996: 351). Notable ethnographies of communication that make direct language policy connections include Hornberger's (1988) study of Quechua in Peru and King's (2001) study of Quichua in Ecuador.

5.5.2 Method

Ethnographies of language policy can take different forms but they must include at least the following characteristics:

1. *a balance between an emic and etic perspective*: While the researcher will go into a research context, cognizant both of language policy theories/frameworks and of particular policies that may be affecting that context, it is crucial to develop an understanding of how the participants view their policy landscape – which policies are most important and what they mean for the participants (see Cincotta-Segi, this volume 3.4 for an example). In turn, it is essential to examine how the empirical data collected line up with already established LPP frameworks and theories. Hymes (1990) describes this process as a dialectic, from etic1→emic→etic2; in other words, the researcher begins with knowledge of theories, frameworks, and policies (etic1), collects ethnographic data to derive findings and test those theories/frameworks (emic) and then, based on the findings, re-tools existing theories/frameworks (etic2);
2. *long-term engagement* with a community or communities in order to establish a thick description of how community members create, interpret, appropriate, and instantiate language policy; and
3. *data triangulation*: Ethnographers triangulate data in order to better evidence their findings. For example, an insider's account about how a particular policy is put into practice in a classroom might be collected in an interview with a teacher but participant observation in that classroom might reveal a different perspective, as might the collection of a document (e.g. school language policy) which states something different than what is claimed by the teacher. It is not the

"objective truth" that the ethnographer is after, just a full account, which is better established with multiple sources of data.

Concept 5.9 Etic and emic

The etic/emic distinction, as introduced by Pike (1954), remains a useful analogy for ethnographic research. Pike based the concepts on the phon*etic*/phon*emic* distinction, analogizing it to the study of human behavior: Phonetics describes all the possible sounds of human language and, similarly, the *etic* approach devises categories of classes, units, and systems. Phonemics, on the other hand, describes how the sounds systematically produce meaning for users and, similarly, an *emic* approach looks for patterns of meaning in human behavior. As Pike (1954: 10) puts it:

> An etic analytical standpoint...might be called "external" or "alien," since for etic purposes the analyst stands "far enough away" from or "outside" of a particular culture to see its separate events, primarily in relation to their similarities and their differences, as compared to the events of other cultures, rather than in reference to the sequences of classes of events within that one particular culture...An emic analytical standpoint, furthermore, might be called "internal" or "domestic" since it classifies behavior in reference to the system of behavior of which it is immediately a part.

While the goal of ethnography is an emic understanding, note Rampton's (2007) criticism that traditional ethnography is in danger of only providing a rudimentary understanding of conventional systems as opposed to really capturing a truly emic perspective.

The following is a heuristic for the scope and data collection focus in ethnography of language policy research. The proposed categories, further delineated in Table 5.3, are neither static nor mutually exclusive. Ethnographies of language policy should develop an understanding of:

1. *agents* – includes both the creators of the policy and those responsible for policy interpretation and appropriation;
2. *goals* – refers to the intentions of the policy as stated in the policy text;
3. *processes* – creation, interpretation, and appropriation of policy text and discourse;

4. *discourses* that engender and perpetuate the policy – the discourses within and without the policy; i.e. the discourses (whether explicit or implicit) within the language policy texts, intertextual and interdiscursive connections to other policy texts and discourses, and the discursive power of a particular policy. Also of interest are the local and societal discourses that interact with policy discourses but these are best captured under the next category.
5. the dynamic social and historical *contexts* in which the policy exists – an ethnography of language policy is interested in the dynamic social, historical, and physical contexts in which language policies are created, interpreted, and appropriated.

Table 5.3 Data collection for ethnography of language policy

Focus	Activities and examples	Data collection
Agents	Creators Interpreters Appropriators	Interviews; participant-observation in policy meetings, classrooms, and community settings; documents created by the agents, including policies, classroom assignments, and media publications
Goals	Promotion Expediency Restriction Null Tolerance (See Table 7.7: Analyzing goals)	Interviews with policymakers; language policy documents, including multiple drafts (if any) of the policy; discourse data of development of policy (e.g. congressional record)
Processes	Creation Interpretation Appropriation	Interviews with creators, interpreters, and appropriators; participant-observation in policy meetings, classrooms, and community settings
Discourses	Dominant and marginal Popular and alternative Macro → Micro National → Local	Formal and informal policy texts and intertextual and interdiscursive links between; participant-observation in meetings, schools, and communities; historical-textual analysis; popular and alternative media
Contexts	Schools, classrooms, speech communities, families, business organizations, health care organizations, places of work	All of the above

5.6 Discourse analysis

A lot of language policy analysis is, essentially, discourse analysis since it involves looking at various policy texts (both spoken and written) and analyzing policy discourses that are instantiated within or engendered by the policy texts. As well, language policy processes are essentially discursive – generated, sustained, and manipulated in spoken interaction and policy documents that, in turn, interact with each other – and may appropriate, resist, and/or possibly change dominant and alternative discourses about language and language policy. Therefore, the increasing prevalence of discourse-analytic studies in LPP is a welcome addition to the field (Bonacina, see 3.3; Cincotta-Segi, see 3.4; Freeman 1998; Hult 2010a; Johnson 2011a; Mortimer 2013; Schmidt, Sr. 2002; Wodak 2006), especially since they address different ways for solving "the perennial challenge" (Hult 2010a) of making connections between the multiple layers of LPP activity.

Discourse analysis is a cover term for a variety of research methods that focus on "discourse." *Discourse* is sometimes used according to the more traditional dictionary definition – stretches of speech, writing, or interaction between participants – and, at other times, its use is more in line with critical theory. Nevertheless, dictionary definitions do not necessarily exclude this meaning, as merriamwebster.online lists the following definition: "a mode of organizing knowledge, ideas, or experience that is rooted in language and its concrete contexts (as history or institutions) <critical *discourse*>." Jaworski and Coupland (1999) compile a useful list of circulating definitions, including this one from Candlin (1997):

Quote 5.2 Defining "discourse"

Discourse...refers to language in use, as a process which is socially situated. However...we may go on to discuss the constructive and dynamic role of either spoken or written discourse in structuring areas of knowledge and the social and institutional practices which are associated with them. In this sense, discourse is a means of talking and writing about and acting upon worlds, a means which both constructs and is constructed by a set of social practices within these worlds, and in so doing both reproduces and constructs afresh particular social-discursive practices, constrained or encouraged by more macro movements in the over-arching social formation.

(Candlin, quoted in Jaworski and Coupland 1999: ix).

Jaworski and Coupland (1999: 3) define discourse as "language use relative to social, political and cultural formations – it is language reflecting social order but also language shaping social order, and shaping individuals' interaction with society." Lemke (1995) distinguishes between discourse as "the social activity of making meaning with language and other symbolic systems in some particular kind of situation or setting" (p. 6) and discourse*s*, which are "produced as a result of certain social habits that we have as a community. There are particular subjects some of us are in the habit of talking about in particular ways, often as part of particular sorts of social activity" (p. 7).

Case 5.9 Foucault (1978) on medical discourse and pathologizing homosexuality

Foucault (1978: 56) offers an analysis of how medical discourse has shaped how we talk and think about sex. By classifying and analyzing "alternative" sexual practices, medical discourse has sought to manage them. He argues that medical discourse (and discoursers, i.e. medical professionals) "constructed around and apropos of sex an immense apparatus for producing truth." However, this medical discourse was not grounded in the actual truth, not in scientific findings, but in an intentional distortion of the truth about human sexuality that appeased and legitimized the state's intolerance. In this way, medical discourse helped marginalize non-heterosexual practices by pathologizing them – depicting them as perverted, unnatural, and a product of illness. By shaping the discourse that surrounds human sexuality, medical professionals controlled how human sexuality was described and which practices were healthy and which were sick. By shaping the discourse, the "truth" was formed. There were of course alternative discourses which, in a sense, created their own reality about sex. However, the power of this medical discourse to marginalize was profound and, while unacceptable in respected scientific communities, still holds sway in many parts of the world where homosexuality is still equated with illness and criminalized (see Ottosson 2008 for a review of state-sponsored homophobia).

Discourse analysis offers the language policy scholar a way to organize and interpret the large number of spoken and written texts collected as data, which can include at least the following: official language policies, documents that act as unofficial language policies, cyber-discourse, media texts, naturally occurring interaction in schools and communities, and interviews with language policy agents. While language policy scholars borrow from different schools of discourse analysis, the uniting characteristic is an interest in connecting macro- , meso- , and micro-level language policy; to put it another way, an interest in language policy creation, interpretation, appropriation, and recontextualization; to put it even another way, the connection between language policy and language practice.

Yet, identifying these connections is challenging. For example, we might ask how teachers interpret and appropriate some macro-level policy but they may only marginally be aware of what is actually in the official policy, or they may be more concerned with district-wide policies, which they consider to be "macro." Unless the teacher says, "Yes, here's how I implement (or do not implement) such and such policy," it may be very difficult to make claims about how classroom practice is related to the language policy. Thus, different forms of discourse analysis offer methods for making connections between spoken and written texts across language policy levels, layers, and spaces. In the following sections, I present a few examples of discourse analysis that may prove useful.

5.6.1 Critical discourse analysis

Critical discourse analysis (CDA) is a label that has been appropriated by a variety of researchers engaged in discourse studies yet it is not characterized by a series of strict methodological guidelines, which has led to the criticism that it is too nebulous (see 5.6.3). It grew out of different intellectual traditions – critical linguistics (Fowler *et al.* 1979), systemic-functional linguistics developed by Michael Halliday (1978), and critical theory (e.g. Foucault 1978) – although current practitioners incorporate these earlier ideas differently and to varying degrees. Power is of primary interest to CDA and a central tenet is that language is shaped by, and *shapes*, the social context; or, as Fairclough (2010: 92) puts it, language "is always a socially and historically situated mode of action, in a dialectical relationship with other facets of 'the social' (its 'social context') – it is socially shaped, but it is also socially shaping, or constitutive." CDA draws connections between the structure of written and spoken texts and the multiple layers of discursive practices and social contexts to illuminate (i.e. 'explain') connections between discourse and power. By exposing how discourse is conditioned by and helps constitute relations of power, CDA attempts to reveal, challenge, and subvert powerful discourses and empower those who have been marginalized by them.

> **Concept 5.10 Wodak's theoretical assumptions underpinning CDA**
>
> Wodak (1996: 17–20) characterizes CDA with a set of theoretical assumptions: (1) CDA is concerned with social problems; (2) power relations have to do with discourse and CDA studies power in and over discourse; (3) language use reproduces and transforms society; (4) language use may be ideological; (5) discourses are historical and intertextually connected to other discourses (historical); (6) interpretations are dynamic.

Fairclough (2010: 10–11) refers to CDA as having multiple "versions" but offers some criteria for what counts as CDA:

1. It is not just analysis of discourse (or more concretely texts), it is part of some form of systematic transdisciplinary analysis of relations between discourse and other elements of the social process.
2. It is not just general commentary on discourse, it includes some form of systematic analysis of texts.
3. It is not just descriptive, it is also normative. It addresses social wrongs in their discursive aspects and possible ways of righting or mitigating them.

Fairclough points out that these criteria do not preclude the possibility of making use of CDA concepts (for example, recontextualization, which both he and Wodak trace to Bernstein 1990) and categories in research which would not necessarily be characterized as CDA.

To analyze how the products of discursive processes, or texts, relate to the sociopolitical and sociocultural contexts from which they emerge, Fairclough offers a three-dimensional model (Figure 5.1). For every discursive event (defined as an "instance of language use, analysed as text, discursive practice, social practice" Fairclough 2010: 95) it is necessary to take into consideration three dimensions:

1. the content and form of the *text* itself, which might include grammar, vocabulary, organization, cohesion, phonology, and/or semantics;

2. the *discourse practices* or the production, distribution, and consumption of a text;
3. the *sociocultural practice*, which refers to the multiple levels of situational, institutional, or social context surrounding the discourse practices.

The analysis of textual features is related to larger discourses or social practices, by way of discourse practices, which are the link between text and sociocultural practices. In other words, how a text is produced, interpreted, and/or consumed (i.e. the discourse practice) depends upon the sociocultural practice(s).

Fairclough's multi-tiered approach lines up nicely with the multi-layered nature of language policy. Any particular language policy text – the written or spoken product of language policy discourse – is a product of discourse practices that should be analyzed within multi-layered (discursive) contexts (of situation) (e.g. institutional and societal discourses about language, language users, language education etc.).

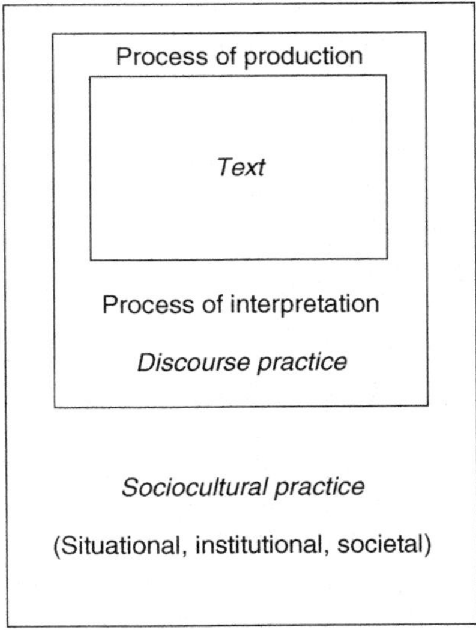

Figure 5.1 Fairclough's dimensions of discourse analysis (2010: 133). From *Critical Discourse Analysis: The Critical Study of Language*, 2nd edition, by Norman Fairclough, ©Pearson Education Limited, reproduced with permission)

Concept 5.11 Applying Fairclough's model: three dimensions of language policy analysis

1. Language policy texts can derive from official and unofficial language policy language; interview transcripts with language policy agents (aka the creators, interpreters, and appropriators of policy); media reports; public signage; transcripts of naturally occurring interaction in meetings, classrooms, communities; public signage, etc.
2. The processes of interpretation and production of these texts, the discourse practices, can be analyzed in a variety of ways including, for example, how participants in a meeting are positioned, the participant structures used in classrooms, and the intertextual relationships between language policies.
3. The multi-leveled sociocultural context(s) of interest include the context of situation – in this room, in this building, in this section of town, in this school, in this city, etc. – and circulating social norms, ideologies, and discourses, which the participants draw upon in the creation, interpretation, appropriation, and recontextualization of language policy.

In a reformulation, Wodak proposes a discourse-historical approach, which uses multiple methods and data sources (e.g. interviews, written texts, speeches, participant observation) to analyze the "historical, political, sociological, and/or psychological dimensions in the analysis and interpretation of a specific discursive occasion" (Wodak 2000: 188). Wodak's model combines ethnographic methods and principles (e.g. the principle of triangulation) and CDA to explore how particular discursive events are embedded within past and current historical and political fields.

In a later publication, Richardson and Wodak (2009: 255) proffer four levels of context as heuristics to guide analysis:

a. The immediate language or text (e.g. slogans of a political campaign)
b. The intertextual and interdiscursive relationship between utterances, texts, genres and discourses; (e.g. history and intertextual references of terms and concepts used)
c. The extra-linguistic social/sociological variables and institutional frames of a specific "context of situation" (e.g. political campaigns)
d. The broader sociopolitical and historical contexts, within which the discursive practices are embedded (e.g. history of a political party).

Concept 5.12 Applying the discourse-historical approach: four levels of context for language policy analysis

a. Text-internal analysis of a language policy text – might include a focus on particular themes, topoi, or linguistic constructions; semantics; deixis; grammar.
b. Intertextual connections to past and present policy texts and discourses – including the multiple drafts, re-authorizations, and/or revisions of a particular language policy, or relations across different language policy documents – and the interdiscursive connections to past and present discourses about language, language users, and/or language education.
c. The extra-linguistic social variables include the institutional and sociolinguistic contexts in which language policies are created, interpreted, and appropriated, i.e. the multiple layers of context in which language policy activity takes place.
d. The sociopolitical and historical contexts include the historical, political, and social impact of a particular language policy, the institution(s) involved in language policy processes, and the beliefs and actions of language policy agents.

CDA lines up well with language policy research because it (1) attends to the multiple layers of sociocultural context in which a text is created, interpreted, and appropriated, and (2) includes both a close analysis of the language within the text and links between the multiple levels of sociocultural practice, which will leave "traces in surface features of the text" (Fairclough 1995b: 97). Strengthening its relevance for language policy research are the commonalities between CDA and critical language policy:

1. Both are influenced by social theory and a Foucauldian conceptualization of discourse.
2. Neither includes a definitive canon of techniques and is instead bound by a philosophical commitment to social justice and an interest in the connections between discourse and power.
3. Both employ strategies to establish connections between the micro-analysis of a text and the sociocultural context in which that text is produced or the "orchestrated and recursive analytic movement between text and context" (Luke 2002: 100).

5.6.2 Intertextuality, interdiscursivity, and recontextualization

Wodak suggests that any discourse-analytic study of language policy should consider all relevant oral and written texts across the multiple "fields of action" (i.e. the multiple layers) across which discourses spread, overlap, or "are in some other way sociofunctionally linked to each other" (Wodak 2006: 177). This flow of discourses, in turn, informs how language policies are interpreted and appropriated by setting constraints on our perceptions and actions. A discourse-analytic study of language policy, then, might seek to explain whether or how a language policy operates as a "mechanism of power" by both examining how a particular policy text relates to the wider sociopolitical context in which it is produced (very similar to the historical-structural approach proposed by Tollefson 1991; see also Schmidt, Sr. 2002), and, examining the connections between the multiple layers of language policy text, discourse, and practice.

Particularly useful within discourse analysis of language policy is the notion of *intertextuality*, which describes how texts derive meaning from other texts. Julia Kristeva (1986, written in 1966) is credited with coining the term in her analyses of Bakhtin's writings on literary semiotics and, particularly relevant, is his notion of dialogism, which he used to describe how works of literature, and their meaning, do not simply exist, but are inextricably "in dialogue" with other works. Bakhtin (1986) proposes that both the texts we write and the speech we create are filled with the echoes of previous speakers and writers and any given utterance can only be understood against the background of other utterances. These echoes, or intertextual connections, imbue texts with dialogic overtones and multiple meanings and any interpretation of a (potentially multi-voiced) text requires an understanding of these intertextual connections. Language policies, by nature, rely on intertextual connections. They are linked to past policy documents (perhaps earlier policies, or versions of the same policy), other types of language policy texts (like a declaration of intent by a school district administrator), and they may be connected to a variety of past and present discourses.

Kristeva (1986) draws upon Bakhtin's notions of *dialogue* – the connections between writer, addressee, and context – and *ambivalence* – as the connection between texts throughout history. Ambivalence describes how a text (under consideration) draws upon other texts in the past but it also "implies the insertion of history (society) into a text and of this text into history" (p. 39), and therefore the meanings of previous works, as well as the present one, are all impacted. Kristeva further distinguishes between *horizontal intertextuality* (based on dialogue), which is meant to capture the relationship between writing subject, addressee, and the "discursive universe" of the text (which includes other texts) and *vertical intertextuality* (based on ambivalence), which is meant to capture the historical connection to other texts. Writing about horizontal intertextuality, she positions the reader or addressee as a part of the discursive universe: "The addressee, however, is included within a book's discursive universe only as discourse itself. He thus fuses with this other discourse, this other book, in relation to which the writer has written his own text" (p. 37). A distinguishing characteristic between Kristeva's notion of horizontal intertextuality and Bakhtin's dialogue is how the reader, for Kristeva, participates in the semiotics of a text which, arguably, opens infinitely more intertextual pathways, including all of the spoken and written texts the reader has ever come across. The emphasis on the reader's agency, and a concomitant de-emphasis on the power of the writer to control the meaning of a text, reflects post-structuralist thought at the time (see Quote 4.6), to which Kristeva was a major contributor.

Fairclough (1992) proposes that the theory of intertextuality should be combined with a theory of power since the meaning of texts is not infinitely innovative but will be socially limited by conditions of power. Particular meanings of a text will be more likely because of how dominant discourses structure social structures and practices. Drawing on the notions of *hétérogeneité montrée* and *hétérogeneité constitutive* (see Authier-Revuz 1982), Fairclough further distinguishes between manifest and constitutive intertextuality, respectively. *Manifest intertextuality* involves other texts being explicitly incorporated into the text in question, for example through the use of quotations or citations. *Constitutive intertextuality*, on the other hand, is "the configuration of discourse conventions that go into [the text's] production" (p. 271) which he describes as *interdiscursivity* (Concept 5.13).

Concept 5.13 Interdiscursivity

The concept of *interdiscursivity* is closely related to intertextuality but, whereas, intertextual analyses largely attend to the lexico-grammatical features of a text – what Candlin refers to as "hugging of the textual ground" (Candlin 2006: 4) – interdiscursivity refers to the connections between discourses or, how "discourse conventions go into a [text's] production" (Fairclough 1992: 271). Candlin and Maley (1997: 212) define it as "the use of elements from one discourse and social practice which carry institutional and social meanings from other discourses and other social practices." Linell (1998) notes that interdiscursivity involves relations between discourse types rather than text tokens, while Fairclough (2010: 234) describes interdiscursivity as an aspect of intertextuality, "a question of which genres, discourses and styles [a text] draws upon, and how it works them into particular articulations."

The discourses that are incorporated in the production of language policy texts (whether spoken or written) rely on the unique sociopolitical context out of which the text emerges and, thus, they are synchronically and diachronically linked to circulating discourses about language, language use, language users, and/or language education. As well, the nature of interpretation and appropriation of language policies is interdiscursively related to the multiple levels of sociopolitical and discursive context, which shape how a language policy will be interpreted (i.e. what it means) and how it will be appropriated (i.e. what it does). While interdiscursivity tends to be depicted as relating to more abstract or global levels (Linell 1998), discourses are not simply macro phenomena – there are meso and micro discourses that play a role in what a language policy means for the community or school in which it is put into action. For example, teachers may appropriate, reject, or ignore discourses about language education that circulate across the district in which they work.

Considering the synchronic and diachronic nature of intertextuality, the multiple agencies of authors and readers, and the innumerable intertextual connections that give rise to a text's meaning, this approach highlights the heterogeneity of texts, the "diverse and often contradictory elements and threads that make up a text" (Fairclough 1992: 272), the multiple potential meanings, and its ambiguity. Furthermore, any text created and interpreted in one particular context (say a language policy in the halls of congress) which is then re-represented in a completely different context (say a teacher meeting in a school district) will be *recontextualized* (Concept 5.14). The process of recontextualization transforms the meaning of a text by either expanding upon or adding to the meaning potential or, perhaps, suppressing and filtering particular meanings. The nature of this transformation relies both on intertextual links to past texts and discourses as well as the current ideological zeitgeist within the new context (see Blackledge 2006).

Concept 5.14 Recontextualization

For policy research, Wodak and Fairclough (2010: 21–22) promote a form of CDA focusing on the category of recontextualization, which illuminates the history and trajectory of texts and their relation to discourse and social change...Spatial and temporal relationships between texts include relations of recontextualization whereby texts (and the discourses and genres which they deploy) move between spatially and temporally different contexts, and are subject to the transformations whose nature depends upon relationships and differences between such contexts."

Linell (1998: 145) defines *recontextualization* as "the dynamic transfer-and-transformation of something from one discourse/text-in-context (the context being in reality a matrix or field of contexts) to another. Recontextualization involves the extrication of some part or aspect from a text or discourse, or from a genre of texts or discourses, and the fitting of this part or aspect into another context, i.e., another text or discourse (or discourse genre) and its use and environment."

Wodak and Fairclough both trace "recontextualization" to Bernstein (1990) who describes a *recontextualizing principle* which "selectively appropriates, relocates, refocuses, and relates other [pedagogic] discourses to constitute its own order and orderings" (p. 184). Bernstein (1990: 60) further defines a *recontextualizing context* in education, "whose positions, agents, and practices are concerned with the movements of texts/practices from the primary context of discursive production to the secondary context of discursive reproduction." The primary contexts engender the primary texts, which are the original sources, so to speak, of educational ideas and discourses. These texts are recontextualized for the secondary context (i.e. schools). Bernstein lists a number of examples of "fields" in which educational discourses are appropriated by recontextualization agents – university colleges of education, departments of education, and media of education (e.g. journals and their readers). He also describes a *principle of decontextualizing* that guides the transformation a text necessarily undergoes during recontextualization and ensures that it is "delocated" and "relocated" and, thus, takes up a new ideological position. "It is the recontextualizing field which generates the positions of pedagogic theory, research, and practice" (Bernstein 1990: 193). The intellectual history of the term may go back even further, however, as Bernstein claims it was introduced in Bernstein (1975) and used in Landsheere (1982).

Intertextual and interdiscursive analysis of language policy can help illuminate the connections across language policy layers and time-scales and helps us to understand how and why a language policy is recontextualized in particular ways in particular contexts. Not only might the intertextual connections influence what some policy means, the idiosyncratic beliefs, ideologies, and discourses circulating in a particular context will influence how it is recontextualized, further influencing the "meaning" of the language policy. This recontextualized meaning may or may not reflect authorial intentions.

Case 5.10 Intertextuality, interdiscursivity and recontextualization of language policy

I propose (Johnson 2011a) a method for studying language policy that combines ethnography with intertextual and interdiscursive analysis. Ethnography is incorporated to understand how research participants interpret and appropriate macro-level language policy texts and discourses, and, create their own language policies. Intertextual and interdiscursive analysis reveals how local policy activities relate to macro-level policy texts and discourses. I argue that, within a community of interaction participants, the meaning of a language policy emerges across a trajectory of speech events and situations. Intertextual and interdiscursive analysis helps illuminate how text production is linked to discursive and sociocultural practices but ethnography uncovers how and why particular policies are recontextualized in particular ways in particular settings. Any text created and interpreted in one context, or level of social organization, will be *recontextualized* in the new context, with the meaning of the original text either expanded upon, added to, filtered, and/or suppressed, and the nature of the recontextualization is shaped by the relationships, beliefs, ideologies, and power relationships, which are indexed in the discursive practices and captured through ethnography.

I analyze how the topoi of *accountability* and *flexibility* are intertextually linked across language policy documents which, in turn, rely on interdiscursive connections to dominant and potentially marginalizing discourses. However, educators in a school district respond to these language policies in varied and unpredictable ways – some help instantiate dominant notions about language, language education, and language policy as inflexibly focused on English education while others resist such notions and, instead, engender local policy text and discourses that celebrate multilingualism, additive bilingual education, and the flexibility of macro-level language policy. Therefore, what a macro-level language policy means for a school district may depend both on the intertextual and interdiscursive links to macro-level policy texts and discourses as well as the practices and beliefs of educators, unique to that particular context.

5.6.3 Criticism of CDA

Some of the more prominent critics of CDA have been Widdowson (1995, 1998), Schegloff (1997), and Blommaert (2001, 2005b), who offers a fairly comprehensive review of these positions (2005b). Here, I summarize, and add to, the main arguments:

1. *Nebulous concepts and methods*. Because there are multiple versions of CDA (Fairclough 2010) and analyses are perhaps guided by a set of theoretical assumptions (Wodak 1996), as opposed to methodological guidelines, what counts as "proper" CDA is a reasonably open question. I would argue that this is a strength of CDA because participation and access to the scholarly community is more egalitarian and accessible, which (a) is not true of its discourse-analytic counterparts (e.g. conversation analysis, linguistic anthropology) which require specialized training in arcane concepts at premier universities, and (b) befits its political leanings towards revealing and fighting social injustice. However, this strength is simultaneously a weakness because without more concise methodological guidance, new scholars struggle to figure out how to do CDA, and it is difficult to determine what counts as a strong or weak CDA analysis.

2. *Biased interpretations*. CDA has often been criticized for presenting the analyst's reading as the sole possible reading of the text, without considering variations in how a text might be interpreted and the plurality of discourses that a single text can generate. Because of this, Widdowson (1995) argues that CDA is interpretation, not analysis, and analysts tend to select portions of the text that support their ideological predispositions and interpret them accordingly. To put it simply, Widdowson (1995: 168) argues that "They read their own reality into it." Similarly, Blommaert (2005b: 32) argues that in CDA analyses "Texts are found to have a certain ideological meaning

that is forced upon the reader" and "particular images of society and social structure are projected onto stretches of discourse, and CDA becomes 'symptomatic' analysis, an analysis aimed at proving the (predefined) presence of a disease on the basis of an analysis of its symptoms."

3. *Lack of agency.* The same criticism that has been leveled against critical theory and critical language policy has been leveled against critical discourse analysis – the "critical" implies a monolithic focus on unequal relations of power, motivated by a characterization of the intractable discourses of power operating and circulating outside of the control of discoursers, which leaves little room for improvisation, subversion, and human creativity – to wit, *agency*. Relationships of power are seen as stable and easily identifiable through simplistic analyses of context. As Blommaert (2001: 15) argues, "Power relations are often predefined and then confirmed by features of discourse...politicians *always* and *intentionally* manipulate their constituencies, doctors are *by definition* and always the powerful party in doctor–patient relationships, etc." While there is a recognition that discourse operates across many levels and analysts should consider local and societal discourses, and the connections between the two, a multi-layered conceptualization of context is less developed. What operates as a "dominant" discourse in one layer may not be the case for another, and what may be viewed as "subversive" (by analysts) in, say, micro-level texts and discourses may be considered quite common, mainstream, or even dominant by the humans responsible for creating and interpreting those texts and discourses, at least in the context they were created.

4. *Inaccurate, under-theorized, or simplistic descriptions of context.* CDA is criticized for a simplistic or under-theorized description of the social context in which the texts are produced, which leads to *a priori* assumptions about which aspects of the context have an influence on text production, and projecting them onto the discourse (Schegloff 1997). This is a criticism that has resonated among CDA analysts, and newer work in the field, sometimes characterized as critical discourse studies (or CDS) is developing more sophisticated understandings of context and thus situating the texts under analysis (see discussion in Krzyżanowski 2011a). For example, ethnography is often combined with CDA to develop a more nuanced and substantive analysis of context (e.g. Cinotta-Segi, see 3.4; see also the theme issue

on CDA and ethnography in Krzyżanowski 2011b). I argue (Johnson 2011a: 277) that "While CDA is effective in establishing intertextual and interdiscursive links between policy texts and discourses, ethnography is essential for contextualizing the data and understanding why language policies are recontextualized in particular ways in particular contexts."

5.6.4 Linguistic anthropology and speech chains

As defined by the Society for Linguistic Anthropology (SLA):

> Linguistic Anthropology is the comparative study of the ways in which language shapes social life. It explores the many ways in which practices of language use shape patterns of communication, formulate categories of social identity and group membership, organize large-scale cultural beliefs and ideologies, and, in conjunction with other semiotic practices, equip people with common cultural representations of their natural and social worlds.

This approach is influenced by Dell Hymes' work (see 2.2.1) and, particularly, his application of anthropological theory and research methods (i.e. ethnography) to the study of both linguistic form and language use (and the interaction between the two). Other influential work includes Ochs and Schiefflin's (1983) research on child language socialization, or how children are enculturated into their community and socialized to and through the use of language; and Silverstein's (1985) research on the connections between ideology and language structure and his argument that ideology influences evolution of linguistic structure.

Much of the work in linguistic anthropology has important implications for language policy, particularly how local agents (say students) are socialized to and through language. For example, in Wortham's (2005) analysis of how a ninth grade student is socialized into academic life, he argues that there are trajectories of socialization – multiple speech events across which the student's identity emerges. Like the student's identity in Wortham's study, the meaning of a language policy often emerges as it is interpreted and appropriated across a series of speech events (and situations) in a community or school. This is not to say that a policy is socialized, of course, but that individuals are socialized to and through language (policy) – and the meaning relies on multiple connected speech events and situations that characterize the policy in a particular way, unique to that context. This approach highlights the intertextual and interdiscursive connections across a trajectory of language policy creation, interpretation, appropriation, and instantiation, which is beneficial for illuminating the connections between language policy layers and contexts. This approach also foregrounds how local actors interpret and appropriate policy in unique ways in unique contexts instead of focusing on original authorial intentions.

Concept 5.15 Agha's "speech chains" (2003: 247)

A *speech chain* is a historical series of speech events linked together by the permutation of individuals across speech-act roles in the following way: the receiver of the message in the (n)th speech event is the sender of the message in the (n+1)th speech event, i.e.

[S→R] [S→R] [S→R] [S→R]...

→ time

The terms 'sender' and 'receiver' (or 'S' and 'R') are variable names for interactional roles, specified in different ways at different points along the speech chain. (Reprinted with permission from Elsevier)

Wortham's (2005) analysis relies, in part, on Agha's (2003) concept of *speech chains*, which he advances as the mechanism for the transmission of cultural messages and linguistic behavior across time and social space. The concept of speech chains helps operationalize intertexuality, so to speak, by revealing a potential mechanism for the link between texts and events. Such a speech chain might be responsible for the interpretation and appropriation of a language policy, as well as how the meaning of a policy emerges in a particular school or community based on a set of intertextually and interdiscursively related speech events and situations.

Case 5.11 Mortimer on language policy in Paraguay

Mortimer (2013) incorporates speech chains to analyze the chain of communicative events that connect macro-level language policy with local educational practice in Paraguay. She traces two distinct meanings of what it means to speak Guaraní, an indigenous Paraguayan language, across macro and micro language policy texts, talk, and practices: (1) that it identifies someone as essentially Paraguayan, and (2) that it identifies someone as ignorant and from the countryside.

5.7 Discussion

This chapter is not an exhaustive review of all of the research methods that can and have been used in LPP research; it certainly represents my own biases in favor of particular research methods that I think have been particularly useful for revealing LPP processes. Methods of note that are not covered include psycho-sociological analysis (Baker 2006), corpus analysis (Fitzsimmons-Doolan, see 3.8), nexus analysis (Hult 2010a), linguistic landscape analysis (Shohamy and Gorter 2009), economic analysis (Grin 2003), interpretive policy analysis (Yanow 2000), and using demography and census data (Zhou 2013). All of these methods and issues (and much more) are covered in detail in the book edited by Hult and Johnson (2013).

The language policy research method adopted will depend on the research questions and the focus of the research. To provide an overarching framework, we can base our research methods on the policy process(es) we are most interested in: creation, interpretation, appropriation, and/or instantiation. Table 5.4 presents an overview.

Table 5.4 An interdisciplinary method for analyzing language policy

LPP activity	Agents of interest	Methods
Creation	Policymakers – examples include lawmakers and other politicians, business leaders, judges and attorneys, multilingual and monolingual activists and advocates; school district administrators; teachers	Historical-textual analysis; ethnographic methods including insider accounts (interviews) and participant-observation during policy creation; discourse analysis of political and policy debate and formation; macro-level document collection

(continued)

Table 5.4 Continued

LPP activity	Agents of interest	Methods
Interpretation	Interpreters of language policy – examples include the policymakers (i.e. how they interpret their creation) as well as those responsible for appropriation, including especially teachers; employers; educational administrators	Discourse analysis of interpretation discourse practices (processes of production and interpretation); interviews and participant-observation; meso-level document collection
Appropriation	Those who appropriate and who are impacted by language policy – primarily teachers and students; employers and employees; parents and children	Participant-observation; interviews; discourse analysis of interaction (collected via audio- and video-recordings); micro-level document collection
Instantiation	Teachers, students, community members	Participant-observation in classrooms and communities; discourse analysis of interaction in classrooms and communities

6
Educational language policy engagement and action research (ELPEAR)

Chapter overview

6.1 Action research
6.2 Language policy action research
6.3 ELPEAR examples
6.4 David Corson's model for critical policymaking in schools
6.5 Language policy engagement: Creation
6.6 Language policy engagement: Interpretation
6.7 Language policy engagement: Appropriation
6.8 Discussion

While Chapter 5 reviewed language policy research methods, this chapter goes into more detail about one in particular – *action research* – and also proposes strategies for engagement and advocacy. This is an attempt to address the epistemological tension and positionality dilemmas engendered when working with marginalized groups (a characterization that includes *all* teachers, since teaching is a marginalized profession). I propose an approach that promotes epistemic solidarity between researchers and educators and critical interrogation of power imbalances in policy processes. Educational language policy engagement and action research (ELPEAR) requires collaboration in policy engagement and research, the goal of which is to challenge deficit discourses and promote social justice in education.

6.1 Action research

Action research was initially proposed by the social psychologist Kurt Lewin (1946: 35), who defined it as "a comparative research on the conditions and effects of various forms of social action and research leading to social action." The application to teaching was developed and further articulated by researchers at Deakin University in Australia, who envisioned action research as a method that put the focus on teachers as self-reflexive researchers in their own classrooms. Important publications include Carr and Kemmis (1986) and, of particular importance for this discussion, *The Action Research Planner* by Kemmis and McTaggart (1988).

Quote 6.1 Action research defined

Action research is a form of *collective* self-reflective enquiry undertaken by participants in social situations in order to improve the rationality and justice of their own social or educational practices, as well as their understanding of these practices and the situations in which these practices are carried out. Groups of participants can be teachers, students, principals, parents and other community members – any group with a shared concern. The approach is only action research when it is *collaborative*, though it is important to realize that the action research of the group is achieved through the *critically examined action* of individual group members.

(Kemmis and McTaggart 1988: 5)

As the definition proposed by Kemmis and McTaggart (Quote 6.1) makes clear, action research involves critical reflection of an individual's own practice, but it is also essentially a collaborative venture, the direction of which is engendered by the shared concerns of a group. An action research project should be open to "as many as possible of those affected by the practices concerned" (Kemmis and McTaggart 1988: 23). Kemmis and McTaggart describe four fundamental aspects of action research (Concept 6.1), that come together to form four linked aspects of an ongoing action research cycle (Figure 6.1). A key aspect is Kemmis and McTaggart's (1988: 23) politically critical engagement and a focus on institutional change and emancipation: "It aims to build communities of people committed to enlightening themselves about the relationship between circumstance, action, and consequence in their own situation, and emancipating themselves from the institutional and personal constraints which limit their power."

Concept 6.1 Fundamental aspects of action research

Group members:

1. *plan* action together
2. *act and observe* individually and collectively
3. *reflect* together
4. *reformulate more critically informed plans*

(Kemmis and McTaggart 1988: 9)

The focus on collaboration and critical engagement leads to another important characteristic of action research – it is not just about changing the educational practices (although this is one essential aspect) but about changing the culture of the collective organization. This involves changes in language and discourses (e.g. how people describe their work); activities and practices (e.g. teaching practices); and social relationships and

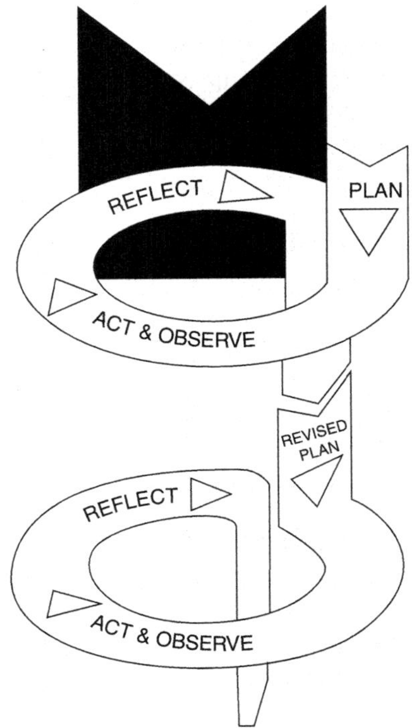

Figure 6.1 The action research spiral (Kemmis and McTaggart 1988: 11)

organization (e.g. the ways people inter-relate). In order to effect change in educational organizations, the collective attempts to improve the educational discourses that govern how they communicate with each other in order to improve organizational and educational practice. Kemmis and McTaggart illustrate the process in terms of a spiral (Figure 6.1).

Kemmis and McTaggart (1988: 22–25) offer key points about action research, which are summarized here. Action research:

1. seeks to improve education by changing it;
2. is both participatory (focused on individual practices) and collaborative (involving those responsible for improving it) and the goal should be to widen the collaborating group to as many as possible of those affected by the practices concerned: "It is not research done on other people" (p. 22);
3. is open-minded about what counts as evidence and includes both qualitative and quantitative data;
4. establishes "self-critical communities" who seek to reveal and resist institutional and personal constraints that limit and marginalize the power of the community and their social values;
5. is a political process that involves critical analysis of the situations, structures, and discourses and, therefore, involves resistance;
6. starts small and then expands, involving as many individuals as possible;
7. builds a reasoned justification of the educational work supported by a body of evidence of the educational practices in question.

Quote 6.2 Action research

AR involves taking a self-reflective, critical, and systematic approach to exploring your own teaching contexts. By critical, I don't mean being negative and derogatory about the way you teach, but taking a questioning and 'problematising' stance towards your teaching. My term, *problematising*, doesn't imply looking at your teaching as ineffective and full of problems. Rather, it means taking an area you feel could be done better, subjecting it to questioning, and then developing new ideas and alternatives. So, in AR, a teacher becomes an 'investigator' or 'explorer' of his or her personal teaching context, while at the same time being one of the participants in it...[T]he central idea of the *action* part of AR is to intervene in a deliberate way in the problematic situation in order to bring about changes.

(Burns 2010: 2)

6.2 Language policy action research

The tenets of AR do not apply neatly to LPP because we are not talking only about teachers and students but about a wide range of language policy agents who are affected by the practices concerned (although teachers are essential for a language policy action research project). It was important in the original formulation of AR to challenge the university scholar's privileged position in conducting research in educational settings; however, university researchers are not necessarily in a similar position when it comes to *language policy* research and engagement. Thus collaboration between a diversity of language policy agents – teachers, students, administrators – *along with* university researchers should be the goal of language policy action research.

Language policy action research is conducted throughout the language policy cycle – creation, interpretation, appropriation, and instantiation – and is used to inform and improve these processes. The focus is:

- how macro-level language policies are interpreted and put into practice
- how micro-level language policies are created, interpreted, and put into practice
- multilingual education and the educational opportunities of minority language users.

It ideally involves teachers and administrators from multiple levels of institutional authority and includes input from students and parents, as well as university scholars. Language policy action research provides the research team with an opportunity to interrogate how they are creating, interpreting, and appropriating language policy and educating students from diverse linguistic and cultural backgrounds, and changing if needed. It also provides the opportunity for the research team to challenge inequalities in schools which emerge from the subordination of minority languages, and thus there is an inherent agenda of social justice. Finally, it provides the research team with the opportunity to critically examine institutional discourses, challenge those aspects that marginalize teachers as mere implementers of language policy and re-position them as policy decision-makers – i.e. *language policy arbiters* (Concept 4.1). In order to challenge marginalizing discourses, the participation frameworks and participation statuses of the participants within meetings often need to be critically examined, challenged, and changed (Concept 6.2).

Concept 6.2 Challenging marginalizing participation frameworks

Goffman (1979) proposes the concept of *footing,* which refers to the participants' alignment or positions in an interaction. The relative footing of participants in an interaction characterizes what Goffman refers to as the *participation framework,* which is engendered by the *participation status* of each of the participants. In Johnson (2011), I argue that non-traditional participation frameworks – in which teachers and administrators engage in egalitarian decision-making and language policy action-research projects – can alter traditional hierarchical power structures and lead to the positioning of teachers as language policy arbiters, not just in policy implementation and classroom teaching, but in bottom-up policy *creation, interpretation,* and *appropriation* of top-down policy. On the other hand, when school district administrators, who are typically invested with more language policy power, rely on hierarchical participation frameworks that position teachers as lacking the expertise to make language policy decisions, teacher agency is stripped (yet resistance becomes more probable).

6.2.1 The language policy action research cycle

Following Kemmis and McTaggart (1988), it is proposed that members of the language policy action research team:

A. *Plan* action together

Language plans, actions, or research foci include:

- the impact of macro-level language policies on educational practices
- the creation, interpretation, and appropriation of micro-level language policies created by and for educators
- educational language plans and research, including:
    - development and implementation of classroom materials for multilingual education (see 6.3.1)
    - multilingual literacy development (see 3.1)
    - impacts of standards and accountability measures on classroom language practices (see Menken 2008)
    - starting and developing bilingual programs (see Freeman 2004, and 6.3.2)
    - implementing practices in "mainstream" classrooms (science, math, etc.) for non-native speakers

B. *Act and observe* individually and collectively
Acting and observing individually and collectively provide an opportunity to examine how language policies are being interpreted and put into practice in classrooms. The focus is how creation, interpretation, and appropriation of language policy and language educational practices impact the educational opportunity of students, particularly from minority language backgrounds.

Actions and observations take place in:

- meetings for language policies, programs, and faculty
- classrooms
- student homes
- school and community spaces where students congregate
- professional development workshops
- parent–teacher conferences

C. *Reflect* together
Reflecting together involves members of the research team reflecting (individually and collectively) on their actions and observations regarding language policy and education. This requires a time to reflect on the progress of the project as a group and these meetings will inform how the group reformulates more critically informed educational language plans and policies.

D. *Reformulate more critically informed educational language plans and policies*
After the group has studied their own practices and reflected together, they may decide to change what they are doing. This provides the group with the opportunity to critically examine their own practices and, then, improve them if necessary. Reformulating educational language plans and policies re-starts the (iterative) cycle and is followed by acting and observing individually and collectively.

Concept 6.3 Research questions for language policy action research

Creation

- Who creates the policies?
- Why are the particular creator(s) invested with this power?
- What are the goals of the policy as evidenced in the policy language?

- What are the goals of the policy as evidenced in the discourse surrounding the creation of policy?
- How are the ideas and language in the policy intertextually and interdiscursively linked to more widely circulating discourses about language, language education and minority language users?
- How can the creation of a language policy be opened up to a wider group of potential policy "authors"?
- How have other schools and school districts developed multilingual education policies?
- How has our school or school district developed language policies in the past? What types of policy-making and implementation processes have been "successful" and "unsuccessful" (however that is defined)?

Interpretation and appropriation

- Who is responsible for the interpretation and appropriation of top-down policies?
- Why are they invested with this authority? That is, why are they *language policy arbiter(s)*? (see Concept 4.1)
- How do their beliefs about language and language education interact with their interpretation and appropriation of the policy?
- How does the interpretation and appropriation in a given context compare with what is happening in other contexts?
- How does the interpretation and appropriation of a language policy open implementational spaces for multilingual education and how does it close them?
- How can the interpretation and appropriation of top-down policies be opened to a wider group of language policy agents?
- How can educators creatively manipulate the implementational spaces in a language policy for multilingual educational practices?

Classroom instantiation

- How do micro and macro language policies impact classroom interaction, pedagogy, and policy within classrooms?
- How do policies help and/or hinder classroom instruction that incorporates minority languages?
- How do standardized tests impact classroom instruction?
- What language policies emerge within a classroom?
- Can language policies that emerge within particular classrooms be utilized in others?

6.2.2 Features of language policy action research

(1) Collaborative and participatory

Language policy action research involves a diverse group of individuals from multiple levels of institutional authority who collaboratively develop research questions, collect and analyze data, and reformulate language plans, policies, and practices based on critical examination. Members of the research team must include teachers and administrators but also could include parents, students, university researchers, and outside consultants. While the research team should include as many of those individuals who are affected by a language policy as possible, a core set of individuals (or even one particular person) needs to shepherd the project until completion. This group, or individual, should be emancipatory leaders (Concept 6.4) who are committed to participation frameworks that encourage collaboration and participation and widen the field of language policy *decision-makers*. Language policy action research is not research done *on* other people.

(2) Acceptance of different types of data as evidence

Quantitative studies focus on the relative effectiveness of different education programs, the implementation of language policies (as reported in surveys), and the attitudes about various language policies and language attitudes. Findings help inform future language plans and policies. Examples include:

- surveys that target how particular polices are interpreted and appropriated by educators and the attitudes towards particular policies and practices (see Dillman *et al.* 2009)
- probability samples of newspaper articles to get a rough count of how many newspaper articles are for and against the policy, or for and against multilingual education (see Concept 5.4)
- standardized test data analysis to determine the relative effectiveness of different language educational programs
- experimental and quasi-experimental studies on the relative effectiveness of language educational programs (e.g. Collier and Thomas 2001)
- meta-analyses of quantitative studies of the relative effectiveness of language educational programs (e.g. Rolstad, Mahoney, and Glass 2005).

Qualitative studies focus on language policy and educational *processes*: How are language policies and programs created, interpreted, and put into practice? How do attitudes about language policies and languages impact classroom instruction? Findings help inform future language plans and policies. Examples include:

- document analysis of the circulating policies in a given context
- document analysis of policies from other contexts (e.g. schools, school districts, states, etc.)
- participant-observation in classrooms and meetings
- audio- and video-recordings in classrooms and meetings
- interviews with teachers, administrators, parents, students, and community members.

(3) Research team members develop an understanding of the macro-level language policies influencing their educational practices and critically examine the language of these policies

While the focus is local – that is, the primary concern is how language policies impact a local community of educators – an understanding of macro-level language policies is crucial. A critical examination of the language in macro-level policies may reveal *implementational* and *ideological spaces* (Concept 4.3) that the research team can utilize to implement the educational strategies and program structures they believe in. As well, when creating local policies, it may be useful to intentionally establish intertextual links between the local policy and macro-level language policy language.

(4) Includes research on past language policy successes and failures and current language policy processes in other parts of the country/world

Every context is unique but there may be similarities in language policy processes across contexts and educators can learn from each other. Such comparisons are vital for developing a fuller understanding of how language policy works and for developing better theories of language policy activity. Language policies developed in other schools and school districts can be analyzed (see 8.5). Connections can be made at conferences (see 8.3), electronic mail lists (see 8.6), and within organizations that focus on language education and policy (see 8.4).

(5) Informed by research in applied linguistics, sociolinguistics, and educational practices

Research teams should be knowledgeable about the research on:

- the relative effectiveness of different language educational programs (e.g. Rolstad *et al.* 2005)

- the impact of testing on language policy and practice (e.g. Menken 2008)
- successful strategies for developing local language policies (see 6.5.2)
- first and second language acquisition (e.g. Lightbown and Spada 2006)
- language learning processes and language teaching methods (e.g. Richards and Rodgers 2006)
- sociolinguistics and language teaching (e.g. Hornberger and McKay 2011)

6.3 ELPEAR examples

Three example ELPEAR projects are discussed here. Neville Alexander and PRAESA's work concerns multilingual education and the promotion of African languages in South Africa. Rebecca Freeman has done research on, and been engaged in, ELPEAR projects around the U.S., advocating for multilingual education and egalitarian discourse communities of policymakers. Richard Hill and Stephen May propose a unique model for doing research in Indigenous communities when the researchers themselves are not from that community. While they focus on Māori, their framework could be usefully applied to many different contexts.

6.3.1 Neville Alexander and PRAESA

Neville Alexander and the Project for the Study of Alternative Education in South Africa (PRAESA) provide inspiration for what ELPEAR can be. Alexander, who died in 2012, was a former revolutionary, who helped found the (South African) National Liberation Front (NLF), and spent ten years at Robben Island prison (with Nelson Mandela). After being released in 1974, he turned his attention towards multilingual education and issues surrounding linguistic human rights in South Africa. He was the director of PRAESA, a language planning and policy organization, which has had a large impact on government, educational, and community structures and entities, including the formulation of a national language plan for South Africa and the Department of Education's language-in-education policy, both of which are committed to promoting multilingualism and, in particular, African languages. In 2011 PRAESA articulated six dimensions of their approach to LPP:

1. close observation and monitoring of the impact of language plans and policies in schools, with subsequent improvements to both policy and practice, based on this research;

2. language in education planning research, including historical analysis of past policies and practices, which can inform contemporary language planning;
3. language mapping and surveys that provide data on the linguistic profiles and attitudes of the students and communities which, in turn, help inform policy and practice;
4. active involvement in debates on language in education issues in South Africa, and increasingly all over the African continent;
5. teacher education and capacity building of teacher educators, education managers, and curriculum developers, with the focus on developing and improving additive bilingual education models;
6. direct liaison with departments of education which leads to influence in language planning and policy processes.

Under the direction of Alexander, PRAESA successfully combined activism and scholarship to the benefit of education in South Africa and many of their publications can be found on their website (http://www.praesa.org.za/). They are very much committed to supporting additive bilingual education that includes African languages, raising the status of African languages (particularly isiXhosa), and they are a resource for educators who work in multilingual classrooms. PRAESA has been involved with many language planning and policy initiatives, including the development and formulation of the National Language Policy Framework and the South African Languages Bill (1999–2004), the evolution, establishment and operationalization of the Pan South African Language Board (1994–2000), and, of particular relevance here, the National Language in Education Policy (1995–1997), which explicitly promotes the linguistic rights of the students, multilingual education, and the promotion of traditionally marginalized languages (Policy text 6.1).

Policy text 6.1 Excerpts from the 1997 South African Language in Education Policy

[T]he government, and thus the Department of Education, recognises that our cultural diversity is a valuable national asset and hence is tasked, amongst other things, to promote multilingualism, the development of the official languages, and respect for all languages used in the country, including South African Sign Language and the languages referred to in the South African Constitution...

This approach is in line with the fact that both societal and individual multilingualism are the global norm today, especially on the African continent. As such, it assumes that the learning of more than one language should be general practice and principle in our society. That is to say, being multilingual should be a defining characteristic of being South African. It is constructed also to counter any particularistic ethnic chauvinism or separatism through mutual understanding...

Recognising that diversity is a valuable asset, which the state is required to respect, the aim of these norms and standards is the promotion, fulfilment and development of the state's overarching language goals in school education in compliance with the Constitution, namely:

1. the protection, promotion, fulfilment and extension of the individual's language rights and means of communication in education; and
2. the facilitation of national and international communication through promotion of bi- or multilingualism through cost-efficient and effective mechanisms;
3. to redress the neglect of the historically disadvantaged languages in school education.

PRAESA's work in ELPEAR follows a multidimensional approach by engaging in language planning and policy development in classrooms, which involves classroom-based research on teaching practices that incorporate African languages. For example, after helping to form the 1997 National Language in Education Policy, PRAESA conducted the Battswood biliteracy project in an English-medium school in Wynberg, Cape Town, the goal of which was to introduce Xhosa–English biliteracy to Xhosa-speaking students and offer Xhosa language classes for English- and Afrikaans-speaking students. A series of approaches that focused on the biliteracy development of the students were introduced and documented. Results revealed positive outcomes related to issues surrounding motivation and identity for the Xhosa-speaking students (and teachers) as well as successful biliteracy development. However, a major challenge was locating reading material, like story books, published in isiXhosa, and those that were found were often (bad) translations from English story books. These findings have informed, and helped motivate, a large-scale project entitled the Early Literacy Unit, which seeks to support the multilingual literacy development of young children, provide teacher training, and develop materials that can support biliteracy.

Throughout their initiatives and projects, PRAESA sticks to the principle that language planning and policy solutions must first be generated "from within, from the ground" and, only thereafter, incorporate what can be learned from without. They are actively engaged in what Alexander (1989: 62–63) proposes as "language planning from below," which includes participation and consent by those affected by policy (students and parents) as well as a historical knowledge of past language planning and policy practices (i.e. what worked and what did not). The alternative, an "imposed policy", is untenable because "any plan that is imposed will be rejected...or it will be subverted and made unworkable by the people" (see *subversive covert policy*, Table 1.1). Alexander argues that while English should continue to serve as a lingua franca, all South Africans should be educated in their mother tongue as a medium of instruction (along with English). He further argues that all South African languages have a right to flourish and should be included in education as part of a "democratically conceived language policy" which "will necessarily bear features that accord with the cultural aspirations and political programmes of those working people, who are the main agents of radical change in South Africa" (p. 51).

Alexander (1989) lays out his plan for South African languages in his book, *Language Policy and National Unity in South Africa/Azania*, which is intended for a wide audience and reads like an inspirational treatise on the importance of multilingualism, multilingual education, and especially African languages. Alexander portrays democratically conceived language policies as essential for national unification and national liberation in South Africa (Quote 6.3).

Quote 6.3 Language policy and national unity in South Africa/Azania

My main aim is to try to show those who read this essay and especially those who are involved in education, community, labour and youth projects, how important the language question is in the conduct of our struggle for national liberation. I want to persuade my readers to my view that, if approached from a historical point of view, language policy can become an instrument to unify our people instead of being the instrument of division which, for the most part, it is today. We

> need to make a democratically conceived language policy an integral part of our programme for national unity and national liberation.
>
> (Alexander 1989: Preface)

6.3.2 Rebecca Freeman

Rebecca Freeman is a sociolinguistic researcher, language policy consultant, and bilingual education advocate in the United States and, through her research and advocacy, she has engendered, promoted, and supported educational programs and policies that incorporate multilingualism as a resource in U.S. schools. Her work is especially remarkable considering the push for English-only or English-focused educational models. She has been a consultant for school districts around the country but her primary research projects have involved Oyster Bilingual School in Washington D.C. and the School District of Philadelphia (SDP). Her major publications from this work include journal articles (e.g. Freeman 2000) and two books. Her first book, *Bilingual Education and Social Change* (1998) is based on an ethnographic and discourse-analytic study conducted in a dual language school (Oyster) and examines how "ideal language-planning goals are realized in actual practice" (p. 87). The book is notable because of its innovative ethnographic and discourse-analytic methodology for studying LPP and making connections between policies and practices.

Case 6.1 Freeman – Building on community bilingualism

I observed Freeman's work in the School District of Philadelphia when she was a consultant and I saw how much power she had on language policy processes therein (for a lengthier discussion, see Johnson 2010a). Based on her own research, Freeman knew that a strictly top-down policy could be met with resistance, and so helped to create a more egalitarian discourse community, in which multiple voices from multiple levels of institutional authority were respected in language policy decisions. She also knew, based on her own research, that developmental or additive models of bilingual education could lead to bilingualism, biliteracy, and academic success and, therefore, promoted these types of programs. And, finally, she knew, based on her research, that an educational language policy succeeds better if it incorporates the needs and wishes of the community. Because of her efforts, multiple dual language programs were created and she played a large role in fostering various additive programs around the district.

Freeman worked for a number of years as a language policy and education consultant to the SDP and conducted ongoing ethnographic and action research projects with teachers and administrators, resulting in her second book, *Building on Community Bilingualism* (2004). Among other things, her book explores language ideologies and identity in Philadelphia neighborhoods, how teachers build on their students' linguistic and cultural expertise (in English and Spanish), and offers a detailed account of a particular language policy and planning initiative (the "dual language initiative") with which she was closely involved. Taken as a whole, the book provides a model for how educators and researchers, working collaboratively, can build on the linguistic and cultural resources in communities by developing and promoting programs and policies that incorporate multilingualism as a resource, even in contexts like the U.S. where monolingual education is the norm.

Based on her research on language planning and policy, Freeman (2004) offers specific guidelines for language planners for developing school language policies that promote multilingualism:

1. Gather information about the sociolinguistic setting, the needs of the target community, and alternative models of education and the research base that informs those models.
2. Consider how different language plans would relate to other socioeconomic and political processes in the target school and community contexts.
3. Define goals, determine outcomes in advance, assess values and attitudes, consider resources and constraints, articulate language plans, and formulate language policies.
4. Make provisions for implementation to ensure that the policy is carried out, including plans and strategies for mobilizing human and material resources, motivating and supervising personnel, and sequencing and coordinating different aspects of the policy.
5. Determine ways to evaluate the language policy on a regular basis, including ways to monitor, adjust, or change the plan and/or policy if either is not successful.

Quote 6.4 The nature of language planning and policy

I see language planning and policy development as dynamic, ideological processes that are shaped by multiple levels of institutional authority. This means that language planners and policy makers must identify and work through the relevant levels of institutional

> authority and/or decision-making structures, which of course vary across schools, school districts, states, and nations over time.
>
> (Freeman 2004: 24)

6.3.3 Richard Hill and Stephen May

The influence of Māori language education on *te reo Māori* (Māori language) revitalization is heralded as a success story for language policies that support Indigenous language revitalization. Much like Indigenous language loss in many parts of the world, Māori language loss in New Zealand was the result of colonization and assimiliationist policies, which put the Māori language at risk of extinction. However, beginning in the 1980's with *Te Kohanga Reo* – full immersion preschool programs – immersion education in Māori has expanded to all educational levels and has been officially incorporated into the New Zealand state educational system. In 1987 the Māori Language Act was passed which recognized *te reo Māori* as one of New Zealand's official languages. May (2005a) argues that the Māori revitalization movement, supported primarily by full immersion education, has aided the process of language reversal, a process by which one of the major languages in a country (here, Māori) becomes more widely and prominently used after a period in which it was declining.

The case of Māori educational language policy is of interest to many different researchers (see the special issue of the *International Journal of Bilingual Education and Bilingualism* on Māori education, edited by May 2005b). Stephen May and Richard Hill have produced a series of publications based on ethnographic accounts of the relationship between national language policy and Māori immersion education. Of particular interest here is their incorporation of a unique research method, *Kaupapa Māori research* (KMR), which "attempts to eliminate the discriminatory practices inherent in many previous research projects involving Māori participants and non-Indigenous researchers" (Hill and May 2011: 163). Instead, the interests of the Māori community are emphasized and all research must conform to Māori cultural values.

KMR provides a model for non-Indigenous researchers who want to conduct studies in Indigenous contexts and Hill and May borrow and build upon their colleagues' work in this area. For example, borrowing from Smith (1997), they propose four questions which need to be addressed before any research project can begin (Hill and May 2013):

1. What difference is this research going to make for the Māori?
2. What meaningful interventions will result?
3. How does the research support Māori cultural and language aspirations?
4. Is the researcher merely telling us what we (Māori) already know?

Only when the research participants deem that these questions have been answered satisfactorily, can a research study proceed. Then, there are seven general guidelines for working in Māori contexts, which are meant to protect the rights and sensitivities of the research participants (cited in Hill and May 2013):

1. Aroha ki te tangata (A respect for people)
2. He kanohi kitea (Meeting people face to face)
3. Titiro, whakarongo... korero (The importance of carefully observing and listening)
4. Manaaki ki te tangata (Sharing, hosting, collaboration, giving back)
5. Kia tūpato (Be cautious)
6. Kaua e takahi te mana o te tangata (Do not trample on the dignity of the person)
7. Kaua e mahaki (Don't flaunt your knowledge).

Finally, borrowing from Bishop and Glynn (1999) and Bishop (2005), they identify five broader KMR principles (Hill and May 2013: 58–62):

- *Initiation:* seeks to incorporate Māori participation during the initiation of the research and, by implication, for Māori participants to play a central role in the research processes as a whole.
- *Benefits:* seeks to ensure that all participants, researcher and researched, work to achieve genuine benefits from their participation and precludes anyone being disadvantaged through the research. As a consequence, this principle limits research that solely serves the interests of the researcher – a criticism of many past research practices towards Māori.
- *Representation:* aims to ensure that the information that is gathered through the research process is an accurate representation of the views of those participants, and their cultural values, beliefs and practices.
- *Legitimation:* where previous research has often belittled Indigenous Māori knowledge, KMR instead embraces and provides status and

credibility to Māori epistemologies because the research contexts are culturally Māori. Hence, this concept attempts to challenge the ideology of cultural superiority that has pervaded much previous research and to ensure power sharing processes are employed. For example, Hill and May assumed that feedback for their ongoing research would be delivered in writing to the participants but, because of the cultural construct of *kanohi kitea* (the seen face), the Māori expectation was oral feedback, which they subsequently delivered.

- *Accountability:* concerns control over the entire research process, the procedures, the means of evaluation, text constructions, and ways of distribution of the new knowledge. From a KMR perspective, the researcher is accountable, not only to the professional research community, but also to all participants. In line with the wider principles of critical ethnography, there is a sharing of power between researcher and participants, which also helps to develop richer accounts (see "joint problematization", Quote 7.1).

6.4 David Corson's model for critical policymaking in schools

David Corson's (1999) *Language Policy in Schools: A Resource for Teachers and Administrators* is meant as an accessible resource and guide for school-based educators who wish to create their own language policy. Corson defines a language policy as a "document compiled by the staff of a school, often assisted by other members of the school community, to which the staff members give their assent and commitment" (p. 1). The goals of such a language policy are to *collaboratively* identify language problems in a school and then agree on solutions.

Quote 6.5 Collaborative critical policymaking

The interests, attitudes, values, and wishes of people with a stake in the policy area provide the basic evidence for critical policymakers. To get access to that evidence, the circle of decision makers in a school widens to include people who are fully in touch with all those things...This means consulting the needs and identifying the interests of relevant teachers, students, parents, community members, and also policymakers working in the wider system.

(Corson 1999: 66)

Corson proposes "critical policymaking", which is inspired by early language planning work (see 2.1) as well as critical theory (e.g. Foucault 1980). As in Kemmis and McTaggart (1988), Corson proposes that school-based policymaking must be collaborative (quote 6.5) and should be inclusive of all of those individuals who are potentially impacted by the policy. This process also relies on what Corson calls "emancipatory leaders" (Concept 6.4) who encourage free and open participation in decision making processes.

Concept 6.4 Emancipatory leaders

Emancipatory leaders:

- rely on the expertise of the community with regards to sociocultural norms and interactional processes in diverse settings and situations
- limit their own presence in debate and decision-making
- encourage democratic decision-making and follow the advice of the democratically developed consensus, thus removing the "effects of their own power from the process of decision making" (p. 62)
- encourage the democratic election of those who will be in charge of implementing the will of the group

Corson's framework for critical policymaking (1999: 64–78) includes four stages, with multiple processes involved in each stage, which are summarized here:

Stage I: Identifying the real problem(s)

- *The problem situation*: Involves determining who will be involved in the language policy process, which should be collaborative (Quote 6.5).
- *The role of expert knowledge*: Includes those traditionally seen as experts (teachers and administrators) as well as those with insight into the local community who can include local knowledge as a resource (parents and other community members)
- *The problem(s)*: The group collaboratively assembles the set of problems which the language policy will address.

Stage II: Trial policies: The views of stakeholders

- *Policy guidelines*: The set of solutions to the policy problems, stated in very clear language so that everyone understands them

- *Controllable changes*: Stages in policy guidelines: Includes evaluation of the policy guidelines by those affected by the policy.

Stage III: Testing policies against the views of participants

- *Testing policies by trial applications*: Trial applications of the policy guidelines are tested and adjustments are made, or are outright rejected
- *Testing policies by research*: Large-scale research projects (e.g. ethnography, naturalistic observation in classrooms, discourse analysis) and small-scale projects (e.g. surveys) are conducted to help determine the impact of a policy.

Stage IV: Policy implementation and evaluations

- The statement of the language policy itself, with the understanding that the language of the policy can adapt to meet the changing needs of the changing participants, problems, and social contexts
- Evaluation involves determining whether the policy solutions meet the needs of the participants and, if not, changing the policy
- Corson implies that the community of evaluators would be as wide as possible: "Everyone's point of view and interpretation of the world would be consulted" (p. 65).

6.5 Language policy engagement: Creation

The focus in the book series of which this is an installment is "Research and Practice in Applied Linguistics." "Practice" in LPP has at least two meanings: the language *practices* in schools and communities that are influenced by language policy; and engaging in language policy processes and *practices*. Both are emphasized in the book but the second is the focus of this section. Engagement and action research go hand in hand, which makes ELPEAR unique – if you are doing action research you will almost necessarily "do" policy work. Furthermore, how to engage in language policy processes should be, in part, inspired by research. This section proposes a model for how researchers, teachers, and other educationists can become actively engaged in language policy processes. I draw on my own action-oriented research in a large U.S. school district to help illustrate some of the main ideas.

Concept 6.5 Language policy engagement

Language policy engagement includes multiple agents – from multiple levels of institutional authority – collectively engaging in *creation* (section 6.5) of micro-level language policies and *interpretation* (6.6) and *appropriation* (6.7) of micro- and macro-level language policies, with the goals being:

- the promotion of minority and Indigenous languages in education
- the promotion of multilingual education
- improving the educational and socioeconomic opportunities for students
- developing excellent education for all students
- promoting a social justice agenda for historically marginalized languages and their users
- expanding the group of language policy arbiters (concept 3.7) to include those historically positioned as mere implementers
- changing institutional discourses that lead to the subjugation or marginalization of minority languages, the students, and their teachers
- changing participation frameworks (Concept 6.2) to empower a diversity of language policy agents as important decision-makers

Getting involved in language policy creation occurs in two contexts, each of which creates two types of language policies – macro-level and micro-level language policies.

Concept 6.6 Macro and micro language policies

Macro-level language policies are language policies that are created outside of the context in which the language policy is interpreted and appropriated.
Micro-level language policies are language policies created within the context in which they are interpreted and appropriated.

Of course, characterizing this as a dichotomy, as only macro and micro, obfuscates what are actually multiple layers of language policy activity. Even within the micro category (say, a school district creating its own policy), the process can be multiply layered. For example, if an administrator creates a policy, the teachers may refer to this as macro-level or top-down policy, even though, in the field of LPP, we would typically count this as an example of micro-level policy creation. Therefore, what is considered "macro" and what is considered "micro" are relative and depends upon the perspective of those being affected by the policy. Figure 6.2 suggests a framework for thinking about language policy layering that is based upon the institutional structure in U.S. education. I divide the levels into nine (although there are certainly more) to show that within any particular context, there are multiple levels, so while a school district administrator works in a MICRO context, they are a Macro-MICRO or Meso-MICRO language policy actor (depending on where they work in the institutional structure) while a teacher is a Micro-MICRO language policy actor.

It is important to note that language policies can potentially be engendered at any of these nine levels but their effects will tend to filter down through the various layers. It is less common for language policies created in micro-contexts to move upward, albeit not impossible (see 6.5.1.2) but what is typically needed is a groundswell of support that encourages or even forces those in higher levels of institutional authority to create a corresponding policy. Also, there are individuals that are not part of the traditional structure of institutional authority, including lobbying groups, researchers, and parents, who may still wield a great deal of influence over language policy. The arbiters of language policy exist in many different contexts and levels of institutional authority and are not necessarily predictable.

6.5.1 Macro-level language policy creation

Macro-level language policy engagement involves citizens taking part in federal, national, or other large-scale language policy initiatives. A good example is the impact Neville Alexander and PRAESA have had on language policy creation in South Africa, working through political channels, such as committees and governing bodies, to influence policy creation. However, how best to engage in macro-level language policy creation will depend in large part on the context in which it is being created and it is difficult to make generalizations about what may work across contexts – what proves to be successful for Alexander and PRAESA in South Africa may not work elsewhere. With that in mind, in this section I will focus on initiatives that have taken place in the context in which I work – the U.S. – in the hopes of reviewing some success stories that may be of value for others, if not directly applicable. Some of these suggestions rely on a successful language education lobbying organization in the United States,

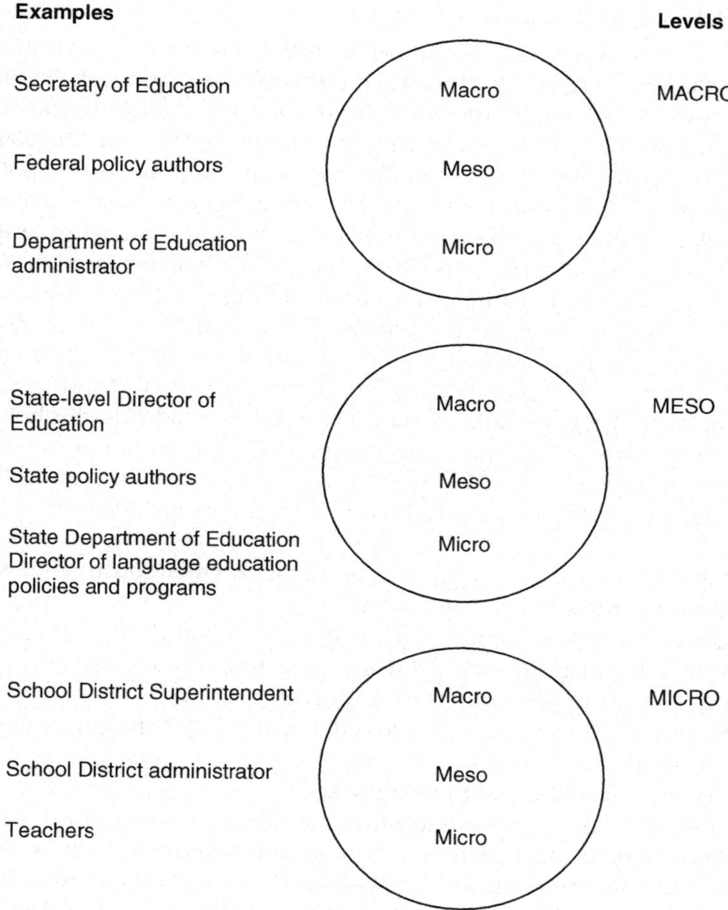

Figure 6.2 Relationships between macro, meso, and micro educational language policy

the Joint National Committee for Languages and The National Council for Languages and International Study (JNCL-NCLIS), which has had an impact on federally created language policies and initiatives aimed primarily at foreign language education for native English speakers (as opposed to English language education or bilingual education for non-native English speakers). However, their techniques could certainly apply to other learners and different kinds of policies.

6.5.1.1 Engaging politicians

JNCL-NCLIS represents a number of other member organizations, including (among many others) the National Association of Bilingual Education (NABE), the Center for Applied Linguistics (CAL), the American Council on the Teaching of Foreign Languages (ACTFL), the Linguistics Society of America (LSA), and the American Association of Applied Linguistics (AAAL) with the combined mission being to ensure that "all Americans must have the opportunity to learn and use English and at least one other language" (JNCL-NCLIS, see this volume, section 8.4). They regularly hold national meetings on language policy issues and invite politicians and other policymakers to be speakers. They also organize an annual Legislative Day and Delegate Assembly in Washington D.C. when JNCL-NCLIS members meet with members of Congress to advocate for language policy issues. They provide guidelines for how to effectively engage legislators, including a video on "making your voice count" (Fontana 2009/2013) that shows example meetings and offers strategies for how to engage legislators. Suggestions include:

- View your advocacy as a teaching moment: Offer constructive suggestions and solutions; be positive.
- Get to know your legislator before the visit: What are their interests? Who influences them? What issues have they been involved in? How can you relate these things to language?
- Statistics and facts are well received: Be prepared with some that you can rattle off.
- Bring a bulleted page of talking points.
- Use proper titles; be flexible with times; dress professionally.
- Ask a question that promotes a commitment to action such as, "Will you support my position?" Or "What can I report back to my group?"
- Follow up with a thank-you letter to congressperson or staffperson, including praise, remind them of issues and how they can help; invite them to conferences; pledge to send them materials (and actually do it).

Concept 6.7 JNCL-NCLIS on writing letters to politicians

Letter writing is probably one of the most effective and efficient ways to express your opinions about an issue. Letters also serve as a means to educate decision-makers about your field and how they can assist you. Responding to constituent mail is a number one priority for most legislators. Letters to policymakers must be brief and to the point (usually no longer than one page). Any letter should include the following major points:

- Identify the issue clearly (with as positive a perspective as possible).
- State your position and why you care about this issue.
- State how the issue will affect you, your school and/or your state.
- Tell the decision-maker what you would like him/her to do.
- Telephone calls: As with letter writing, telephone calls are a good way to contact policymakers. Be sure to give the following information during the call:
    - Your name, address, and phone number
    - The issue that has prompted your call
    - What action you would like to see on this issue.

(http://languagepolicy.org/advocacy/popup4_advocacy_workshop.html)

6.5.1.2 Grassroots organization and political activism

While establishing connections with politicians who will support multilingual language policies may be challenging, maintaining and utilizing those connections is crucial. Warhol (2011) recounts the development of the 1990 Native American Languages Act (NALA), which was notable for its support of Native languages and Native language education in the U.S. Such support was unprecedented for a federal government that had predominantly passed policies leading to the eradication of those same languages NALA helped to protect: "The status of the cultures and languages of Native Americans is unique and the United States has the responsibility to act together with Native Americans to ensure the survival of these unique cultures and languages" (cited in Warhol 2011: 282).

Warhol explains how the confluence of a variety of grassroots organizations built the groundwork for NALA. First, the advent of bilingual education in the U.S. led to collaborations between linguists and Native educators who, in turn, joined forces with a network of Native language educationists and activists across many Native American communities. Such collaborations helped spawn institutes and organizations like the Native American Language Issues (NALI) Institute and the American Indian Language Development Institute (AILDI) who co-hosted a conference in June of 1988, out of which NALA emerged. Meanwhile educators involved in Hawai'ian language revitalization efforts and language education programs took an interest in, and joined forces with, the Native language activists on the mainland U.S. This connection proved essential because one of the staffers on the Senate Committee on Indian Affairs (Lurline McGregor), who introduced NALA to congress, was from Hawai'i. McGregor and Robert Arnold (from Alaska) promoted NALA, which was introduced by Senator Inouye from Hawai'i in September of 1988. However, perhaps because of a push for English-focused and English-only educational programs at the time, NALA did not enjoy widespread support and political maneuvering proved necessary to pass it through congress. Eventually, NALA was attached to a bill that *had nothing to do with language,* which allowed the resolution to, as McGregor put it, "fly under the radar" (quoted in Warhol 2011: 288). The passage of NALA relied on some opportunism and a bit of luck; however, it was only passed because of a unique confluence of grassroots organizations that were mobilized and organized – *with a language policy ready and waiting* – and thus able to maximize the benefit of their political contacts.

NALA's passage is, in some ways, related to Māori language education and revitalization efforts in New Zealand and the connection reveals the network of Indigenous language educationists, activists, and others committed to language policy around the world. Central to the passage of NALA were Hawai'ian educators and the congressional connection, McGregor, also from Hawai'i. But the Hawai'ian parents who started the early immersion Hawai'ian language preschool were initially inspired by Māori language education and revitalization efforts, which also began with full immersion pre-school programs (*Te Kohanga Reo*). The Hawai'ian language education movement and organizations like NALI have naturally focused on more local and micro-level educational and policy initiatives but the passage of NALA reveals how grassroots organizations can combine and mobilize to have a major impact on macro-level language policy as well.

Quote 6.6 Schools as sites for social change

It seems reasonable to believe that if people from minority groups collectively and continually refuse negative positioning in the micro-level face-to-face interaction, and if people from majority groups become aware of the discriminatory practices that prevail in mainstream U.S. institutional and societal discourse, that eventually

> people's knowledge schemas (minority and majority alike) will slowly change to expect more or less equal participation of people, regardless of background. Given the powerful role that schools have in socializing students into understanding what social identities exist in society, what the attributes associated with these identities are, and what activities these identities can and should participate in, schools can be considered a rich ground for social change. If educators recognize the discriminatory practices that are prevalent in mainstream U.S. schools and society, and if they work together to construct alternative educational discourses, schools can help students find opportunities to define who they are relative to each other in a way that all students, regardless of background, have more options available to them.
>
> (Freeman 1998: 81)

6.5.1.3 The courts

The impact that courts have had on language policy is covered in 5.3.1 but here I focus on how both scholars and parents have had an influence on the courts. For example, Labov (1982) recounts his experience with a trial that began on July 28 1977 when the parents of African American students brought suit against the Ann Arbor School District for failing to "take into account the cultural, social, and economic factors that would prevent them from making normal progress in the school" (Labov 1982: 168). While this case, officially entitled "Martin Luther King Junior Elementary School Children et al. v. Ann Arbor School District", was not initially about language, after a consideration of the motions to dismiss the charges, Judge Joiner decided that the only legitimate cause of action was that the defendants (the Ann Arbor School District) had perhaps failed to account for language barriers – because the children spoke "Black English" – thus denying equal educational opportunity to those students. While the lawyers for the plaintiffs had prepared a case based on the economic and social problems faced by the students, not a case focused on language, they had to act on what they were given.

Accordingly, they recruited Geneva Smitherman, a linguist with expertise in what was then called Black English Vernacular (BEV) who assembled the bulk of the evidence and testimony. Labov himself testified, as did a number of other linguists, on behalf of the plaintiffs and even though the defense suggested that they too would call linguists as witnesses, they never did, and in fact called no witnesses at all. Joiner decided for the plaintiffs and ordered the school district to submit a plan to develop appropriate pedagogical strategies for their students who spoke BEV. While this case only accounted for a few students in one school, as Labov argues, it "stands as a decision in this Federal District Court that may be cited in other cases where parents have reason to think that there is a language barrier between their children and the standard language at school" (Labov 1982: 193). Indeed, even though they may only represent a handful of individuals, court decisions can have a dramatic impact on language policy and can be, and have been, a venue for parents and students to challenge the power of schools to deny linguistic accommodations for students.

Concept 6.8 JNCL-NCLIS on testifying

Testifying before a congressional hearing, your state legislature, or the local school board, is yet another way to let your voice be heard. Hearings give policy-makers necessary information to accurately assess, write, and vote on laws and policies.

- Know why the hearing is being called so your testimony is appropriate.
- Meet with committee members and staff in advance.
- Prepare and provide your written testimony as far in advance as possible.
- Arrive early.
- Be brief – don't read – maintain eye contact.
- If you don't know the answer, say so.
- Be courteous and tell the truth.
- In most cases, you do not have to be present in order to submit written testimony for the record.
- Call the appropriate office for details.

6.5.1.4 Engaging the media

Another linguist who has been visible in the public debate on African American Language (AAL) in the U.S. is John Rickford, a linguist at Stanford University. After the Oakland School Board (OSB) passed a resolution recognizing the dialectal differences between what was used by their African American students (i.e. "Ebonics", see Table 6.1) and what was traditionally promoted in mainstream U.S. classrooms (Standard

Table 6.1 Terminological history of "Ebonics"

Era	Terms commonly used
1960's	Negro speech, Negro dialect, Negro English
1970's	Black English, Black English Vernacular (BEV)
1990's–2000's	African American Vernacular English (AAVE)
Late 1996	Ebonics (as a result of the OSB resolution, which used the term)
Mid 1990's–present	African American Language (AAL), African American English (AAE)

American English), a media firestorm erupted, which led to a national debate (see Rickford 1999 for a detailed account).

Once again, linguists were asked to testify, this time before the Congressional Subcommittee on Education and they were unanimous in their advocacy for AAL as well as the OSB resolution. While Rickford did not testify, he did send a letter of support for the OSB resolution (see 8.7) to the chair of the committee, Arlen Specter. In his analysis of the OSB resolution, the ensuing media attention, and public debate, Rickford (1999) avers that engaging newspapers and television media was ineffective because the views of linguists – i.e. findings in linguistics – often conflict with mainstream ideas. In this way, as Rickford (1999) argues, the media *manufacture consent* about issues pertaining to language diversity and education by ignoring dissenting information (Quote 6.7).

Quote 6.7 Manufacturing consent in the media

One of the lessons that struck me early on is the extent to which the media really do "manufacture consent" (Herman and Chomsky 1988), serving to promote mainstream "facts" and interpretations, and to prevent dissenting information and viewpoints from reaching the public. In the case at hand, the mainstream view was that Ebonics itself was street slang, and that Oakland teachers were going to teach in it, or allow students to talk or write in it instead of in English. It was in response to *this* misrepresentation of Ebonics and the Oakland resolutions that editorials, Op-Ed pieces, letters to the editor, cartoons, and agitated calls to radio talk shows were directed, and attempts to get alternative viewpoints aired were often very difficult, especially in the most prestigious media.

(Rickford 1999: 270)

What has frustrated many linguists and educationists with regard to public debates about AAL and bilingual education is that using evidence to counter widely held misconceptions about language, especially when they are popularly held language myths (Table 6.2 on page 206), is largely ineffective. As Rickford (1999: 271) further argues, "[W]e seem to have forgotten what advertisers of Colgate toothpaste and other products never forget: that the message has to be repeated over and over, anew for each generation and each different audience type, and preferably in simple, direct and arresting language which the public can understand and appreciate." As well, the way academics argue – by relying on a review of the available evidence, collected in research studies, and presented in arcane academic journals and conferences – is different from how public policy debates tend to take place, which are sometimes won with effective use of propaganda tactics including repetition (ad nauseam), oversimplification, glittering generalities, and appeals to emotion rather than logic and evidence (pathos rather than logos).

Propaganda provides only partial information, selectively presenting ideas that support the cause, while the intentions of Rickford, Labov, Chomsky, and Smitherman are to illuminate, educate, and liberate. This approach, however, has not proven as effective as others – for example, the more politically strategic campaign to retain bilingual education in Colorado. The initiative to restrict bilingual education in the state of Colorado was engendered by Ron Unz, an anti-bilingual education activist, who had spearheaded similar successful campaigns in California (Proposition 227), Massachusetts (Question 2), and Arizona (Proposition 203). However, Colorado's Amendment 31 was defeated, thus giving Unz's anti-bilingual education campaign its first defeat. Escamilla *et al.* (2003) review the processes and initiatives that led up to the defeat of Amendment 31, which must be described as an incredibly remarkable feat of political savvy considering that 80% of voters supported the proposal in a July 2002 survey, just four months before Amendment 31 was voted down by a 56% to 44% margin. How did they do it? First, opponents of the anti-bilingual education measure built a broad bi-partisan coalition, which included high-profile spokespersons, including the Republican governor Bill Owens. Second, one of the organizations that was against the measure, the Colarado Association for Bilingual Education, hired a consultant firm (Welchert & Britz) to help develop and deliver their message against Amendment 31. Based on their research, Welchert & Britz advised the campaign to appeal to a broad constituency by developing a cohesive message that:

1. was *not* about bilingual education. The campaign did not focus much on trying to educate the public about the merits of bilingual education;
2. did *not* focus on Latinos, Latino culture, or educational rights for minorities and instead focused on "Coloradoans" in general. In the *Rocky Mountain News*, Welchert said "If this is about being Mexican, about Mexicans, it is gone. It's got to be about Coloradoans" and Britz said "Our polling shows no sensitivity to the Latino culture in Colorado" (Mitchell 2002: 29a);
3. was very disciplined about ignoring racist comments from the opposition and not framing the debate in terms of race, culture, or educational rights;
4. instead emphasized that Amendment 31 would reduce parental choice, be costly, and be punitive because it threatened the jobs of teachers.

Media discourse played a crucial role in facilitating the debate and disseminating the bilingual education advocates' message. The pro-bilingual education organizations like Padres Unidos and English Plus launched vigorous media campaigns targeted at white middle-class voters, which focused on two cohesive and consistent messages: (1) Amendment 31 would restrict local educational choice, a long-held value by political conservatives; and (2) When ELLs are mainstreamed, the teachers' attention may be directed away from native English-speaking students. These television ads were widely criticized. For example, one television spot promoted the unseemly idea that if Amendment 31 were enacted, ELLs would disrupt the education of "your children" (Mitchell 2002), apparently in an attempt to ignite any segregationist and/or xenophobic tendencies among white voters. Even though dissenting voices in the movement wanted to frame the debate in terms of minority rights, a minority rights message did not reach the mainstream media because everyone agreed to stay on message (Padres Unidos 2003). This message was encouraged by Welchert & Britz, who report having an "a-ha" moment when interviewing a white Republican who expressed concern that Amendment 31 might cause her children's teachers to be distracted by the non-English speaking children who would be entering "their" classrooms. Thus, "chaos in the classroom" became a key slogan in the campaign and was frequently used in television ads. In meeting with Latino leaders who expressed concern with the direction of the campaign, Welchert reports saying to them "Do you want to win? Or do you want to be right?" (Mitchell 2002).

The ethicality of the campaign to retain bilingual education in Colorado is questionable and one wonders if appealing to, and therefore implicitly legitimizing, xenophobic and racist sentiments provides long-term stability and strength for multilingual educational programs. Nevertheless, the anti-Amendment 31 campaign's success is instructive for how to successfully engage with the media concerning language policy issues:

- Have a coherent, simple, and consistent message.
- Repeat the same message over and over again.
- Appeal to emotion and use modes of persuasion based on pathos not logos.
- Use language that is easily understood and rely less on nuanced scholarly findings that necessitate lengthy explanation.
- Direct the argument at a large constituency including those who are not necessarily in favor of multilingual education.

While many scholars and educationists will be unwilling to utilize such tactics, the U.S. media have not proven to be a particularly good venue for nuanced scholarly debates about the evidentiary bases for different pedagogical models and we will need to develop alternative strategies if we are to be successful in countering the dominant myths about language that circulate in the media, public opinion, departments of education, and legal bodies.

Concept 6.9 JNCL-NCLIS on establishing media contacts

Local newspapers, radio and television stations will offer publicity for an issue if they are convinced that the issue merits attention, and if you are willing to offer assistance. Remember to utilize your school newspapers and association newsletters as well. Include relevant policy-makers on your mailing lists. Publicity may include:

- Press releases on noteworthy programs (your school's National Foreign Language Week program)
- Notices of meetings (your state language association's annual meeting)
- Editorials

- Letters to the Editor
- Networking: Other organizations can be a source of collaborative strength. Expand your network to include areas where you may never have expected to find support:
  Businesses with trade concerns
  Social organizations with international dimensions (Rotary, 4H, etc.)

By combining resources, skills, ideas, and networking lists, you can generate hundreds of letters and calls, positive support, and effective political action. Through joint meetings, coalitions can focus on common goals and priorities, target specific issues, and develop effective strategies.

Concept 6.10 JNCL-NCLIS on how to write a press release

Purpose:

- Announce event and invite the media, or issue statement and inform the media
- Release statement/take a position on an issue
- Provide background information

What to include:

- Who, What, When, Where and Why are essential to any press release. The information stands out if it is highlighted and set apart from the rest of the text if it is a press event.
- If it is a press release, include this information, but there is no need to have it highlighted. The first two paragraphs should include this information, as well as some material about your organization.
- The second or third paragraph should elaborate on the issue. Give a brief background and including talking points. The reporter should be able to write a story by just using this press release. (More often than not, this is how they will write a story.)

Convey the message in a reportorial style:

- Use short declarative sentences.
- Keep acronyms to a minimum.

- Do not bury the lead.
- Avoid subordinated sentences.
- Do not editorialize.
- Include memorable quotes.
- Be concise. Keep to 400 words (1.5 pages).
- Use letterhead. It looks more professional, while also giving the reader an address and phone number of where you can be reached.
- Compose using Associated Press Stylebook.
- Include the title and organization of any person mentioned.

One scholar who actively engages in language policy debates is Stephen Krashen. He is mostly known for his research on second language acquisition (Krashen 1985) but he is also well known for his research on and advocacy for bilingual education (Krashen 1996). Since the advent of the No Child Left Behind education policy, he has also fought against rampant and increasingly ubiquitous standardized testing in the United States. The following is a letter to the editor, published in *The Santa Monica Daily Press*.

Case 6.2 Letter to the editor from Stephen Krashen

Editor:

I have done my best to read all 50th Assembly District candidates' positions on education. None have discussed what I consider to be the most important issue: California's acceptance of the Common Core Standards and Tests for language arts and math.

Are any of the candidates aware of what this will mean? Our students are already deluged with tests thanks to No Child Left Behind, as well as additional tests required by the state (e.g. the High School Exit Examination). We now test reading and math, but there are plans to add history and science. We now test students only at the end of the school year, but there are plans to add "interim tests," tests given during the course of the year.

There is also interest in measuring improvement, which could mean pre-tests given in the fall, and there is discussion of expanding testing

> to the lower grades, starting at kindergarten. All of these tests will be closely linked to very rigorous (I would say brutal) standards, making individualization and creative teaching nearly impossible.
>
> There is no evidence that any of this will improve educational attainment. In fact, there is good evidence that it won't: The research tell us that adding standardized tests does not even improve performance on standardized tests.
>
> This increase in testing is going to cost a lot of money. The new tests will be administered online, which means every student has to be connected to the Internet. According to the NY Times last year, New York City was planning to budget over a half billion just to connect all students to the Internet so they could take the new tests. We will be increasing expenditures on testing while firing teachers due to lack of funds.
>
> It isn't too late to stop all this. I will support the candidate who pledges to take a good look at this issue.
>
> Stephen Krashen
> Professor emeritus University of Southern California
>
> (Krashen 2012a)

In a follow-up blog post on a website called At the Chalk Face (http://atthechalkface.com/), Krashen (2012b) reports that he also sent the letter to the three Democratic party candidates, one of whom (Tori Osborn) responded that she "agreed totally" and wanted to meet with Krashen after the election.

The question of how to successfully advocate for multilingual language policies, especially in the face of circulating myths about language, language education, and language users (see Case 5.8) is challenging and one with which language scholars grapple. Table 6.2 presents some of the popular myths about language, many of which are represented in two books, the first an edited volume *Language Myths* (Bauer and Trudgill 1998) and the second a book by Samway and McKeon (2007) called *Myths and Realities: Best Practices for English Language Learners*. Despite the lack of research evidence to support these assertions, they are often taken up as accepted fact, conventional wisdom, or just

Table 6.2 Some popular myths about language (education)

Myth	Resources
1. Women talk more than men	Holmes 1998 Cameron 2007
2. Some languages have no, or less complicated, grammar	Bauer 1998 Pinker 1994
3. Some languages are more complex and harder to learn	Andersson 1998
4. Some children, especially poor children, are verbally deprived	Labov 1972a Wolfram 1998
5. The most effective way to learn a language is to be immersed in a classroom that only uses that language	Samway and McKeon 2007
6. Bilingual education is less effective than monolingual education at teaching English	Rolstad *et al.* 2005
7. Double negatives (in English) are illogical	Labov 1972a Case 1.1, this volume

common sense and their durability supports Rickford's (1999) claim that the media manufacture consent about language issues. Yet, JNCL-NCLIS, Stephen Krashen, and even the Colorado campaign provide lessons for how to utilize the media to advocate for minority language users, multilingual education, and educational programs and policies that are supported by research evidence. The question going forward will be: If we want to challenge popular notions about language that do a disservice to minority language and dialect users, how do we develop a message that reflects and disseminates research evidence and yet still has an impact in the media and, ultimately, on the development of language policies?

6.5.2 Micro-level language policy creation

Micro-level language policy engagement involves community members, teachers, administrators, and other educators creating a language policy for their own students or community. In ELPEAR, this is ideally done with input from individuals across multiple contexts and levels of institutional authority. Of course, this is not always how it happens – often, education administrators and officials will make policy without teacher input – but for any policy to be successful, there needs to be buy-in and *ownership* by those intended to implement the policy and, without it, problems will surface, including outright resistance to the policy.

Building on Corson (1999), Freeman (2004), Hill and May (2013), the work of Neville Alexander (1989) and PRAESA, and based on my own study of the development of a language policy in a large U.S. school district (Johnson 2007), the following is a set of criteria for creating micro-level language policies in ELPEAR, in no particular order:

(1) Include contributors with diverse areas of expertise

In a school, school district, or other educational setting, this would entail teachers who work in different disciplines and should necessarily involve teachers who work in different language education programs. It is also important to include teachers from the subject or content areas (science, history, math etc.) who do not specialize in language education – their support can help ensure the success of the implementation of the language policy and if they, themselves, will be impacted by the policy, their input is required.

(2) Incorporate research findings as support

It is important to be able to defend your language policy to various stakeholders and some of them may be interested in the evidentiary basis that supports the policy. It is useful to have a set of talking points that succinctly summarize the research supporting the direction of the language policy as well as numbers, statistics, and accessible visual images (in the form of charts and graphs) that show the effectiveness of the chosen programs. Upper-level policymakers and those involved in politics tend to be less interested in nuanced qualitative descriptions than numbers, statistics, and more generalizable findings.

(3) Plan meetings that support egalitarian participation frameworks

Goffman (1979) proposes the concept of *footing* (see 4.1.2) which refers to the participants' alignment or positions in an interaction. The relative footing of participants in an interaction characterizes what Goffman calls the *participation framework*, which is engendered by the 'participation status' of each of the participants. More traditional participation frameworks in classrooms and meetings position a small set of experts – or perhaps only one – as the sole distributor of knowledge. In meetings that rely more on egalitarian participation frameworks, interaction among the participants is encouraged, expertise is shared, and power is distributed. Participants must feel like their input is valued, their voices heard, and their concerns respectfully considered.

(4) Include contributors from multiple levels of institutional authority including emancipatory leaders

To help ensure a more egalitarian participation framework, participants from multiple levels of institutional authority should be invited to participate. The group to which invitations should be sent should be the widest possible and represent all of those who may be impacted by the language policy. Still, meetings may be organized and run by emancipatory leaders (Concept 6.4) who are committed to shepherding the language policy to completion.

(5) Emancipatory leaders must be knowledgeable about other language policies

This is evident in the work of PRAESA, who make it part of their mission to research the history of language policy and, specifically, what has worked and what has not. As well, a language policy developed at the local level may interact in expected and unexpected ways with meso- and macro-level language policies and it will be important to be knowledgeable about the nature of this interaction. For example, the language within the policy might be borrowed from other meso- and macro-level language policies; these intentional intertextual connections help support the credibility of the policy to upper-level policymakers. Some macro-level language policies outline funding structures for language educational programs and it is important to *not* craft a policy that will jeopardize that funding. Concomitantly, it may be advantageous to craft policy language that draws on the implementational and ideological spaces for multilingualism within those macro-level language policies.

(6) A core group of committed creators must stay involved and take ownership

Kemmis and McTaggart (1988: 23) argue that action research involves "widening the collaborating group to as many as possible of those affected by the practices concerned." This is true for developing language policies as well but there also needs to be a core group of committed creators who take ownership for shepherding the policy to completion. This group should ideally be representative of the wide range of individuals who will be affected by the policy but, whatever the makeup of the group, they must stay involved until the end. This is especially important when the development of language policies is not a part of the participants' job description and the activities require additional work on top of an often overburdened work schedule. Without this core group of committed creators, the original intentions may be lost as multiple drafts are developed, or worse, the policy may die.

(7) Top-down language policy sometimes does not work

Alexander (1989) argues that an imposed policy is untenable; therefore, a locally developed language policy should not be imposed. However, even if it is not imposed, and no matter how thoughtfully prepared it is, language policies sometimes just do not work. Not everyone who will be affected can always be included, especially when preparing language policies for large organizations like school districts in which hundreds, thousands, or tens of thousands of individuals will be affected. Therefore, backlash is always possible and alterations may need to be made. This should not be viewed as failure but as part of the language policy process that, in the end, results in a better language policy.

(8) Create an egalitarian discourse community of policymakers

The notion of *egalitarian discourse community* (see Case 6.1) is inspired by my ethnographic observation of the development of a school district language policy and Freeman's description of the "discourse community" in her ethnographic portrayal of Oyster Bilingual School (Freeman 1998). She argues that Oyster resisted and rejected dominant monolingual ideologies that promoted English-only pedagogy and instead forged a unique identity committed to bilingualism and pluralistic educational practices. This provided opportunities for Oyster students to "create alternative social identities that are not readily available in mainstream US schools and society" (p. 79). This rejection of dominant societal discourses relies on collaboration between minority and majority individuals and a shift in institutional discourse (the institution in this case being Oyster School) away from traditional hierarchical models and towards more egalitarian models of interaction within institutions.

Quote 6.8 Challenging discriminatory practices in education

If we assume that discrimination is jointly constructed through communication, then changing discriminatory practices requires minority and majority individuals and groups to recognize and refuse those practices. When both groups agree through their actions to challenge discourse practices that marginalize, exclude, or stereotype minority individuals and groups, then positively evaluated minority social identities whose differences are expected, tolerated, and respected can emerge within the discourse community.

(Freeman 1998: 79)

In ELPEAR, it is important to create an egalitarian discourse community of language policy developers who are empowered, have diverse expertise, are from multiple levels of institutional authority, and take ownership of the policy. Such a community will help challenge discriminatory discourse and practices and disempowering participation structures which unfairly cede a disproportionate amount of power to particular individuals.

6.6 Language policy engagement: Interpretation

Whether an educator is interpreting a micro- or macro-level language policy, ELPEAR involves active interpretation of policy language, which sometimes will explicitly promote or prohibit particular languages or language education programs; however, policies – especially when created by multiple authors – are often a product of compromise and revision (see 4.5.3) and, therefore, the resultant policy text can be characterized by competing intentions and heterogeneity (see 4.5.1). While some policies aim at (and perhaps are successful at) restricting implementational space (see Concept 4.3) for multilingualism and multilingual education, a language policy is not always a monolithic doctrine that precludes interpretive agency. Interpretation is a creative enterprise and it should be the goal of ELPEAR for individuals across multiple levels of institutional authority to become engaged in creative and critical interpretation of language policy.

Concept 6.11 LPEAR interpretation

LPEAR interpretation involves searching for implementational spaces in the language of a policy that allow for educational practices that promote a diversity of languages as resources for the education of all students and provide educational and social equality for linguistic minorities.

Case 6.3 Interpreting federal language policy

In my own research, I have seen how the same policy can be interpreted in very different ways and here the cases of Emily Dixon-Marquez and Lucia Sánchez are offered as examples of interpretative agency. Both were key administrators (at different times) of the ESOL/bilingual education office for the school district in which I did research. The administrators in this office oversaw the interpretation and appropriation of federal and state-level language policies and funding as well as the development of language education policies and programs within the district. During my ethnographic fieldwork, an important federal policy shift took place when Title VII of the Elementary and Secondary Education Act (ESEA), also known as the Bilingual Education Act, was replaced by Title III, which was titled "Language Instruction for Limited English Proficient and Immigrant Students." A lot has been written about this shift (Wiley and Wright 2004; Menken 2008) and the newly invigorated focus away from bilingual education programs and towards transitional and English-only programs. Still, I have argued (Johnson 2011a) that such a shift relies, not just on the language of the new policy, but on the interpretation by language policy agents.

Dixon-Marquez and Sánchez interpreted Title III in very different ways, which led to different forms of implementation of the policy. In a discussion about NCLB in 2003, which was then a new policy, Dixon-Marquez said, "There's an emphasis on English language acquisition [in NCLB] but it doesn't mean that's all they're going to fund – we haven't changed our programs dramatically – we're pretty much going to do what we've been doing" (11 April 2003). What they "had been doing" was further developing the additive bilingual programs in the district. Dixon-Marquez made this quite clear in her proposal to the Federal Department of Education, *and,* she got the money. So, it appears that her interpretation of Title III was not rejected by the Department of Education even though her intention was to use Title III money to support additive bilingual education programs.

During the 2003–2004 school year, there was a shake-up of the administrative personnel in the ESOL/bilingual office and Lucia Sánchez stepped in as the head of the office. Her ideas about language education, in general, and her interpretation of Title III and the goals of NCLB, in particular, were very different than her predecessors. In a discussion about Title III, she said: "Title III was created to improve English language acquisition programs by increasing the services or creating situations where the students would be getting supplemental services to move them into English language acquisition situations" (13 June 2005). Sánchez' interpretation of Title III is much different than Dixon-Marquez' and this interpretation helped guide the implementation of Title III and radically changed the direction of language education in the school district. While Dixon-Marquez and her colleagues had interpreted and utilized implementational space in Title III that allowed them to agentively develop additive bilingual policies and programs, Sánchez saw no such implementational space and instead interpreted Title III as an English-only doctrine – a document with homogenous intentions that forced her hand when it came to language education. Sánchez implemented the policy accordingly.

6.7 Language policy engagement: Appropriation

I use the term *appropriation* instead of implementation because the latter implies a linear process with little agency while the former refers to the creative and agentive ways that language policy agents put a policy into action.

Concept 6.12 ELPEAR appropriation

ELPEAR appropriation is *critical* because it involves challenging deficit discourses, while utilizing the implementational spaces of circulating macro-level language policies, to engender educational practices that promote a diversity of languages as resources in the education of all students. Critical appropriation includes championing educational equity and principles of social justice by exploiting the spaces in policy language to meet the multilingual needs, and build on the multilingual resources, of students.

Case 6.3 cont. Appropriating Title III

During my fieldwork, the district language policy began to shift toward English-focused programs; however, this educational transformation relied on Sánchez' interpretation of Title III and her own beliefs about language education. Dixon-Marquez, on the other hand, created and supported ideological and implementational spaces for additive bilingualism. *Both used Title III money.* In order for the effects of Title III to be truly monolingual, at least in this district, administrators must be conscripted by its monolingual leanings. Local educators are not helplessly caught in the ebb and flow of shifting ideologies in language policies – they help develop, maintain, and change that flow.

Sánchez' interpretation of Title III had the following impacts on appropriation: (1) Official policy language shifted to allow and even promote transitional policies, diminishing the possibility of additive bilingual programs; (2) Many bilingual teachers felt disempowered because they felt they no longer had control over the language policy in their schools which led to conflict; (3) One particular conflict occurred at a bilingual middle school where, clandestinely motivated by their teachers, bilingual education students planned a protest of the new policies and practices of Sánchez; (4) Some programs began to adapt to the official policy language promoted by Sánchez and follow a transitional model instead of a developmental bilingual education model.

Dixon-Marquez' and Sánchez' beliefs about bilingual education and interpretations of Title III impacted the appropriation of Title III. Dixon-Marquez' interpretation that Title III is as flexible as it claims, and her beliefs about bilingual education research, created and supported ideological and implementational spaces for additive bilingualism and teacher agency. The shift in district language policy toward transitional programs relied on Sanchez' interpretation of Title III as rigidly English-dominant and appropriation followed suit.

6.8 Discussion

Collaborative language planning and policymaking is often referred to as grassroots or bottom-up and refers to language policy made by and for the community to be affected. The type and amount of collaboration varies widely and, thus, so does how much a policy is actually "grassroots". For example, a language policy can be enacted at a macro-level after the community to be impacted is merely consulted, as is the case when national educational language policymakers consult teachers and teacher organizations. Or, a language policy can be made by and for a community, as is the case when a school district creates its own language policy to guide language education for their students. Even at the most "grassroots", however, policymaking can still be a multi-layered process with some policy agents wielding a disproportionate amount of power in the language policy process.

By working collaboratively, teams of researchers and educators who understand both the local context and larger body of research, can work together to promote local ideological spaces that foster multilingual language policies. This might involve outright resistance to macro-level policies that restrict the use of multiple languages, or perhaps simply creative forms of interpretation of these policies. In ELPEAR, both language policy research and language policy *action* are targeted and, in particular, language policy actions that advocate for the educational rights of linguistic minorities.

This orientation to language policy research entails a paradigmatic shift. A reconceptualization is needed if researchers really believe in the power of discourse, because they themselves help to develop those discourses. Focusing exclusively on the subjugating power of policy helps perpetuate the idea that language policy is a necessarily monolithic mechanism for cultural and linguistic hegemony in education and helps reify critical conceptualizations as disempowering realities. We need to balance our critical analyses of policy power while simultaneously finding, examining, and exploiting spaces for educator agency because if the arc of our research bends toward continued analyses which emphasize single-noted hegemony, the arc of language policy may bend in the same direction.

7
Research direction(s) and model projects

Chapter overview

7.1 Topics and contexts
7.2 Access and positionality
7.3 Research questions and organizing data collection
7.4 Data collection and analysis
7.5 Example analyses
7.6 Discussion

> Any research which is aimed at discovery (rather than confirmation or verification of findings by other researchers) needs to be both systematic and flexible. It needs to be systematic in order that the chances of discovery are maximized and not left solely to luck or 'happy accidents'. However, it also needs to be flexible so that it can respond to the unanticipated problems and detours that will almost inevitably accompany exploratory research (Layder 1993: 121).

Layder's advice is especially true for language policy research – it is important to go into a research setting knowledgeable of the existing LPP theories, concepts, and methods; however, because unanticipated problems and detours are inevitable (and not always unwelcome), it is also very important to be flexible. This chapter is designed to offer some guidance on conducting an LPP research project. Chapter 5 reviewed some of the prominent research methodologies used to study language policy products and processes and Chapter 6 detailed one particular method – language policy action research – and proposed ways to engage in language policy processes. Chapter 7 is designed as a guide to doing an LPP research project and it follows a typical trajectory, from developing a topic and choosing a context to designing research questions, and collecting and analyzing data. This is not proposed as a statically rigid framework but as a pliable heuristic.

7.1 Topics and contexts

The first step in a study of language policy is to decide what topic to focus on within the field. In other words, what kinds of language

Table 7.1 LPP topics according to discipline

Discipline	Topics
K-12 Educational	Educational language policies – federal, state, and local policies that impact language teaching, learning, and/or use in schools; classroom interaction and language policy; local language policy creation; language shift and revitalization
Applied linguistics	Language learning and teaching in diverse contexts: second and foreign language learning classrooms; citizenship classes; business contexts; etc. etc.
Anthropology	Language learning, socialization, attitudes, and use in communities and classrooms; "language policy" as practice, in action – that is, as attitudes, ideologies, and discourses about language and language use; family language policy; Indigenous language revitalization
Linguistics	The impact of language policies and plans on the forms and functions of languages over time; the impact of language policies on social and regional variation in language use
Political science	Policy texts and discourses incorporated into political organizations, movements, and campaigns; voter-approved language policies; language policy decisions made by governmental bodies and leaders; language policy and political debate
Communications studies	Media discourse and language policy; media reports of particular language policies; media discourse and language ideology; language use and policy on social networking sites
Law	Impact of language policy on judicial processes; impact of judgments on language policies; voter-approved language policies; language policies for citizenship and voting; forensic linguistics; courtroom interaction; police reports and interviews; language rights and laws

(*continued*)

Table 7.1 Continued

Discipline	Topics
Healthcare	Medical discourse and language policy – doctor–patient consultation; doctor–doctor and doctor–nurse interaction; objectivist epistemology and medical rhetoric; linguistic resources offered by healthcare providers (e.g. translation services); hospice, end of life treatment, and the language of dying; disease prevention (e.g. AIDS) and language; genetic counseling; drug and alcohol abuse counseling and language (i.e. the language policy of rehab); drug companies and the solicitation and marketization of health; language ideology and speech pathology; the language of pain (patient descriptions and medical policies concerning treatment of pain)
Business and management	Professional discourse, practice ("institutional and organizational rules and procedures" Sarangi and Candlin 2010: 3) and language policy: performance criteria and language; workplace interaction; conflict resolution in mediation; employee coercion and language; the language politics of unions and anti-union lobbyists; employment interviews
Social welfare	Counseling interaction; language practices in childcare organizations (educational practices, language attitudes, childcare worker–parent interactions, language socialization and gender)
Theology	Religion and language policy – language and ritual activities (marriages, funerals, confirmations, prayers); interaction in religious institutions (churches, synagogues, mosques, temples, etc.); oratory style (priests, clerics, monks etc. etc.); banned linguistic practices; genesis of language according to religious belief; language ideology and religious dogma; deviancy, anti-theism, and language practices

policies and policy processes should be studied? What is considered to be "language policy" and how one approaches it are often determined by discipline. Table 7.1 offers some examples of LPP topics by discipline.

The next step is to determine the context(s) for studying the particular topic chosen, as in Table 7.2. The contexts for collecting data will be determined by the topic and projects that attempt to connect theory and practice and will require empirical data collection of language policy in action.

The topics and contexts chosen for a study will depend on gaps in the LPP literature. While LPP research is not focused exclusively on

Table 7.2 LPP contexts according to topic

General topics	Contexts
Educational language policy (see 2.7)	Classrooms, school(s), or a school district; administrative offices across multiple levels (district, state, and federal); second and foreign language classrooms; governmental organizations that influence second and foreign language education; college and university language programs; student homes
Indigenous language revitalization and education (see 1.3.2)	Indigenous communities, schools
Macro-level language policy and planning	The impact of language planning and policy on use across cities, regions, and countries; in churches, businesses, schools, courtrooms, and legislative domains
Language socialization (see 5.6.4)	Speech communities, communities of practice, families, and schools
Political movements and campaigns (see 6.5.1)	Governmental and political bodies that attempt to change language policy; communities of activists; organizations of educators
Citizenship policies (see 5.3.3)	Newcomer and citizenship centers that assist immigrants with language learning and prepare them for citizenship tests
Business language policies	Restaurants, call centers, software companies, and any other corporate entities that enact language policies; language learning classes in business contexts.

Table 7.3 Countries receiving little or no attention in the LPP literature to date

Region	Countries receiving little or no attention
Africa	Angola, Chad, Equatorial Guinea, Libya, Gabon, Liberia, Rwanda
Asia	Syria, Yemen, Afghanistan, Mongolia, Bangladesh, Myanmar, Laos, Tibet, United Arab Emirates, Turkmenistan
Central America	Belize, Costa Rica, Honduras, El Salvador, Panama
Australasia	Samoa, Guam, French Polynesia
Europe	Malta, Albania
South America	Guyana, Venezuela
North America	A few U.S. states (namely California, New York, Florida, Arizona, and Texas) have received a majority of the attention. Quebec, in general, and the city of Toronto have received much of the attention in Canada.

countries, some contexts have received much more attention than others. As a reference, Table 7.3 gives a list of countries that have enjoyed little or no attention in the LPP literature.

Example Project 7.1 Oil and language policy in Equatorial Guinea

Topic: Governmental and business language policy

Context: Equatorial Guinea (EG) is one of a number of African countries that has experienced rapidly increasing oil production in recent years. However, unlike neighboring Nigeria, which has been producing oil since 1956, EG is a relative newcomer, having discovered vast off-shore oil fields in 1995. In fact, it was probably not the EG government but foreign oil companies, notably Exxon Mobil, that "discovered" the oil fields; regardless, the influence of foreign oil companies on EG's political and economic policy remains very important as oil production has become, by far, the most important income source for the nation's economy. Yet, the economic boon to EG is lost on most of its citizens since the president, Teodoro Obiang Nguema Mbasogo, and his advisors retain most of the wealth generated by the oil fields. The massive and secure compounds reserved for Exxon Mobil employees are also financed by the oil. The economic and political changes engendered by oil have also influenced language use in the country because many of the foreign oil companies are from English-speaking parts of the world.

Research question: How has the discovery of oil influenced language policy in EG?

Procedure:

Part 1: Historical-textual analysis (see 5.2)

(i) Do an historical-textual analysis of the language policy history of EG to determine how governmental and educational policy treats each of the official languages (French and Spanish), the native African languages (Bubi and Fang), and English.
(ii) Do an historical-textual analysis of the oil company language policies. Analyze the official and unofficial language policies of the various oil companies to determine which languages are promoted and valued, and which are not.

(iii) Analyze the intertextual and interdiscursive connections between the findings for (i) and (ii). For example, have educational and governmental language policies changed to meet the needs of the oil companies?

Part 2: Ethnography of language policy (see 5.5)

The study described in Part 1 is a fairly large undertaking and could be conducted outside of EG. However, to examine what these language policies mean in the lives of EG citizens:

(i) Interview (Method 7.1) employees and employers at Exxon Mobil about which languages are promoted/allowed at work. (You will not be able to interview government officials.)
(ii) Conduct participant-observation (Method 7.3) in classrooms at the University of Equatorial Guinea to discover which languages are used and for which subjects; as well as which languages are taught, promoted, and allowed.
(iii) Conduct a linguistic landscape analysis (Shohamy and Gorter 2009) of the signage in Malabo to see which languages are used and in what contexts.
(iv) Collect official and unofficial documents from the oil companies, university, and government that pertain to language policy to determine which languages are promoted, allowed, and/or prohibited, and for what contexts.

Note: This project could be applied to other oil-rich African countries as well, like Nigeria, Libya, Algeria, or Gabon.

7.2 Access and positionality

Context and access often depend on each other. That is, which context you choose to study may depend on what kind of access you have to a particular context. Doing research locally carries with it the primary advantage that you, already, are somewhat familiar with the context. Positionality requires that we critically examine our subjectivity and "attend to how our subjectivity *in relation to others* informs and is informed by our engagement and representation of the Other" (Madison, 2012: 10). A good starting point are the principles of linguistic research proposed by William Labov (Concept 7.1), who offers a framework for thinking about our responsibility as language scholars. Labov has built a career on studying and supporting minority dialects and their speakers in the U.S. and has been asked to provide expert testimony in congress about dialect education issues (see 6.5.1.3). He proffers four principles to guide the responsibilities of the researcher to the researched.

Concept 7.1 Labov's (1982) principles of research

Principle of error correction: A scientist who becomes aware of a widespread idea or social practice with important consequences that is invalidated by his own data is obligated to bring this error to the attention of the widest possible audience (p. 172).

Principle of debt incurred: An investigator who has obtained linguistic data from members of a speech community has an obligation to use the knowledge based on that data for the benefit of the community (p. 173).

Principle of linguistic democracy: Linguists support the use of a standard dialect in so far as it is an instrument of wider communication for the general population, but oppose its use as a barrier to social mobility (p. 186).

Principle of linguistic autonomy: The choice of what language or dialect is to be used in a given domain of a speech community is reserved to members of that community (p. 186).

While Labov's framework offers some general guidelines, other research guidelines have been proposed by Hill and May (2013, see 6.3.3). *Kaupapa Māori Research* (KMR) places restrictions on what the researcher can do and say because there is a history of non-Indigenous (and non-minority) language users doing research that benefits their own agendas, while ignoring the wishes of the community under study. This continues a colonial legacy that has objectified and subjugated Indigenous communities and othered their languages and cultures as exotic interests for the non-Indigenous.

Quote 7.1 Joint problematization

What is the role of the applied linguist? Is it to marshal the array of applied linguistic tools...and in some sense "bring" them to the [research participants] as a way of documenting the linguistic

> aspects of evidential data?...Or, is it rather to engage in a process of *joint problematisation* which evolves a "common discourse" for identifying and characterising such evidence (Sarangi 2007)? In our view attaining the latter would be a hoped-for goal for applied linguistics, emphasising the strengths of inter-professionality.
>
> (Sarangi and Candlin 2011: 19)

The principles of KMR are specific to the Māori but, like the Māori, many communities or schools will view an outside researcher as a potential threat and good intentions may not count for much. Teachers, especially, are often under heavy surveillance from supervisors, administrators, parents, etc. and one more "observer", even if they are a *participant*-observer, might not be welcome. Added to this is the potentially contentious nature of what the teachers are doing; i.e., working to preserve multilingualism in multilingual settings is often politically contentious and teachers and schools may not want to attract any more attention than they already receive! Be prepared for anyone being observed to withdraw their permission at any point during the research process, even right at the end. Tenuous access in LPP research is to be expected but can be improved by a critical engagement with researcher positionality and how the research goals interact with the goals of the community.

Concept 7.2 Access and positionality in schools

Gaining access in schools and classrooms can be challenging because (1) the research may be working with, or around, children and the school districts have a responsibility to protect their students from harm; and (2) these students often come from marginalized communities. It is impossible to remain objective in such situations. Gaining access to schools and classrooms often means working for free. For example, participant-observation in classrooms might involve helping the teachers with busy-work (e.g. filing and organizing student work) and assisting in student group work. Outside researchers may also be asked to do things they find ethically questionable (e.g. testing, evaluating programs). Positionality in schools is always a challenge and it is difficult to balance a critical perspective – the aim of which is to expose unequal power structures – with a desire to promote the efforts of the school. The researcher must make difficult decisions about the impacts of what they 'expose'. To help improve access when working in schools, the following may help:

- Volunteer in offices and classrooms.
- Create research questions based on the interests of the teachers and administrators.
- Engage in, what Sarangi and Candlin (2011), refer to as "joint problematization", which involves developing a common discourse between researchers and research participants in jointly inspired reflexive research (see Quote 7.1).
- If you want to do multi-leveled work, across various levels of institutional authority, be careful about taking sides – teachers and administrators are often at odds.
- When conducting interviews, work around the interviewee's schedule, and offer to buy coffee, tea, or lunch, etc.
- Share your findings with research participants.
- Be completely up front and open about your research interests and intentions.
- Language policy research is not always "evaluative," in the sense that it does not compare the relative effectiveness of different language education programs. It may be important to emphasize this because educators are sometimes tired and leary of more evaluation.
- Two great references for helping navigate access in schools include David Corson's (1999) *Language Policy in Schools* (see 6.4) and Rebecca Freeman's (2004) *Building on Community Bilingualism* (see 6.3.2).

Concept 7.3 Researcher roles in Sarangi and Candlin (2003)

Researcher as insider/outsider

"In the ethnographic tradition, the role for the researcher is either to blend in or to keep a distance, with the aim in either case to least influence the activity under observation" (p. 278).

Researcher as resource

"Resource can be interpreted in terms of researcher contribution to professional practices at the research site" (p. 279). For example, researchers are often asked to help out with classroom teaching practices.

Researcher as befriender

Researchers are encouraged to develop rapport with participants and interviewees. However, interviews can also be opportunities for respondents to clarify and develop their ideas. They provide a forum for invention of new ideas not merely the production of ideas already formed.

Researcher as target audience and assessor of performance

Researchers are sometimes asked to provide feedback on the practices and policies within their research sites. On the other hand, such an evaluation may not be desired, especially when the researcher is viewed as "the visible hand of the establishment" (p. 280).

Researcher as expert/consultant and agent of change

Being perceived as an expert carries with it the onus that the researcher may feel like they must perform as one.

7.3 Research questions and organizing data collection

Whichever context is decided upon, the research questions should emerge from a review of the pertinent literature and the challenges, problems, or foci found in practice. One perennial challenge is capturing the multiple layers or levels of LPP activity, from the macro to the micro, between policy and practice. Here, a heuristic is offered for asking language policy research questions, which focuses on three language policy processes: *creation, interpretation,* and *appropriation*. Together, these cover a wide range of language policy activities, and can be used as prompts for research questions, organizing descriptors for data collection, and even codes for data analysis.

7.3.1 Creation

The creation category covers how and why language policies are created and for what purpose.

Sample research questions (see also Concept 6.3)

- What were the sociopolitical and historical processes that led to the creation of a language policy?
- Who are the policymakers and what were their intentions?
- What is the goal of the language policy?

- How is a particular language policy intertextually linked to previous policies? How is it not?
- How is a particular language policy interdiscursively linked to present and past discourses?
- What language ideologies engender, or are engendered by, this language policy?

This last question is not as much about the creation process of a policy, as it is about the final text, but analyses of the language policy text are also included in this category. So, one might ask:

- What are the discourses circulating, dominating, or competing in this policy? or
- How does the policy text reflect the purported intentions of its creator(s)? And, how does it *not*?

Answering the research questions

The categories listed in Table 7.4 are meant to help organize the search around the language policy activity of creation. Examples are included from my own work, which looks at the creation of Title III of the No Child Left Behind Act and the Washington State Transitional Bilingual Instructional Policy in the USA.

Table 7.4 Creation activities

Creation category	Activity
Drafts of language policy	Many language policies go through a drafting process and the multiple drafts may be available for inspection. Language policies that are created by governments, especially, will be the product of multiple edits and revisions. The variations in language, insertions, deletions, and intertextual connections/disconnects are often quite revealing.
Policy re-authorization	Language policies are often the product of earlier versions of the same policy, especially those created by governments as laws. These policies are often re-authorized to suit the aims/needs of a new set of politicians. The edits and revisions between the re-authorizations can tell you something about the political climate in which it was authorized and re-authorized. For example, in 1984, the Washington State legislature re-authorized its Transitional Bilingual Instructional Policy (TBIP), the language policy that governs all language education in Washington State, U.S. Key changes were made in the 1984 authorization that focused

(*continued*)

Table 7.4 Continued

Creation category	Activity
	on transitional bilingual education and opened up the possibility for "alternative programs" under the TBIP policy that are neither transitional nor bilingual and, in fact, focus exclusively on English. This creates the odd result that the TBIP funds English-only programs (see Policy text 7.1).
Policy debate	Many language policies undergo debate before enactment and these meetings are sometimes recorded. Audio-recordings of such debates make terrific data but written reproductions (as is the case with political debate in a congress or parliament for example) are good too. Interviews with debate participants can be conducted; however, these may or may not be accurate characterizations of the debate and need to be analyzed as a *perspective* about the debate and not the debate itself. Still, the participants' perspectives about the debate make for interesting data in and of themselves. One might ask, how do the varying participants view the debate that led up to the creation of a language policy? How do they characterize their intentions? And, how does what they say reflect or contradict what is in the policy text?
Sociopolitical and historical context	A language policy is a product of the sociopolitical and historical context in which it is created. This is the point made by Tollefson (1991) when he argues for a historical-structural approach (discussed in Chapter 2) and his analysis of increasingly restrictive language policies under increasingly despotic rule in the former Yugoslavia is a good example (see Tollefson 2002c, and 4.2.1).

To take each of these categories in turn (repeated from Table 7.4):

Drafts of language policy: Many language policies go through a drafting process and the multiple drafts may be available for inspection. Language policies that are created by governments, especially, will be the product of multiple edits and revisions. The variations in language, insertions, deletions, and intertextual connections/disconnects are often quite revealing.

Case 7.1 Drafting Title III of the No Child Left Behind Act

Title VII of the U.S. Elementary and Secondary Education Act (ESEA) was enacted in 1968. Known as the Bilingual Education Act (BEA), it was the first U.S. federal policy to support bilingual education in public [i.e. non-private] schools. It was revised and reauthorized multiple times until 2002 when it was replaced by Title III of the No Child Left Behind Act. When the first version of Title III, then called House Resolution 1 (HR 1), was introduced in the House of Representatives, it began, like the BEA did, with "findings", which provide an introduction and rationale for the policy:

> (a) FINDINGS – The congress finds as follows: (1) English is the common language of the United States and every citizen and other person residing in the United States should have a command of the English language in order to develop their full potential (H.R.1., Title III, Sec. 3102)

Compare this with the beginning of the BEA:

> (a) FINDINGS – The congress finds that: (1) language minority Americans speak virtually all world languages plus many that are indigenous to the United States (Title VII, Part A, Sec. 7102, 1)

Instead of the BEA's recognition that the U.S. is a multilingual country, HR1 instead emphasizes that everyone should command English in order to develop "their full potential". HR 1's myopic focus on English education was coupled with a three-year time limit on L1 instruction (HR1, Title III, Sec. 3102). It passed on May 23, 2001 and was sent to the Senate, who then defanged Title III's focus on English.

By June 14 2001, the Senate had completely revamped HR 1 including the title – "*English* Language Acquisition, Language Enhancement, and Language Acquisition Programs" was changed to "*Bilingual* Education, Language Enhancement..." James Jeffords (I-NH) introduced an amendment which re-inserted BEA language including "Part A – *Bilingual Education*," declaring "This part may be cited as the Bilingual Education Act" (HR1, Engrossed Amendment as Agreed to by Senate). The three-year time limit and the jingoistic "findings" that U.S. citizens need English to realize their full potential were abandoned in the Senate's version, which in describing the purpose of the act, instead quotes the BEA:

> [Purpose] (2) developing bilingual skills and multicultural understanding: (3) developing the English of limited English proficient children and youth and, to the extent possible, the native language skills of such children and youth.

While the final version of Title III would eventually replace *bilingual* skills with *language* skills, these Senate revisions maintained the possibility of additive bilingual education in the U.S. The multiple drafts of Title III reveal the divergent views and voices that, ultimately, created the final draft (see Johnson 2007 for full discussion).

Policy re-authorizations: Language policies are often the product of earlier versions of the same policy, especially those created by governments as laws. These policies are often re-authorized to suit the aims/needs of a new set of politicians. The edits and revisions between the re-authorizations can tell you something about the political climate in which it was authorized and reauthorized. For example, in 1984, the Washington State legislature re-authorized its Transitional Bilingual Instructional Act (TBIA), the language policy that governs all language education in Washington State. Key changes were made in the 1984 authorization that focused on transitional bilingual education and opened up the possibility for "alternative programs" that are neither transitional nor bilingual and, in fact, focus exclusively on English.

Policy text 7.1 1984 Re-authorization of the Washington State Transitional Bilingual Instructional Act

1979	1984
Classes which are taught in English are inadequate to meet the needs of [ELLs]. The legislature finds that a bilingual education program can meet the needs of these children...it is the purpose of this act to provide for the implementation of bilingual education programs	Classes which are taught in English are inadequate to meet the needs of [ELLs]. The legislature finds that a <u>transitional</u> bilingual education program can meet the needs of these children...it is the purpose of this act to provide for the implementation of <u>transitional</u> bilingual education programs
Every school district board of directors shall make available to each eligible pupil bilingual instruction	Every school district board of directors shall make available to each eligible pupil <u>transitional</u> bilingual instruction <u>to achieve competency in English</u>

Transitional bilingual instruction means a system of instruction which uses two languages	Transitional bilingual instruction means a system of instruction which uses two languages...In those cases in which the use of two languages is not practicable...an alternative system of instruction which may include English as a second language

Policy debate: Many language policies undergo debate before enactment and these meetings are sometimes recorded. Audio-recordings of such debates make terrific data but written reproductions (as is the case with political debate in a congress or parliament for example) are good too. Interviews with debate participants can be conducted; however, these may or may not be accurate characterizations of the debate and need to be analyzed as a *perspective* about the debate and not the debate itself. Still, the participants' perspectives about the debate make for interesting data in and of themselves. One might ask: How do the varying participants view the debate that led up to the creation of a language policy? How do they characterize their intentions? And, how does what they say reflect or contradict what is in the policy text? These questions are closely related to the interpretation category.

Case 7.2 Debating Title III (from Johnson 2007)

During U.S. legislative debate of federal education policy, both proponents and opponents of bilingual education supported Title III because both thought it met their aims. For example, on the floor of the house Silvestre Reyes (D-TX) celebrated Title III's passage:

> H.R. 1 [Title III] will extend bilingual education to millions of eligible students who currently do not receive bilingual education services. (Congressional record 20 December 2001)

And, Ted Kennedy (D-MA), who helped steer NCLB through the Senate, said the following on the Senate Floor:

> [NCLB] improves bilingual education for students with limited proficiency in English. (Congressional record 17 December 2001)

Both Kennedy, and especially Reyes, felt that Title III would improve upon current bilingual education policy by, as Reyes says, allocating more money to bilingual education.

While supporters like Kennedy and Reyes saw Title III as a victory for bilingual education, opponents of bilingual education also felt victorious. Orating on the Senate floor, Senator Gregg (R-NH) seems to envision a restructuring of bilingual education with a renewed emphasis on learning English because, as he argues, students did not learn English in bilingual education in the past:

> [W]e know what happened to bilingual education. It got off track. Instead of kids learning English, we ended up isolating kids, took them on a train track that took them to their language and left them there...[R]etaining one's language, yes, that is essential, but they come through as a result of their ethnic background, and they need to learn English...So we change the bilingual program so now the stress in bilingual education is going to be teaching kids to learn English (Congressional record 17 December 2001).

Gregg, at least, acknowledges the value of native language maintenance and suggests that Title III does not abandon bilingual education but changes the focus. On the other hand, in one of his press releases, Representative Boehner (R-OH) thinks Title III will effectively end bilingual education:

> As a result of the No Child Left Behind Act (H.R. 1), the bipartisan education reform legislation signed in January by President Bush, bilingual education programs across the country are being transformed to give new tools to parents and to focus on helping limited English proficient (LEP) children learn English. (News from the committee on Education and the Workforce, 17 October 2002)

All of these legislators eventually voted for the bill. All could be considered "policymakers" and, yet they have very different ideas about the intentions of their creation.

Sociopolitical and historical context: A language policy is a product of the sociopolitical and historical context in which it is created. This is the point made by Tollefson (1991) when he argues for a historical-structural approach (discussed in Chapter 2) and his analysis of increasingly restrictive language policies under increasingly despotic rule in the former Yugoslavia is a good example.

Example Project 7.2 Circulating notions of one nation-one language (1N1L) ideology in language policy

Consider the two quotes (Concept box 5.2), the first from David Cameron, Prime Minister of the UK, and the second from a 1917 speech given by Theodore Roosevelt, President of the United States. The one nation-one language ideology is not terribly new but its resilience in the face of increased globalization is remarkable. It might be argued that Cameron's and Roosevelt's ideas arose out of a war-time context, in which allegiance to one's country (and language) became paramount. However, this raises other questions:

Research questions: (1) Where else has the one nation-one language ideology arisen? (2) What types of sociopolitical contexts give rise to this ideology? (3) What, if any, impact does this have on language policy? And, (4) Are there alternatives?

Procedure:

Part 1: Historical-textual analysis (see 5.2), critical discourse analysis (5.6.1), media discourse analysis (5.4)

(i) Posting a question to electronic mailing lists (see 8.6) may be a good starting point. Ask list members about their experiences with this topic. They may have experience with, or know about, language policy activities that instantiate the one nation-one language ideology.
(ii) Choose a few countries/contexts that seem to best exemplify the ideology and a few that seem to oppose it.
(iii) Follow up with library database and internet research that focuses on (a) the sociopolitical climate of the countries in question as indexed in political speeches, political debate, and media discourse, and (b) official and unofficial language policies published by governmental, legal, educational, and business organizations.

Focus analysis on the following questions:

- Are there similarities among the sociopolitical contexts that give rise to this ideology and to policy that instantiates it? Are there similarities among the countries that do not?

- What intertextual and interdiscursive connections can be found between political and media discourse and the language policies? To answer this question, choose themes or topoi and see how they manifest across the policy texts.
- In the contexts where 1N1L seems to be a dominant ideology, what alternative discourses circulate?

Part 2: Ethnography of LPP (see 2.4)

After Part 1 is completed, one could enter one of the contexts of interest and collect data on the ground. There are many communities and sites in which this data collection could take place. You may want to follow a particular policy, you may wish to follow a particular agency, political body, or speech community, or you may want to enter one particular site. One option might include:

> *Schools*: Is there evidence that 1N1L ends up in school curricula or is it countered in school curriculum? Is there evidence that 1N1L fueled language policies impact schools? Collect data in a school or schools, in classrooms and teacher meetings. Interview teachers and administrators.

See Example project 7.4 for more detail about research on educational language policy.

It is important to evidence any claims about the intentions of a policy. Often, the intentions will be multiple and the creation (as is especially the case with policies created by political bodies) will be characterized by disagreement, contention, and compromise. This mediation is typical of language policy discourse and sometimes means that the creators do not agree about what it is they created.

7.3.2 Interpretation

Interpretation and appropriation are closely tied together in the sense that appropriation falls out of interpretation; that is, how a policy is appropriated depends on how it is interpreted. However, interpretation deserves its own category for at least two reasons. First, while there are varying levels of appropriative power – from the school district superintendent, for example, who wields a great deal of power, to the substitute teacher who wields much less – there is no level of power, so to speak, when it comes to interpretation. Everyone has equal rights at interpreting language policy even though some interpretations will be privileged during appropriation. Second, appropriation is something that happens after the policy is enacted but interpretation occurs on both sides of the creation of policy; that is, the creators interpret what they are creating before it is put into practice and, then, the creators and everyone else interpret the product.

Sample research questions

- How do policymakers interpret their creation? What do the policymakers perceive as the intention(s) of the language policy? How are their interpretations the same and how are they different?
- How do administrators, teachers, and/or students interpret the parameters of a language policy? What do they perceive as promoted, allowed, and/or prohibited under a particular language policy? How do their interpretations line up with the interpretations of the policymakers?
- What interpretations of a language policy circulate in the media? How do those interpretations line up with the language of the policy? How do media interpretations line up with the interpretations of the policymakers?
- How do community members (e.g. Indigenous and minority language speakers) interpret the impact of a given policy on their school and/or community?
- How do business leaders and employees interpret the impact of a given language policy on their business practices?

Addressing the research questions

Table 7.5 is meant to help guide data collection and organization for answering questions pertaining to language policy interpretation by offering some examples of agents, the interpretation activities they engage in, and sources for data collection.

Table 7.5 Interpretation of LPP: Activities and data sources

Agents	Activities	Data sources
Policymakers(s)	The creators and authors of a language policy will have their own interpretations of the goals or intentions of their creation.	Interviews with the authors; other publications from the authors (e.g. press releases about the policy in question); quotes in the media; participant observation during policy creation; legislative records

(*continued*)

Table 7.5 Continued

Agents	Activities	Data sources
Media	Major language policies will often receive media scrutiny and how newspapers and news programs portray the language policy can have an impact on public perceptions.	Reports and portrayals of a language policy in newspapers and on television; opinion pieces about the language policy
Educators	Educator interpretations vary across multiple levels of institutional context. The perspectives of educators and administrators in state departments of education, school district offices, and schools may be of interest.	Interviews; participant-observation; school and school district publications, including materials for parents; published curricula; classroom observation and recording; observation and recordings in curriculum and policy meetings
Community members	Macro- and micro-level language policies impact the status, education, and revitalization of Indigenous and minority languages. Community members will have their own interpretations about the goals and impact of such policies.	Participant-observation in community centers, churches, parks, restaurants, bars, etc. etc.; interviews; local media publications; educational materials distributed to parents
Organizational workers, employers, and employees	Whether created internally (e.g. business language policy) or externally (e.g. federal language policy that impacts a business), employers and employees in business, healthcare, and social service organizations will have interpretations about the impact and goals of language policies on their work.	Macro (externally created) and micro (internally created) language policy document collection; interviews with workers; participant-observation in businesses (via employment or volunteering); audio- and video-recorded meetings

Example Project 7.3 Media discourse and language policy

Media interpretation of language policies and the resultant circulation of dominant and, less commonly, alternative ideologies and discourses about language, language users, and language education is a part of the sociocultural context in which language policies operate.

Newspaper articles and television reports can have an impact on what the public knows, and thinks, about a particular policy or policies, language(s), language users, and language education.

Research questions: How is the language policy interpreted and, then, characterized in the media? What ideologies about language are drawn upon in the reporting of language policy issues? Do the range of media reports create a particular climate (either for or against) a language policy?

Procedure:

(i) Search library databases (such as lexusnexus) for all of the newspaper articles published about a particular language policy.
(ii) Use probability sampling (Concept 5.4) to collect a representative sample of all of the media reports.
(iii) Perform a rough calculation of the number of articles which are positive or negative in their depiction of the language policy. Based on the sample, you can generalize to the larger population.
(iv) As you are reading the articles, code them for themes or textual elements you want to analyze. Examples: the depiction of language minorities; the depiction of bilingual education; dominant ideologies about language and/or language education; metaphors pertaining to language and language minorities.
(v) Use discourse analysis (see 5.6) to analyze the themes or textual elements chosen.

Example Project 7.4 Examining interpretation of educational language policy among powerful arbiters

A perennial challenge in the field is making connections across the multiple layers of language policy activity. Ricento and Hornberger (1996) present the LPP onion as a metaphorical representation of the complexity of language policy layering (see Quote 4.2) and argue that LPP research has been unsuccessful in accounting for activity throughout the layers. Much research since then has addressed this gap in the literature (see Chapters 3 and 4 for examples and findings) with book-length volumes devoted to language policy at the micro-level (e.g. McCarty 2011a; Menken and García 2010). However, showing these connections in the data remains a methodological challenge for the field. There are at least two potential solutions: (1) Doing multi-layered LPP work requires collecting data in multiple contexts and, because a single researcher cannot be everywhere at once, multiple researchers looking at the same policy can provide a depth of coverage that a single researcher cannot. Denzin (1978) refers to this as *investigator triangulation*. (2) Focus on *language policy arbiters* (see Concept 4.1), who are defined as language policy agents who wield a disproportionate amount of power in how policies get interpreted and appropriated.

Research questions: Who are the key decision-makers in creating, interpreting, and appropriating language policy for a school or school district? How do these language policy arbiters impact the appropriation of macro-level language policy for language education in schools? Do different interpretations lead to varied appropriation?

Procedure: Ethnography of LPP (5.5), critical discourse analysis (5.6.1)

(i) Focus on one particular macro-level educational language policy that has an impact on the education of language minorities and analyze the various versions, drafts, authorizations, and re-authorizations to determine which language educational activities are allowed, prohibited, and promoted.
(ii) Participant-observation in schools and classrooms.
(iii) Conduct interviews with language policy creators and appropriators across multiple layers of institutional authority, beginning with the level that engendered the policy and continuing with interviews with school (district) administrators.
(iv) Focus on the language policy arbiters. These individuals will wield a disproportionate amount of power over how language policy is interpreted and appropriated for students.
(v) Analyze the relationship between the policy as interpreted by the language policy arbiters and the appropriation in schools and classrooms.

7.3.3 Appropriation

As discussed in 4.1, "appropriation" is used instead of "implementation" to describe what happens when a language policy is put into action at the local level. Traditional policy studies have tended to look at implementation from a technocratic perspective, conceptualizing policy as a top-down process and foregrounding the intentions of policymakers. This type of research seeks to understand whether or not a policy has been successfully implemented and, if not, how the policy might be changed to ensure successful implementation. Appropriation, on the other hand, includes a variety of activities, including implementation, re-crafting, ignoring, and resisting (see Table 7.6).

Table 7.6 Appropriation of LPP

Appropriation activities	Examples
Explicit rejection	A school district, business, or other organization refuses to obey a particular language policy. This can come about if a state or other meso-level agency, for example, challenges the legality of a national policy in courts. Teachers may explicitly reject the demands of a policy as well. For example, if they are prohibited from using minority languages in their classrooms, they may reject this policy and incorporate those languages as resources anyway.
Implicit rejection	A school district, business, or other organization gives the appearance of obeying a particular language policy while not actually adopting it; teachers might give the appearance to administrators that they are following a particular language policy while rejecting it in classroom practice.
Adoption: Changing educational practices	Hiring/firing teachers; curriculum adaptations including incorporating and/or prohibiting minority and Indigenous languages in classrooms; testing adaptations, including offering tests in particular languages only; creating or cutting language education programs; creating local policy to meet the demands of macro policy; creating language educational programs to accommodate a change in national language policy.
Adoption: Changing business practices or services	Hiring/firing employees based on language proficiency; hiring/firing translators; prohibiting, promoting, or allowing particular languages in the workplace; adding language requirements in hiring practices.
Creative adoption	Because of implementational spaces in language policies which allow for varying amounts of interpretative agency, teachers, administrators, and business leaders sometimes can creatively appropriate a language policy, or particular pieces of a policy, to allow for a continuation of already existing practices.

Example Project 7.5 Appropriating naturalization language policies at citizenship centers

Piller (2001) has argued that policies that require language testing for naturalization can be discriminatory attempts to weed out particular undesirables in certain countries, and points to Germany as one example (see Case 5.5). Shohamy (2006) argues that language tests are mechanisms for de facto language policies which conceal a covert agenda that prioritizes majority languages and their users.

Research questions: How are language tests for citizenship conducted in various countries? Countries which require language tests include the U.S., Canada, Australia, France, the U.K. (among others) and we know very little about what goes on in these naturalization offices and citizenship centers. How are the language testing requirements administered within a given polity and are there differences across contexts within that polity?

Furthermore, many of the immigrants who will take these tests engage in language education and, in the case of the U.S., history lessons (and other "citizenship" training) in not-for-profit centers, such as El Centro de la Raza of Seattle, Washington. How do these organizations prepare immigrants for citizenship? What types of English language learning services are offered? Finally, perhaps the biggest unknown in this process is the experience of the immigrants: What is the experience of immigrants who must go through this naturalization process? How do they prepare and how do they interpret the legitimacy/rationality/motivation for citizenship language policies in their new home?

Procedure:

(i) Volunteer to teach or tutor a language at a newcomer or citizenship center.
(ii) Recruit some of your students as case studies and track their progress through their language learning to determine how languages are learned in a newcomer/citizenship center.
(iii) Interview students and teachers about how they interpret the effectiveness, usefulness, and/or ideological nature of the language learning as it pertains to the citizenship process.
(iv) Follow these students to their citizenship interviews and observe the interactions there. If such observations are impossible, elicit post-test interviews with both the testers and the test-takers.
(v) Conduct interviews with students to learn about their experiences after either passing or failing the citizenship test.

7.4 Data collection and analysis

The categories of creation, interpretation, and appropriation can help engender research questions and they can also be organizing categories for data collection. However, an expanded heuristic is offered here for guiding data collection, and it begins with a thesis proposed in an article in *Language Policy* (Johnson 2009). For any language policy, one must consider the *agents, goals, processes,* and *discourses* which engender and perpetuate the policy, and the dynamic social and historical contexts in which the policy exists, keeping in mind that these categories are neither static nor mutually exclusive.

Agents: Because the effects of a policy rely on human agents who interpret and appropriate policies in potentially unpredictable ways, this approach foregrounds language policy *agency*. Language policy *agents* are the individuals responsible for creation, interpretation, appropriation, and instantiation of language policy. Language policy agents will have varying amounts of power within language policy processes and those who wield a disproportionate amount of power relative to other individuals within the same language policy layer are *language policy arbiters* (Concept 4.1). Creators of a policy are good candidates but arbiters can exist across various contexts and levels of institutional authority. Determining who these arbiters are requires on-the-ground data collection. However, the arbiters are not the only individuals of interest and anyone impacted by a language policy, even those who wield little or no power over its appropriation, is also a language policy agent. For example, even if students have little say over how, or if, their languages are incorporated into classrooms, they are still language policy agents. The best methods for understanding the actions of language policy agents include interviews with those who are involved with, or impacted by, language policy processes, and, participant-observation. It is important to determine the scope of the agency of the language policy agents – that is, how their beliefs and actions impact the creation, interpretation, and appropriation.

Concept 7.4 Talmy's (2011) contrasting conceptualizations of the research interview

In a special issue on interview methodology in applied linguistics (Talmy and Richards 2011), Talmy argues that the interview should be theorized, not as a *research instrument* that reveals objective facts or truths about the respondents, but as a *social practice* in which meaning is co-constructed between interviewer and interviewee. He offers the following heuristic (reproduced here with the permission of Oxford University Press):

	Interview as research instrument	**Research interview as social practice**
Status of interview	• A resource for collecting or eliciting information.	• Involves participation in social practices. • A site for investigation.
Status of interview data	• Data are reports of truths, facts, and/or the attitudes, beliefs, and mental states of self-disclosing respondents.	• Just as with knowledge in general, data are viewed as socially constructed. • Data are thus *representations* or *accounts* of truths, facts, attitudes, beliefs, mental states, etc., co-constructed between interviewer and interviewee.
Voice	• Interviews give voice to interviewees.	• Voice is situationally contingent and discursively co-constructed.
Bias	• Interviewers must work against contaminating data.	• Reflexive recognition that data are collaboratively produced (and analysis of how they are); data cannot therefore be contaminated.
Analytic approaches	• Decontextualized content or thematic analysis, summaries of data, and/or straightforward quotation, either abridged or verbatim. • Often minimal discussion of analytic procedures used to identify themes, beyond that they 'emerged'.	• Data analysis focuses not just on content, but on how meaning is negotiated, knowledge co-constructed, and the interview is locally accomplished. • Any analytic approach that acknowledges the sociality of the interview, including, but not limited to various forms of discourse analysis.
Analytic focus	• Product-oriented • 'What'	• Process-oriented • 'What' *and* 'how'

Method 7.1 Insider accounts: Language policy interviews

Interviews can help reveal how the beliefs and actions of language policy agents impact the creation, interpretation, appropriation, and instantiation of language policy. It is important to keep in mind, however, that the answers given by interview participants are a reflection of their perceptions of events, or of what they want the interviewer to believe, rather than an objective description of reality. Therefore, insider accounts may provide as much information about the interviewee as they do about the processes to which the respondent is referring. Interview responses may tell us about the beliefs, ideologies, and discourses circulating in the contexts being studied. As Hammersly and Atkinson (1995: 126) put it, "[Insider accounts] can be used both as a source of information about events, and as revealing the perspectives and discursive practices of those who produced them." This balance is important in language policy interviewing because the perspectives of the *agents*, the *discourses* that circulate in a given context, and the actual *processes* are all of note. Multiple interviews with multiple participants and incorporating other data collection techniques (i.e. triangulation) helps support findings.

When preparing for language policy interviews, the following are some things to consider.

Logistics and etiquette:

- Set a time limit and stick to it.
- Offer to send an interview protocol before the interview.
- Accommodate the interviewees' schedule.
- Always ask before audio-recording and obtain consent (i.e. fill out a consent form) before beginning.
- Allow the interviewee to choose the interview location. Interviewing in a comfortable setting may help them open up.
- Follow the interview with a thank-you email or letter.

Technique:

- Be a good listener. Do not rush to your next question.
- Ask follow-up questions that might elicit good information.
- Try to avoid loud locations that can hurt the quality of audio-recordings.
- Ask questions if you do not understand something in a response.

- Prepare questions but allow the interviewee to carry the conversation in unexpected directions. Often the best information is gathered when interviewees veer away from the prepared questions.
- Transcribe the interview as soon after completion as possible. The longer you wait to transcribe, the less you will remember about the conversation and context of the interview.
- Select a wide variety of interview participants, across multiple contexts and levels of institutional authority. As the study progresses, use "theoretical sampling" (Glaser and Strauss 1967), which steers the selection of informants in the direction of emerging analytic ideas.

Keep in mind:

- An interview is not a neutral instrument for gathering unadulterated attitudes and beliefs or a "conduit into what interviewees really think, feel, or believe" (Talmy and Richards 2011: 4); it is its own speech event "in which intervewer(s) and interviewee(s) make meaning, co-construct knowledge, and participate in social practices" (Talmy and Richards 2011: 2).
- The interview is not a neutral context. It is a unique speech event with its own sociolinguistic norms of interaction. The potential imbalance of power in an interview can influence interviewee answers.
- The *observer's paradox* as proposed by Labov (1972b: 181; Concept 3.1): "The aim of linguistic research in the community must be to find out how people talk when they are not being systematically observed; yet we can only obtain this data by systematic observation." Retrieving natural speech in interviews is extremely difficult since the interviewer's presence will often impact the naturalness of the speech.
- Interviews are not just instruments for gathering the perspectives of interviewees but can be sites of interactive *production* of meaning, in which ideas are collaboratively produced between interviewer and interviewee (see discussion of *active interview* in Mann 2011: 8).

Example Project 7.6 Independent music labels, bands, and language policy

Studies of the punk rock subculture (e.g. Hebdige 1979; Laing 1985; Roman 1993; Savage 2002) have been around almost as long as punk rock has. This work tends to focus on the fashion, visual art, ideology and musical style associated with this youth subculture. Yet, no research to date has examined language use among punks from a sociolinguistic or language policy perspective. The proposed study here, however, extends beyond "punk" and could include any number of musical subcultures existing in what is known as independent rock or indy rock and could also include alternative hip hop, afrobeat, or any other type of music community that openly rejects mainstream notions about music, the music business, and/or dominant political structures. Of interest would be the sociolinguistic norms, discourses, and ideologies about language that manifest in both the production of the art (music lyrics, album covers, advertising materials, style of dress, musical instruments, etc.) and the interaction among the members of the community, which might include explicit political activity (as it did with the afrobeat musician Fela Kuti). Someone who is already involved in this community in some way (either as a publicist, booking agent, record label employee, or musician) would be ideally suited but, if not, access may still be possible.

Research questions: What are the sociolinguistic norms, discourses, and ideologies about language that manifest in both the production of independent music (lyrics, album covers, advertising materials, style of dress, musical instruments, etc.) and the interaction among the members of the independent musical community? What are the dominant language policies that govern the production of mainstream music and what alternatives are offered in independent music communities? How are these discourses interpreted and appropriated by consumers of this music?

Procedure: Ethnography of language policy (see 5.5), discourse analysis (see 5.6)

(i) Become a participant-observer within the community in concert venues, recording studios, record label offices, bars and restaurants, record stores (if you can find one) etc.
(ii) Interview community members for insider accounts.
(iii) Collect multiple documents including album covers, advertising material including ads in periodicals, concert promotion material, online social media postings (facebook, myspace).
(iv) Conduct audio- and video-recordings of group conversations at concerts and in meetings.
(v) Analyze the textual data to determine the dominant and marginalized ideologies about language and discourses, official and unofficial language policies, and how both are interpreted and appropriated by musicians and audiences.

Goals: This category refers to the intentions of the policy as stated in the policy document(s). The beliefs and actions of language policy agents can quite powerfully sculpt how language policies are appropriated; still, the bounds of their agency might be limited by the goals of a policy as expressed within the document(s). This requires close attention to the language of the policies in question as well as any earlier drafts or versions. I present in Table 7.7 a framework for characterizing the goals of a language policy, which I've adapted from Wiley (2002) and Kloss (1977) and incorporated Ruiz (1984) (see Table 2.2 and Concept 2.3).

Table 7.7 Analyzing goals

Policy orientation Kloss 1977/ Wiley 2002	**Orientation toward minority languages (Ruiz 1984)**	**Goals**
Promotion: The government/state/ agency allocates resources to support the official use of minority languages.	Language as resource	Development, maintenance, and revitalization of Indigenous and minority languages as a resource to both minority and majority language users.
	Language as right	Development, maintenance, and revitalization of Indigenous and minority languages as a resource and right for minority language users.
Expediency: A weaker version of promotion laws not intended to expand the use of minority language, but typically used only for short-term accommodations.	Language as problem	Using minority languages as springboards toward the acquisition and use of majority languages; i.e. transitional bilingual education.
Restrictive: Legal prohibitions or curtailments on the use of minority languages; age requirements dictating when a child may study a minority/ foreign language.	Language as problem	Curtailment and/or eradication of minority and Indigenous languages. Promotion of the hegemony of a majority language.

(*continued*)

Table 7.7 Continued

Policy orientation Kloss 1977/ Wiley 2002	Orientation toward minority languages (Ruiz 1984)	Goals
Null: The significant absence of policy recognizing minority languages or language varieties.	Language as problem	A null policy can indicate an honest ignorance about linguistic diversity or the potential role of minority and Indigenous languages in schools and society. A de jure null policy can also be a de facto restrictive policy with the actual goal being curtailment of minority language use. A null policy can lead to submersion of minority language speakers into majority language contexts with no additional assistance.
Tolerance: Characterized by the noticeable absence of state intervention in the linguistic life of the language minority community.	Depends on local policy	Tolerance policies allow for local communities to develop, for example, private language schools, without interfering. Tolerance may take the form of a null policy, with a de jure tolerance toward minority languages, or tolerance-oriented policies may indicate implicit acceptance of the expansion and use of minority and Indigenous languages.

While some policies fit neatly into this framework – for example, the U.S. restriction on Native American Indian languages in boarding schools is clearly a restrictive policy – there may be evidence of more than one orientation/goal in the policy language. The goals of a policy may be implicit or covert, or, not clearly articulated, homogenous, or consistent. Language policies are often multi-authored documents and the authors themselves may not agree about the goals of their creation. The document may reflect multiple, perhaps conflicting, goals and/or be the result of negotiation and compromise, creating a document that is ideologically heterogeneous.

Method 7.2 Intertextual analysis in language policy

Intertextual analysis attends to how lexico-grammatical features, circulate across multiple language policy texts or multiple versions of the same language policy. For example, in Washington State language policy, "alternative system of instruction" is a phrase that was added in 1984, used in the re-authorizations that followed, and it also circulates across a variety of school district policies throughout the state of Washington (see Policy text 7.1). This diagram attempts to show what intertextual analysis might look like in LPP research. The recursive nature of intertextual borrowings means that there are actually many more boxes and arrows pointing in every direction.

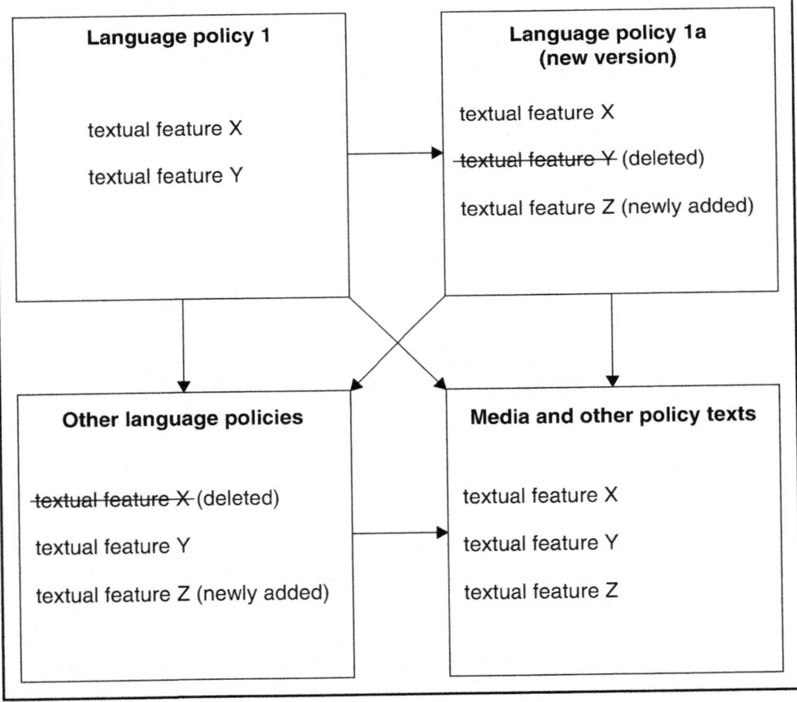

Processes: Processes of interest include creation, interpretation, appropriation, and instantiation, as set out in Table 7.8.

Table 7.8 Primary data collection methods for LPP processes

Processes	Primary data collection methods
Creation	• Historical-textual analysis • Intertextual analysis • Participant-observation during creation • Interviews with policymakers • Recordings of creation process (e.g. legislative record)
Interpretation	• Interviews • Participant-observation • Surveys
Appropriation	• Participant-observation • Audio- and video-recordings • Interviews • Surveys
Instantiation	• Participant-observation in classrooms • Audio- and video-recordings in classrooms

Method 7.3 Participant observation and fieldnotes

Participant observation is a valuable tool for any project that investigates LPP processes. The balance between *participation* and *observation* will depend on the researcher and the research context – some contexts may require more participation, especially in under-resourced areas/schools where the helping hand of the researcher is very much needed. This implies that the researcher is not merely an objective observer but a participant to, and co-constructor of, interaction and activities in the context being observed. During participant-observation, the researcher makes notes of what they see and hear and these *fieldnotes* "consist of relatively concrete descriptions of social processes and their contexts" (Hammersley and Atkinson 1995: 175). By "concrete", Hammersley and Atkinson mean that fieldnotes should *describe* what is being observed without interpreting. Only later, when reviewing the fieldnotes, does the process of interpretation begin. Some researchers create two columns in a notebook, the first for the descriptions, and the second for the interpretations of the events, motivations, actions, language use, etc. etc. Fieldnotes are typically handwritten (although this might be changing) and, if so, they need to be typed up as soon as possible after the observations. Human memory is very fallible and typing up the fieldnotes soon after observations will help strengthen the validity of the observations.

As Table 7.8 shows, participant-observation can be incorporated in all phases of the language policy process. Participant-observation during the *creation* of a policy is not as common as the other activities but provides excellent insight into a part of the policy process that is often difficult to gain access to. While it is difficult to get access to the macro-level contexts of policy creation, local language policy creation is much more accessible; a good example is the work of Rebecca Freeman (2004), who worked on the development of a policy with the School District of Philadelphia. Being a participant-observer to *interpretation* requires observing activities (meetings, classroom instruction) in which language policy agents negotiate and interpret the meaning of a language policy. While interviews are a necessary component of uncovering interpretations, participant-observation might reveal other interpretations not expressed in the interviews. Participant-observation is essential for examining *appropriation* and *instantiation*, especially when examining how teachers appropriate and/or instantiate language policies in their classrooms.

Method 7.4 Audio- and video-recordings

As Hammersly and Atkinson (1995: 186) note, the "pen and notebook approach to fieldwork inevitably means the loss of much detailed information. The fine grain of speech and non-verbal communication is not easily reconstructed." An audio-recording will provide *more* data – because a tape or digital recorder does not need to focus on only one or two conversations in a social interaction like a human observer does. And it provides better data, because it is impossible to write down everything that is said while it is being said. Observing while audio-recording is still important, especially because audio data do not capture important information about the physical context and non-verbal behavior. Some sort of audio-recording is essential for all forms of discourse analysis, although decisions about how much of the data to transcribe and which transcription techniques to use will depend on the form of discourse analysis (see Jaworski and Coupland 1999 and Johnstone 2008 for examples). For example, critical discourse analysis (CDA) typically relies less on fine-grained descriptions of things like the length of intervals between utterances, prosody, and gaze direction than conversation analysis (CA). Video-recordings do capture non-verbal behavior which makes them necessary for some forms of research, like ethnographic microanalysis, which examines potentially very brief segments of interaction and the non-verbal behaviors of listeners and speakers – "what the listener is doing while the speaker is speaking", as Erickson (1996: 290) puts it.

Humans act and speak differently when they are being recorded, and introducing microphones, audio-recorders, and video-recorders into a setting may create challenges in collecting naturally occurring speech data. Labov (1972b) describes a challenge in collecting natural speech, in unnatural situations, as the *observer's paradox* (Concept 3.1). Some ways to mitigate the problem arising from the observer's paradox include placing any microphones in unobtrusive areas, utilizing small digital recorders, and recording over time so that the participants become accustomed to the presence of the recording device.

Discourse: The category is meant to capture the discourses within a policy text, the interdiscursive connections to past discourses, the interdiscursive connections to societal discourses, and the discursive power of a policy.

Method 7.5 Interdiscursive analysis

Language policy interdiscursive analysis involves tracing how discourses get instantiated in policy texts and how these texts, in turn, engender new policy discourses. It also involves examining how both societal and policy actors impact the interpretation and appropriation of language policy. For example, a teacher may draw upon elements of circulating societal and/or policy discourses in their teaching practices or they may reject them. Sometimes local policy discourses, which provide implementational space for minority language use, are not enough to overcome societal discourses; on the other hand, local policy discourses may create ideological space not present in societal discourses for the incorporation of minority languages. Discourses vary across contexts and layers of LPP activity, with macro-discourses interacting with meso- and micro-discourses.

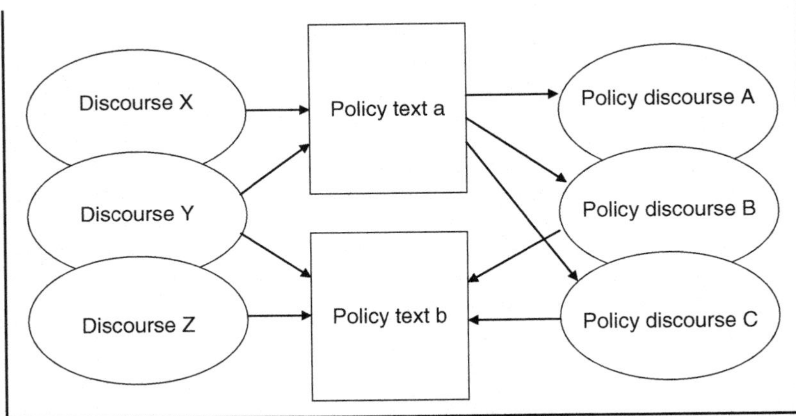

Contexts: Finally, one should consider the dynamic social, historical, and physical *contexts* in which language policies are created, interpreted, and appropriated. In analyzing a language policy text, whether spoken or written, deciding which aspect of the multiple layers of context is most relevant is one of the central tasks of the analysis. Each context and layer – supranational, national, state, district, school etc. etc. – contains its own policy texts, a multiplicity of agents who engage with those texts, and multiple discourses. Each context carries its own set of dominant and alternative ideologies about language education and language policy. Blommaert (2013) refers to this as a layering of ideological hegemony (Quote 7.2).

Quote 7.2 Layering of ideological hegemony

There is rarely just one ideological hegemony governing actual social events; more often there are a number of hegemonies that co-occur in a social event, but their co-occurrence is layered, with macro-hegemonies (e.g. the official language policy) playing into and against meso- and micro-hegemonies (e.g. one's own ways of organizing practice, or more local pressures on performance).

(Blommaert 2013: 133)

Method 7.6 Historical-textual analysis

Language policies are a product of the socio-historical context in which they are created and an analysis of these contexts is necessary for an understanding of the language policy goals, processes, and actions of the agents. Historical-textual analysis involves examining policy texts and other historical documents that shed light on the language policy or policies under investigation. The purpose is similar to Tollefson's historical-structural approach, for which the major goal is "to discover the historical and structural pressures that lead to particular policies and plans and that constrain individual choice" (Tollefson 1991: 32), with a major difference being that the focus is not only on how a language policy acts as a "mechanism by which the interests of dominant sociopolitical groups are maintained" (Tollefson 1991: 32) but also how they can be mechanisms for opening implementational and ideological spaces for minority languages and, thus, for furthering the interests of marginalized sociopolitical groups.

All language policy research requires some historical-textual analysis. At the very least, the language of the policy document(s) in question must be read and analyzed. However, a variety of historical and policy texts may be of interest including media accounts, political publications, advertising materials, employee/teacher handbooks, education curricula, public relations materials, letters to students' parents, historical accounts, etc. etc. Together, these texts shed light on the historical trajectory that led to the creation of the policy in question.

Example Project 7.7 Discourse of technology and enterprise in Bangalore, India

The imposition of English in India by the British colonizers created yet another stronghold for the English language as well as a unique nativized variety of English, Indian English. Yet, India remains a very multilingual country with Hindi being the primary official language according to the Constitution ("The official language of the Union shall be Hindi in Devanagari script" Part XVII, Ch.1, 343.1), English occupying a sort of secondary official status ("The English language shall continue to be used for all the official purposes of the Union" Part XVII, Ch. 1, 343.2), with each state designating its own official languages ("The Legislature of a State may by law adopt any one or more of the languages in use in the State or Hindi as the language or languages to be used for all or any of the official purposes of that State" Part XVII, Ch. 2, 345). There are 22 official state languages, which are listed in the Eighth schedule of the constitution and are often referred to as national languages. Of interest here is Karnataka state and its capital, Bangalore where Kannada and English are the official languages but Tulu is widely used in spoken conversation (see discussion in Sridhar 1996). Bangalore has experienced a high-tech boom in recent years marked by a dramatic growth of information technology companies and software companies, some of which are organized into "parks", for example the International Tech Park, Bangalore (http://www.itpbangalore.com/). Many multinational companies (from the U.S., Europe, and Japan) involved with technological innovation have set up design and development centers in Bangalore, alongside Indian companies. The development of infrastrcutre has led to modern-looking buildings, high-end commercial zones, and very western-looking shopping malls. However, when leaving the modern shopping mall parking lot, a driver may still have to dodge a cow wandering the street. The co-existence of old and new India creates a unique cityscape and a potential change in the linguistic ecology of the city.

Research question: How does the computer and technological business development impact the linguistic ecology of Bangalore?

Procedure:

(i) Linguistic landscape analysis.
(ii) Do a document analysis of language policies of IT, software, and other computing companies to determine which languages are promoted, allowed, and prohibited in workplaces.
(iii) Do a document analysis and conduct interviews to determine which languages are required for employment.
(iv) Interview employers to determine how they interpret and appropriate the language policies of the companies.
(v) Interview employees to determine how they interpret and appropriate the language policies of the companies they work at; as well as how this might impact the languages they use at home.
(vi) Undertake participant observation in Bangalore schools to determine if the high-tech boom has impacted educational language policy and/or practice.
(vii) Interview administrators and teachers to determine if the high-tech boom has impacted educational language policy and/or practice.
(viii) Interview city officials to determine how the high-tech boom has impacted city-wide language policy and linguistic practices.

Example Project 7.8 Ecotourism and language policy in Costa Rica

The official language of Costa Rica is Spanish. The literacy rate in Costa Rica is 96%, one of the highest in Latin America and education is free and obligatory according to the Costa Rican constitution. With pristine rainforests, cloud forests, active volcanoes, very diverse flora and fauna, and beaches that attract visitors from far and wide, Costa Rica enjoys a lot of tourism, especially ecotourism. Yet the demand for ecotourism would seem to impact the linguistic ecology and, perhaps, language policy of the country.

Research question: How does the demand for ecotourism impact the language ecology and language policy of Costa Rica?

Procedure:

(i) Visit (or even better volunteer in) eco-tourist destinations (e.g. Monteverde cloud forest, Manuel Antonio beach, Arenal Volcano, Corcovado rain forest) to determine which language(s) are used and for what purposes. Take guided tours, rafting expeditions, etc.
(ii) Interview eco-tourist workers (guides, travel agents, biologists) to determine what languages they use and for what purposes.
(iii) Collect and analyze eco-tourist advertising literature to determine what languages are used and for what purposes.
(iv) Interview professors at the University of Costa Rica to determine what they interpret the impact of ecotourism to be on the language ecology of Costa Rica.
(v) Observe in hotels and other accommodations for eco-tourists to determine which languages are used and for what purposes. Interview employers and employees to determine which language(s) are promoted, allowed, and/or prohibited.

7.5 Example analyses

Data collection in language policy might include interview transcripts, documents, audio- recordings, pages and pages of fieldnotes, newspaper articles, photographs, videos etc. Most scholars rely on other disciplines to provide techniques for data analysis and there are no established methods for LPP data analysis yet. Here, I offer three examples (Texts 1–3).

Text 1: Bar sign in Pasco, Washington

The photo of Text 1 was taken on a busy street in Pasco, Washington (pop: 32,000), which is very active with business – restaurants, bakeries, hair salons, grocery stores, bars, clothing stores. One quickly notices that all of the public signage for these businesses is bilingual at least, and maybe only in Spanish and on a typical day, you may not hear one word of English. So, the sign is a good representation of what Schiffman (1996) calls the linguistic culture of the community – largely Mexican and Spanish-speaking.

So, while the sign is not a language policy, in and of itself, it does reflect an implicit language policy within this community: any business that wants to attract customers needs to use Spanish in their public signage. Almost everything on the sign is in Spanish except for the price ($7.99+tax), indexing the use of U.S. currency and offering a reminder that the tax dollars go to the U.S. government. However, this sign is actually trilingual because of the word "karaeoke," (misspelled) which is a Japanese word now widely borrowed by other languages and cultures. The language of this sign is a reflection of the global flow of cultural and linguistic practices – in a small town in rural Washington, United States, a Spanish-language dominant bar hosts a Japanese singing contest, and in order to attract customers, the bar owners create a trilingual sign.

Text 2: Lucia Sánchez

Text 2 is an excerpt from an audio-recording of a language policy and bilingual education program meeting in a large U.S. school district (see Johnson 2011a). There were a series of major language policy changes leading up to this transaction between Lucia Sánchez and a bilingual education teacher. First, a major language policy shift had occurred nationally – the 1968 Bilingual Education Act (Title VII of the Elementary and Secondary Education Act) was replaced with Title III and re-titled the "Language Instruction for Limited English Proficient and Immigrant Students Program", marking a shift towards a focus on English instead of bilingual education. However, locally, a dual language education initiative had been in progress for a while, with the goal of increasing the number of dual language education, and other additive bilingual education, programs in the district. Also, a district-wide language policy had been created by teachers and administrators (see Johnson 2010b), which supported dual language education. Finally, amidst these language policy initiatives and processes, a new director of ESOL/bilingual education programs was hired, Lucia Sánchez, and unlike her predecessor, she was not as supportive of initiatives or local policies that promoted additive bilingualism, and instead favored transitional programs that encouraged the transition of non-native English speakers into all-English instructional settings. Sánchez led a series of meetings, intended to explain the new direction in the district and, not surprisingly, some of the bilingual teachers – many of whom taught in and supported dual language programs – challenged Sanchez:

Teacher1: Who or where did the decision make...come from to [transition students]?

Sánchez: Because, because, number 1, we looked at all the programs that are effective based on Krashen's research...and the beginning of Title III of the No Child Left Behind Act, which is long, and there's nothing we can do to change that. (tape-recorded 1 December 2005)

And, later, while defending her decisions:

> *Sánchez*: Everyone knows about Stephen Krashen – he's a linguist that has devoted most of his research to education, but he's a *linguist*. He's a scientist that studies different linguistic patterns but he really – we heard about the silent period through Krashen, we heard about comprehensible input, that's Krashen. We heard about the lowering the affective filter, that's Krashen, error correction, that's Krashen, so all of that is good research that we all as language teachers need to know. And he said, *he* is the expert, and he said that, yes, you can introduce English right away – Yes it is important that we know what the research says (tape-recorded 12 January 2005).

Is this a language policy? I would argue that it is. Here, Sánchez' utterance has the power of a declarative speech act, in the sense that it changed policy and pedagogy simply by being uttered. So, how would we analyze this language policy?

First, it's very important to contextualize this text, some of which is provided above, but a more full analysis might include a description of the sociopolitical and language policy climate, macro-level policies (like Title III), local sociopolitical climate and policies, the beliefs and actions of Sánchez, and education initiatives leading up to this meeting. It might also be necessary to analyze the context of the meeting itself and, indeed, it is noteworthy that this meeting had a very specific structure – it was largely a lecture given by Sánchez. This is perhaps not that unusual elsewhere, but in the past, similar meetings established a more egalitarian participation framework (Concept 6.2), with lots of group work and input from teachers and other educators from varying levels of institutional authority. The discursive practice at this meeting was hierarchical and positioned Sanchez, along with Krashen, as the expert and the other meeting participants (teachers) as novices, reflecting a traditional hierarchical form of policy creation and implementation.

So, when Teacher 1 violated the rules established within this participation framework (disregarding the participation status imposed upon her), Sánchez became defensive, and proceeded to justify both her policy decisions and the nature of the speech event. Sánchez portrays Title III and the research, here embodied by Stephen Krashen, as setting rigid standards to which district language policy, and the teachers, must adapt. By conferring language policy decisions to Stephen Krashen (with which he would disagree, see Krashen 1996) and Title III, Sánchez deflects responsibility to outside experts and outside language policy, both of which rigidly dictate a transitional bilingual language policy and "there's nothing we can do to change that." Even though she claims that she and the teachers are powerless against the will of the research and Title III, Sánchez is, in fact, exerting a great deal of agentive power. Wodak and Fairclough (2010) describe this discursive strategy as a *fallacy* because it shifts blame to outside and abstract entities, thus allowing for positive self-presentation (and preservation). Sánchez positions herself as one of them while concomitantly disregarding the teachers' wishes.

As well, Sánchez emphasizes Krashen's role as a *linguist* and a *scientist* (emphasis hers) and by legitimating Krashen's decision-making ability because of his standing as a linguist and a scientist, the teachers are stripped of their expertise and agency in making language policy decisions – since they are neither linguists nor scientists, at least not according to Sánchez. Thus, through Sánchez, dominant discourses about language and language education are implemented in the school district and they shape what is educationally feasible. Sanchez selectively draws upon Title III and macro-level policy text and discourse to support her own interpretations of the research and what she feels are the best pedagogical models, and in doing so, she potentially marginalizes minority language students.

Text 3 Title III, No Child Left Behind (NCLB)

The final text is an extract from Title III, the policy of note in the previous discussion. This is a policy text I have referred to throughout the book to illustrate the doctrine of last antecedent (see Case 5.7) and as evidence that the intentions behind a policy are especially difficult to determine, especially when based solely on readings of policy language. In this section, the policy describes the types of language instructional programs for ELLs that would be eligible for Title III monies, portrayed as "purposes":

> The purposes of [Title III] are to...provide State agencies and local agencies with the flexibility to implement language instructional educational programs, based on scientifically-based research on teaching limited English proficient children, that the agencies believe to be the most effective for teaching English (Title III, Part A, Sec. 3102 (9))

It would be important to consider context, agents, processes, or discourses, within and without this text (see Johnson 2007), but, here let's focus on the goals as expressed in the text itself. Based on the text alone, what can we say about what it *means*? First, one notices the use of the word "flexibility," giving the impression that state agencies and local agencies (i.e. school districts) are given some latitude and, indeed, one finds the word "flexibility" repeated 119 times throughout NCLB. Further supporting this interpretation, the text emphasizes that program decisions must also be based on the *beliefs* of the agencies. However, inserted between is a clause that specifies the bounds of this flexibility – the programs must be based on "scientifically-based research" (another oft-used phrase in NCLB – 115 instances) although a definition of "scientifically-based" is not mentioned nor is a description of what this research does, in fact, support. Which leaves an interpretive quandary. First, what does the scientifically-based research support? And, what is "believe" referring to? The use of multiple clauses creates some ambiguity around the word "believe" since it could be referring to either language instructional education programs or scientifically-based research, or both. A more traditional interpretation might suggest that the final clause is referring to beliefs about programs but, at least in terms of the structure of the text, beliefs could be referring to research – that is, what the districts *believe* the research says about programs – and, supporting this interpretation, we do not find any specification about what the research supports. Furthermore, as argued in Case 5.7, if we strictly follow the doctrine of last antecedent in interpreting this piece of statutory language, we must assume that "believe" is referring to scientifically-based research, not programs. This passage is ambiguous and the interpreters and appropriators of this policy text are left to their own devices in deciding what the research supports.

Was this the intent of this language policy? Was its goal to provide that much flexibility? I don't know. It is of note that the "flexibility" theme is intertextually and interdiscursively linked to debates in congress and federal administrators who defended the increased oversight in federal education policy, including a vast increase in accountability (i.e. standardized tests), by repeatedly portraying it as flexible. It is also of note that both supporters of bilingual education and detractors were advocates and voted for this policy. Therefore, the goals of the policy, at least based on this text alone, are vague. However, it does reveal something about the genre of language policy, especially when it emerges from political wrangling and compromise – it can be characterized by an ambiguity that attracts the most supporters (i.e. congressional voters) possible and multiple creators can see within it their intentions reflected, even though those intentions are heterogeneous and perhaps in conflict.

7.6 Discussion

This chapter has attempted to develop a useable framework for language policy research by outlining contexts, research questions, and data collection and analysis techniques. Many techniques and methods are not covered (too many to list) and it reflects my biases; however, it is the chapter I wanted to read when I was working on my first LPP research project and that's how I wrote it – as an over-arching design that could be followed from beginning to end. More specific descriptions of individual methods can be found in the edited volume by Hult and Johnson (2013b), which includes chapters addressing the practicalities of data collection and analysis. Each chapter is written by a leading LPP expert and offers a how-to guide on applying a particular approach to gathering and analyzing data.

Part IV
Resources

8
Further resources

Chapter overview

8.1 Books
8.2 Journals
8.3 Professional organizations and conferences
8.4 Organizations and projects concerning language policy and education
8.5 Example language policies
8.6 Electronic mailing lists
8.7 Websites

8.1 Books

Edited volumes featuring early language planning work

Cobarrubias, J. and Fishman, J.A. (eds.) (1983). *Progress in Language Planning: International Perspectives*. Berlin: Walter De Gruyter & Co.

Fishman, J., Ferguson, C.A., and Das Gupta, J. (eds.) (1968). *Language Problems of Developing Nations*. New York: John Wiley & Sons.

Rubin, J. and Jernudd, B. H. (eds.) (1971). *Can Language Be Planned? Sociolinguistic Theory and Practice for Developing Nations*. Honolulu: The University Press of Hawaii.

Rubin, J., Jernudd, B. H., Das Gupta, J., Fishman, J.A., and Ferguson, C.A. (1977). *Language Planning Processes*. The Hague: Mouton Publishers.

Book-length reports of longitudinal research

Chimbutane, F. (2011). *Rethinking Bilingual Education in Postcolonial Contexts*. Clevedon: Multilingual Matters.

Davis, K. (1994). *Language Planning in Multilingual Contexts: Policies, Communities, and Schools in Luxembourg*. Philadelphia, PA: John Benjamins.

Freeman, R.D. (1998). *Bilingual Education and Social Change*. Clevedon: Multilingual Matters.
Hornberger, N.H. (1988). *Bilingual Education and Language Maintenance*. Dordrecht: Foris Publications.
King, K.A. (2001). *Language Revitalization Processes and Prospects: Quichua in the Ecuadorian Andes*. Clevedon: Multilingual Matters.
Menken, K. (2008). *English Learners Left Behind: Standardized Testing as Language Policy*. Clevedon: Multilingual Matters.
Stritikus, T. (2002). *Immigrant Children and the Politics of English-only*. New York: LFB Scholarly Publishing LLC.

Edited volumes

Hornberger, N.H. (ed.) (1997). *Indigenous Literacies in the Americas: Language Planning from the Bottom Up*. Berlin: Mouton de Gruyter.
Hornberger, N.H. (ed.) (2008). *Can Schools Save Indigenous Languages? Policy and Practice on Four Continents*. Basingstoke and New York: Palgrave Macmillan.
Huebner, T. and Davis, K.A. (eds.) (1999). *Sociopolitical Perspectives on Language Policy and Planning in the USA*. Amsterdam/Philadelphia: John Benjamins Publishing Company.
McCarty, T.L. (ed.) (2011). *Ethnography and Language Policy*. New York and London: Routledge.
Menken, K., and García, O. (eds.) (2010). *Negotiating Language Policies in Schools: Educators as Policymakers*. New York: Routledge.
Ricento , T. (ed.) (2000). *Ideology, Politics, and Language Policies: Focus on English*. Amsterdam/Philadelphia: John Benjamins Publishing Company.
Ricento, T. (ed.) (2006). *An Introduction to Language Policy: Theory and Method*. Malden, MA: Blackwell Publishing.
Tollefson, J.W. (ed.) (2013a). *Language Policies in Education: Critical Issues*. Mahwah, NJ: Lawrence Erlbaum Publishers.
Tollefson, J.W. and Tsui, A.B.M. (eds.) (2003). *Medium of Instruction Policies: Which Agenda? Whose Agenda?* Mahwah, NJ: Lawrence Erlbaum Associates.

Important contributions by single authors

Ager, D. (2001). *Motivation in Language Planning and Language Policy*. Clevedon: Multilingual Matters.
Cooper, R.L. (1989). *Language Planning and Social Change*. Cambridge University Press.
Corson, D. (1999). *Language Policy in Schools: A Resource for Teachers and Administrators*. Mahwah, NJ: Lawrence Erlbaum Associates.
Fishman, J.A. (1991). *Reversing Language Shift: Theoretical and Empirical Foundations of Assistance to Threatened Languages*. Clevedon: Multilingual Matters.
Freeman, R. (2004). *Building on Community Bilingualism*. Philadelphia, PA: Caslon.
Grin, F. (2003). *Language Policy Evaluation and the European Charter for Regional or Minority Languages*. Basingstoke and New York: Palgrave Macmillan.
Kaplan, R.B. and Baldauf Jr., R.B. (1997). *Language Planning: From Practice to Theory*. Clevedon: Multilingual Matters.
Kloss, H. (1977). *The American Bilingual Tradition*. Washington DC: Center for Applied Linguistics.

Krashen, S.D. (1996). *Under Attack: The Case Against Bilingual Education*. Culver City, CA: Language Education Associates.
Phillipson, R. (2003). *English-Only Europe? Challenging Language Policy*. London and New York: Routledge.
Reagan, T. (2010). *Language Policy and Planning for Sign Languages*. Washington, DC: Gallaudet University Press.
Schiffman, H.G. (1996). *Linguistic Culture and Language Policy*. London and New York: Routledge.
Shohamy, E. (2006). *Language Policy: Hidden Agendas and New Approaches*. London and New York: Routledge.
Spolsky, B. (2004). *Language Policy*. Cambridge University Press.
Spolsky, B. (2009). *Language Management*. Cambridge University Press.
Tollefson, J.W. (1991). *Planning Language, Planning Inequality: Language Policy in the Community*. London: Longman.

8.2 Journals

LPP Journals

Current Issues in Language Planning
http://www.tandf.co.uk/journals/rclp

Language Policy
http://www.springerlink.com/content/108796/

Language Problems and Language Planning
http://benjamins.com/#catalog/journals/lplp

The following lists of journals publish articles from time to time on language policy and planning issues

Sociolinguistics, Applied Linguistics, and Educational Linguistics journals

Annual Review of Applied Linguistics
http://journals.cambridge.org/action/displayJournal?jid=APL

Applied Linguistics
http://applij.oxfordjournals.org/

International Journal of Multilingualism
http://www.tandf.co.uk/journals/1479-0718

International Journal of the Sociology of Language
http://www.degruyter.com/view/j/ijsl

International Multilingual Research Journal
http://www.tandf.co.uk/journals/titles/19313152.asp

Journal of Language, Identity, and Education
http://www.tandf.co.uk/journals/titles/15348458.asp

Journal of Multilingual and Multicultural Development
http://www.tandf.co.uk/journals/rmmm

Journal of Sociolinguistics
http://www.blackwellpublishing.com/journal.asp?ref=1360-6441

Language, Culture, and Curriculum
http://www.tandf.co.uk/journals/0790-8318

Language in Society
http://journals.cambridge.org/action/displayJournal?jid=LSY

Language Learning
http://www.wiley.com/WileyCDA/WileyTitle/productCd-LANG.html

Language Testing
http://ltj.sagepub.com/

Linguistics and Education
http://www.journals.elsevier.com/linguistics-and-education/

TESOL Quarterly
http://www.tesol.org/s_tesol/seccss.asp?cid=209&did=1679

Working Papers in Educational Linguistics
http://www.gse.upenn.edu/wpel/

Education journals

Anthropology and Education Quarterly
http://www.wiley.com/WileyCDA/WileyTitle/productCd-AEQ.html

Compare
http://www.tandf.co.uk/journals/CCOM

Educational Policy
http://epx.sagepub.com/

eJournal of Education Policy
https://www4.nau.edu/cee/jep/

International Journal of Bilingual Education and Bilingualism
http://www.tandf.co.uk/journals/rbeb

Journal of Education Policy
http://www.tandf.co.uk/journals/tedp

Language and Education
http://www.tandf.co.uk/journals/0950-0782

Discourse and language studies

Critical Discourse Studies
http://www.tandf.co.uk/journals/titles/17405904.asp

Critical Inquiry in Language Studies
http://www.tandf.co.uk/journals/HCIL

Discourse
http://www.tandf.co.uk/journals/cdis

Discourse and Society
http://das.sagepub.com/

Discourse Studies
http://dis.sagepub.com/

Journal of Language and Politics
http://benjamins.com/#catalog/journals/jlp

Journal of Linguistic Anthropology
http://www.wiley.com/WileyCDA/WileyTitle/productCd-JOLA.html

8.3 Professional organizations and conferences

Professional organizations that hold annual conferences containing presentations on language planning and policy issues

AAA (American Anthropological Association)
http://www.aaanet.org/

AAAL (American Association of Applied Linguistics)
http://www.aaal.org/

AERA (American Educational Research Association)
http://www.aera.net/

AILA (Association Internationale de Linguistique Appliquée)
http://www.aila.info/

Bilingual Education Special Interest Group
http://www.aera.net/SIG012/BilingualEducationResearchSIG12/tabid/11604/Default.aspx

BAAL (British Association for Applied Linguistics)
http://www.baal.org.uk

Council on Anthropology and Education Special Interest Group
http://www.aaanet.org/sections/cae/

ISLS (International Society for Language Studies)
http://www.isls.co/

NABE (National Association of Bilingual Education)
http://www.nabe.org/

TESOL
http://www.tesol.org/s_tesol/index.asp

Other conferences that feature LPP work

Ethnography in Education Research Forum
http://www.gse.upenn.edu/cue/forum

LED (Language, Education, and Diversity)
http://www.led.education.auckland.ac.nz/

Multidisciplinary Approaches in Language Policy and Planning
http://www.educ.ucalgary.ca/lpp/

Sociolinguistics Symposium
http://www.sociolinguistics-symposium-2012.de/

8.4 Organizations and projects concerning language policy and education

Asia-Pacific Economic Cooperation and the Human Resources Development Working Group
http://hrd.apec.org/index.php/Language_Policy

Center for Applied Linguistics
http://www.cal.org/

Center for Multilingual, Multicultural Research
http://www-bcf.usc.edu/~cmmr/Policy.html

Consortium for Language Policy and Planning
http://ccat.sas.upenn.edu/plc/clpp/

La Coordinación General de Educación Intercultural y Bilingüe (CGEIB, Mexico)
http://eib.sep.gob.mx/cgeib/index.php

Council of Europe (Language Policy Division)
http://www.coe.int/t/dg4/linguistic/

Ethnologue: Languages of the World
http://www.ethnologue.com/show_subject.asp?code=LPL

European Commission on Languages
http://ec.europa.eu/languages/index_en.htm

Hablamos Juntos: Language policy and practice in health care
http://www.hablamosjuntos.org/

The Hans Rausing Endangered Language Project
http://www.hrelp.org/

Institute for the Languages of Finland
http://www.kotus.fi/index.phtml?l=en

JNCL-NCLIS (Joint National Committee for Languages and the National Council for Languages and International Studies)
http://www.languagepolicy.org/

Language Policy Research Center
http://www.biu.ac.il/hu/lprc/home/index.html

Language Policy Research Network
http://www.cal.org/lpren/index.html

Māori Language Commission
http://www.tetaurawhiri.govt.nz/english/

PRAESA (Project for the Study of Alternative Education in South Africa)
http://web.uct.ac.za/depts/praesa/

PROEIB Andes
http://www.proeibandes.org/

Te Waka Reo: National Language Policy Network (of New Zealand)
http://www.hrc.co.nz/race-relations/te-ngira-the-nz-diversity-action-programme/te-waka-reo-national-language-policy-network

8.5 Example language policies

Chicago, IL (U.S.) Public Schools Language Policy
http://policy.cps.k12.il.us/documents/603.1.pdf

Conference on College Composition and Communication
http://www.ncte.org/cccc/resources/positions/nationallangpolicy

European Union language policies
http://ec.europa.eu/languages/languages-of-europe/index_en.htm

Federated States of Micronesia
http://www.fsmed.fm/pdf/FSM%20language%20Policy.pdf

Gaelic language policy
http://www.arts.ed.ac.uk/celtic/poileasaidh/ipcamacpherson2.pdf

International Federation of Library Associations
http://www.ifla.org/language-policy

Jamaica: Language Education Policy
http://www.moec.gov.jm/policies/languagepolicy.pdf

The Māori Language Act of 1987
http://www.tetaurawhiri.govt.nz/act87/index.shtml

NALA (Native American Languages Act) of 1990
http://www2.nau.edu/jar/SIL/NALAct.pdf

Plurilingual Education in Europe
http://www.coe.int/t/dg4/linguistic/Source/PlurinlingalEducation_En.pdf

Politique Linguistique du Quebec (Quebec Language Policy)
http://www.spl.gouv.qc.ca/languefrancaise/politiquelinguistique/

The School District of Philadelphia
http://webgui.phila.k12.pa.us/uploads/0P/SC/0PSCe4tbSVP2R3Izq2HRiw/2011-12-Handbook-Revised-August-I.pdf

South Africa's 1997 Language in Education Policy
http://www.education.gov.za/LinkClick.aspx?fileticket=XpJ7gz4rPT0%3D&tabid=390&mid=1125

Transitional Bilingual Instructional Program (Washington, U.S.)
http://apps.leg.wa.gov/rcw/default.aspx?cite=28A.180&full=true#28A.180.010

UNESCO's "Language Vitality and Endangerment"
http://www.unesco.org/culture/ich/doc/src/00120-EN.pdf

West Palm Beach Transportation Language Policy
http://www.8-80cities.org/Articles/City%20Transportation%20Language%20Policy.pdf

8.6 Electronic mailing lists which feature LPP information

Language Policy List
http://ccat.sas.upenn.edu/plc/clpp/

Linguistlist
http://linguistlist.org/

The Educational Linguistics List
https://lists.sis.utsa.edu/mailman/listinfo/edling

8.7 Websites

I Love Languages
http://www.ilovelanguages.com/

The Human Languages Page
http://www.june29.com/hlp/h-linfo.html

James Crawford's Language Policy Website and Emporium
http://www.languagepolicy.net/

Language Futures Europe
http://www.ttt.org/lingsem/old/eulang.html

TESOL's Language Policy page
http://www.tesol.org/s_tesol/seccss.asp?cid=922&did=4042

Wikipedia Page
http://en.wikipedia.org/wiki/Language_policy

John Rickford's writings on policy concerning African American English
http://www.stanford.edu/~rickford/ebonics/

References

Agar, M. (1983/1996). *The Professional Stranger: An Informal Introduction to Ethnography*. New York: Academic Press.

Ager, D. (2001). *Motivation in Language Planning and Language Policy*. Clevedon: Multilingual Matters.

Agha, A. (2003). The social life of cultural value. *Language and Communication* 23: 231–273.

Alexander, N. (1989). *Language Policy and National Unity in South Africa/Azania*. Cape Town: Buchu Books.

Allwright, D. and Hanks, J. (2009). *The Developing Language Learner: An Introduction to Exploratory Practice*. Basingstoke and New York: Palgrave Macmillan.

Althusser, L. (1971). *Lenin and Philosophy and Other Essays*. London: New Left Books.

Andersson, L-G. (1998). Some languages are harder than others. In L. Bauer and P. Trudgill (eds.) *Language Myths*, pp. 50–57. London: Penguin Books.

Antaki, C. (ed.) (2011). *Applied Conversation Analysis: Intervention and Change in Institutional Talk*. Basingstoke and New York: Palgrave Macmillan.

Authier-Revuz, J. (1982). Hétérogénéité montrée et hétérogénéité constitutive: Elements pour une approche de l'autre dans le discours [Manifest and constitutive intertextuality: The other discourse]. *DRLAV* 32.

Baker, C. (2003). Education as a site of language contact. *Annual Review of Applied Linguistics* 23: 95–112.

Baker, C. (2006). Psycho-sociological analysis in language policy. In T. Ricento (ed.) *An Introduction to Language Policy: Theory and Method*. Malden, MA: Balckwell.

Bakhtin, M.M. (1986). *Speech Genres & Other Late Essays*. Austin: The University of Texas Press.

Ball, S.J. (1993). What is policy? Texts, trajectories and toolboxes. *Discourse* 13(2): 10–17.

Ball, S.J. (2006). *Education Policy and Social Class: The Selected Works of Stephen J. Ball*. London and New York: Routledge.

Baltodano, M. (2004). Latino immigrant parents and the hegemony of Proposition 227. *Latino Studies*, 2(2): 246–253.

Barthes, R. (1967). The death of the author. Aspen 5+6, item 3. Web version: http://www.ubu.com/aspen/aspen5and6/threeEssays.html#barthes.

Bauer, L. (1998). Some languages have no grammar. In L. Bauer and P. Trudgill (eds.) *Language Myths*, pp. 77–84. London: Penguin Books.

Bauer, L. and Trudgill, P. (eds.) (1998). *Language Myths*. London: Penguin Books.

Bekerman, Z. (2005). Complex contexts and ideologies: Bilingual education in conflict-ridden areas. *Journal of Language, Identity, and Education* 4: 1–20.

Bernstein, B. (1975). *Class, Codes and Control. Volume III: Towards a Theory of Educational Transmission*. London: Routledge.

Bernstein, B. (1990). *Class, Codes and Control. Volume IV: The Structuring of Pedagogic Discourse*. London: Routledge.

Bishop, R. (2005). Freeing ourselves from neo-colonial domination in research: A Kaupapa Mâori approach to creating knowledge. In N. Denzin and Y. Lincoln (eds.) *The SAGE Handbook of Qualitative Research,* pp. 109–138. Thousand Oaks, CA: SAGE Publications.

Bishop, R. and Glynn, T. (1999). *Culture Counts: Changing Power Relations in Education.* Palmerston North: Dunmore Press.

Blackledge, A. (2006). The magical frontier between the dominant and the dominated: Sociolinguistics and social justice in a multilingual world. *Journal of Multilingual and Multicultural Development* 27(1): 22–41.

Blommaert, J. (2001). Context is/as critique. *Critique of Anthropology* 21(1): 13–32.

Blommaert, J. (2005a). Situating language rights: English and Swahili in Tanzania revisited. *Journal of Sociolinguistics* 9(3): 390–417.

Blommaert, J. (2005b). *Discourse: A Critical Introduction.* Cambridge University Press.

Blommaert, J. (2013). Policy, policing and the ecology of social norms: Ethnographic monitoring revisited. *International Journal of the Sociology of Language* 219: 123–140.

Blommaert, J. and Jie, D. (2010). *Ethnographic Fieldwork: A Beginner's Guide.* Bristol: Multilingual Matters.

Bonacina, F. (2008). Fieldwork on 'taboo' practices: Multilingual practiced language policies in a monolingual educational environment. Poster presentation, The University of Birmingham, 8 April.

Bonacina, F. (2010). *A Conversation Analytic Approach to Practiced Language Policies: The example of an induction classroom for newly-arrived immigrant children in France.* Ph.D thesis, The University of Edinburgh.

Bourdieu, P. (1991). *Language and Symbolic Power.* Cambridge, MA: Harvard University Press.

Bowe, R. and Ball, S.J. (1992). *Reforming Education and Changing Schools: Case Studies in Policy Sociology.* London and New York: Routledge.

Burns, A. (2010). *Doing Action Research in English Language Teaching: A Guide for Practitioners.* New York and London: Routledge.

Cameron, D. (2007). *The Myth of Mars and Venus: Do Men and Women Really Speak Different Languages?* Oxford University Press.

Canagarajah, S. (1995). Functions of codeswitching in the ESL classroom: Socialising bilingualism in Jaffna. *Journal of Multilingual and Multicultural Development* 16(3): 173–196.

Canagarajah, A. S. (ed.) (2005). *Reclaiming the Local in Language Policy and Practice.* Mahwah, NJ: Lawrence Erlbaum.

Canagarajah, S. (2006). Ethnographic methods in language policy. In T. Ricento (ed.) *An Introduction to Language Policy: Theory and Method,* pp. 153–169. Malden, MA: Blackwell.

Candlin, C. (1997). General editor's preface. In B.L. Gunnarsson, P. Linell, and B. Nordberg (eds.) *The Construction of Professional Discourse,* pp. ix–xiv. London: Longman.

Candlin, C. (2006). Accounting for interdiscursivity: Challenges to professional expertise. In M. Gotti and D. Giannoni (eds.) *New Trends in Specialized Discourse Analysis,* pp. 21–45. Bern: Peter Lang Verlag.

Candlin, C. and Candlin, S. (2003). Health care communication: A problematic site for applied linguistics research. *Annual Review of Applied Linguistics* 23: 134–154.

Candlin, C.N. and Maley, Y. (1997). Intertextuality and interdiscursivity in the discourse of alternative dispute resolution. In B.L. Gunnarsson, P. Linnel and B. Nordberg (eds.) *The Construction of Professional Discourse*, pp. 201–222. London: Longman.

Carr, W. and Kemmis, S. (1986). *Becoming Critical: Knowing Through Action Research*. London: The Falmer Press.

Chimbutane, F. (2011). *Rethinking Bilingual Education in Postcolonial Contexts*. Clevedon: Multilingual Matters.

Chomsky, N. (1965). *Aspects of the Theory of Syntax*. Cambridge, MA: MIT Press.

Cincotta-Segi, A. (2009). *'The big ones swallow the small ones.' Or do they? The Language Policy and Practice of Ethnic Minority Education in the Lao PDR: A case study from Nalae*. Ph.D thesis, The Australian National University, Canberra.

Cincotta-Segi, A. (2011a). Talking in, talking around and talking about the L2: three literacy teaching responses to L2 medium of instruction in the Lao PDR. *Compare* 41(2): 195–209.

Cincotta-Segi, A. (2011b). Signalling L2 centrality, maintaining L1 dominance: Teacher language choice in an ethnic minority primary classroom in the Lao PDR. *Language and Education* 25(1): 19–31.

Cincotta-SEgi, A. (2011c). 'The big ones swallow the small ones'. Or do they? Language-in-education policy and ethnic minority education in the Lao PDR. *Journal of Multilingual and Multicultural Development* 32(1): 1–15.

Cincotta-Segi, A. (forthcoming). Language/ing in education: Policy discourse, classroom talk and ethnic identities in the Lao PDR. In P. Sercombe and R. Tupas (eds.) *Languages, Identities and Education in Southeast Asia*. Basingstoke and New York: Palgrave Macmillan.

Cobarrubias, J. (1983a). Language planning: The state of the art. In J. Cobarrubias and J.A. Fishman (eds.) *Progress in Language Planning: International Perspectives*, pp. 3–26. Berlin: Mouton de Gruyter.

Cobarrubias, J. (1983b). Ethical issues in status planning. In J. Cobarrubias and J.A. Fishman (eds.) *Progress in Language Planning: International Perspectives*, pp. 41–86. Berlin: Mouton de Gruyter.

Cobarrubias, J. and Fishman, J.A. (eds.) (1983). *Progress in Language Planning: International Perspectives*. Berlin: Mouton de Gruyter.

Collier, V. and Thomas, W.P. (1997). *School Effectiveness for Language Minority Children*. Washington, DC: National Clearinghouse for Bilingual Education.

Collier, V.P. and Thomas, W.P. (2001). *A National Study of School Effectiveness for Language Minority Students' Long-term Academic Achievement*. Berkeley, CA: CREDE.

Collier, V.P. and Thomas, W.P. (2004). The astounding effectiveness of dual language education for all. *NABE Journal of Research and Practice* 2(1): 1–20.

Cooper, R.L. (1989). *Language Planning and Social Change*. Cambridge University Press.

Corson, D. (1999). *Language Policy in Schools: A Resource for Teachers and Administrators*. Mahwah, NJ: Lawrence Erlbaum Associates.

Cowie, C. (2007). The accents of outsourcing: the meanings of "neutral" in the Indian call centre industry. *World Englishes* 26(3): 316–330.

Crawford, J. (1992). *Language Loyalties: A Source Book on the Official English Controversy*. The University of Chicago Press.

Creswell, J.W. 1998. *Qualitative Inquiry and Research Design: Choosing among Five Traditions*. Thousand Oaks, CA: SAGE Publications.

Das Gupta, J. (1971). Religion, language, and political mobilization. In. J. Rubin and B.H. Jernudd (eds.) *Can Language Be Planned: Sociolinguistic Theory and Practice for Developing Nations*, pp. 293–305. Honolulu: The University Press of Hawaii.

Davies, A. (1996). Review article: Ironising the myth of linguicism. *Journal of Multilingual and Multicultural Development* 17(6): 485–496.

Davis, K. (1994). *Language Planning in Multilingual Contexts: Policies, Communities, and Schools in Luxembourg*. Amsterdam/Philadelphia: John Benjamins.

Davis, K.A. (1999). Dynamics of indigenous language maintenance. In T. Huebner and K.A. Davis (eds.) *Sociopolitical Perspectives on Language Policy and Planning in the USA*, pp. 67–98. Amsterdam/Philadelphia: John Benjamins.

De los Heros, S. (2009). Linguistic pluralism or prescriptivism? A CDA of language ideologies in *Talento*, Peru's official textbook for the first-year of high school. *Linguistics and Education* 20: 172–199.

Denzin, N. (2006). *Sociological Methods: A Sourcebook*, 5th edition. New Brunswick, NJ: Aldine Transaction.

Dillman, D.A., Smyth, J.D., and Christian, L.M. (2009). *Internet, Mail, and Mixed-Mode Surveys: The Tailored Design Method*. Hoboken, NJ: John Wiley & Sons Inc.

Ellis, A.J. (1863). *The Only English Proclamation of Henry III, 18 October 1258, and its Treatment by Former Editors and Translators, Considered and Illustrated*. London: Asher and Co.

Erickson, F. (1996). Ethnographic microanalysis. In. N.H. Hornberger and S.L. McKay (eds.) *Sociolinguistics and Language Teaching*, pp. 283–306. Cambridge University Press.

Escamilla, K., Shannon, S., Carlos, S., and García, J. (2003). Breaking the code: Colorado's defeat of the anti-bilingual education initiative (Amendment 31). *Bilingual Research Journal* 27(3): 357–382.

Esch, E. (2010). Epistemic injustice and the power to define: Interviewing Cameroonian primary school teachers about language education. In C. Candlin and J. Crichton (eds.) *Discourses of Deficit*, pp. 235–255. Basingstoke and New York: Palgrave Macmillan.

Fairclough, N. (1989). *Language and Power*. London and New York: Longman.

Fairclough, N. (1992). Intertextuality in critical discourse analysis. *Linguistics and Education* 4: 269–293.

Fairclough, N. (1995a). *Media Discourse*. London: Edward Arnold.

Fairclough, N. (1995b). *Critical Discourse Analysis: The Critical Study of Language*. London and New York: Longman.

Fairclough, N. (2010). *Critical Discourse Analysis: The Critical Study of Language*, 2nd edition. Harlow: Pearson.

Ferguson, C.A. (1968). Language development. In J. Fishman, C.A. Ferguson, and J. Das Gupta (eds.) *Language Problems of Developing Nations*, pp. 27–35. New York: John Wiley & Sons.

Fishman, J.A., Das Gupta, J., Jernudd, B.H., and Rubin, J. (1971). Research outline for comparative studies of language planning. In. J. Rubin and B.H. Jernudd (eds.) *Can Language Be Planned? Sociolinguistic Theory and Practice for Developing Nations*, pp. 293–305. Honolulu: The University Press of Hawaii.

Fishman, J.A. (1977). Comparative study of language planning: Introducing a survey. In J. Rubin, B.H. Jernudd, J. Das Gupta, J.A. Fishman, and C.A. Ferguson (eds.) *Language Planning Processes*, pp. 31–40. The Hague: Mouton.

Fishman, J.A. (1979). Bilingual education, language planning and English. *English World-Wide* 1(1): 11–24.

Fishman, J.A. (1991). *Reversing Language Shift: Theoretical and Empirical Foundations of Assistance to Threatened Languages*. Clevedon: Multilingual Matters.

Fishman, J. (1993). Reversing language shift: Successes, failures, doubts and dilemmas. In E. Jahr (ed.) *Language Conflict and Language Planning* (pp. 69–81). Berlin: Mouton de Gruyter.

Fishman, J.A. (1994). Critiques of language planning: A minority languages perspective. *Journal Of Multilingual & Multicultural Development* 15(2–3): 91–99.

Fishman, J., Ferguson, C.A., and Das Gupta, J. (eds.) (1968). *Language Problems of Developing Nations*. New York: John Wiley & Sons.

Fitzsimmons-Doolan, S. (2009). Is public discourse about language policy really public discourse about immigration? A corpus-based study. *Language Policy* 8: 377–402.

Fitzsimmons-Doolan, S. (2013). Applying corpus linguistics. In F.M. Hult and D.C. Johnson (eds.) *Research Methods in Language Policy and Planning: A Practical Guide*. Hoboken, NJ: Wiley-Blackwell.

Fontana, V. (2009/2013). *Language Advocacy: Making your voice count!* [Video file]. Retrieved 2013 from: http://www.languagepolicy.org/advocacy/legday_simluation_video.html.

Foucault, M. (1978). *The History of Sexuality*. New York: Random House.

Foucault, M. (1979). *Discipline and Punish*. Harmondsworth: Penguin.

Foucault, M. (1980). *Power/Knowledge: Selected Interviews and Other Writings 1971–1977*. New York: Pantheon.

Foucault, M. (1982). The subject and power. *Critical Inquiry 8* (Summer): 777–795.

Foucault, M. (1991). Governmentality. In G. Burchell, C. Gordon, and P. Miller (eds.) *The Foucault Effect: Studies in Governmentality*, pp. 87–104. The University of Chicago Press.

Fowler, R., Hodge, B., Kress, G., and Trew, T. (1979). *Language and Control*. London: Routledge and Kegan Paul.

Freeman, R.D. (1998). *Bilingual Education and Social Change*. Clevedon: Multilingual Matters.

Freeman, R. (2000). Contextual challenges to dual-language education: A case study of a developing middle school program. *Anthropology and Education Quarterly* 21(2): 202–229.

Freeman, R. (2004). *Building on Community Bilingualism*. Philadelphia, PA: Caslon.

Freedom House (2011). *Worst of the Worst 2011: The Worlds' Most Repressive Societies*. Washington, DC: Freedom House.

García, S. (1997). European Union identity and citizenship: Some challenges. In M. Roche and R. van Berkel (eds.) *European Citizenship and Social Exclusion*, pp. 201–212. Aldershot: Ashgate.

García, O. and Menken, K. (2010). Stirring the onion: Educators and the dynamics of language education policies (looking ahead). In K. Menken and O. García (eds.) *Negotiating Language Policies in Schools: Educators as Policymakers*, pp. 249–261. London and New York: Routledge.

García, O., Skutnabb-Kangas, T., and Torres-Guzmán, M. (eds.) (2006). *Imagining Multilingual Schools: Languages in Education and Glocalization*. Clevedon: Multilingual Matters.

Giddens, A. (1971). *Capitalism and Modern Social Theory: An Analysis of the Writings of Marx, Durkheim, and Max Weber*. Cambridge University Press.

Geertz, C. 1973. *The Interpretation of Cultures: Selected Essays*. New York: Basic Books.

Glaser, B.G. (1978). *Theoretical Sensitivity: Advances in the Methodology of Grounded Theory*. Mill Valley, CA: Sociology Press.

Glaser, B. and Strauss, A. (1967). *The Discovery of Grounded Theory*. Chicago: Aldine.

Goffman, E. (1979). Footing. *Semiotica* 25(1–2).

Gram, D. (2004, October 9). Scalia talks up 'originalism' in UVM speech. *The Barre Montpelier Times Argus*. Retrieved from http://www.timesargus.com/apps/pbcs.dll/article?AID=/20041009/NEWS/410090381/1002.

Gramsci, A. (1971). *Selections from the Prison Notebooks of Antonio Gramsci*. London: Lawrence and Wishart.

Gramsci, A. (1992/2007). *Prison Notebooks*. New York: Columbia University Press.

Greenberg, S. (2010, Aug 25). *in*Context Blog: Ya Salam: Breaking the language barrier. Washington, DC: The Jewish Policy Center. Retrieved from http://www.jewishpolicycenter.org/blog/2010/08/ya-salam-breaking-the-language-barrier

Grin, F. (2003). Language planning and economics. *Current Issues in Language Planning* 4(1): 1–66.

Gutmann, A. (1997). Preface in Scalia, A. *A Matter of Interpretation: Federal Courts and the Law*. Princeton University Press.

Habermas, J. (1973). *Theory and Practice*. Boston: Beacon Press.

Hall, J.K. and Eggington, W.G. (eds.) (2000). *The Sociopolitics of English Language Teaching*. Clevedon: Multilingual Matters.

Hammersley, M. and Atkinson, P. (1995). *Ethnography: Principles in Practice*, 2nd edition. London and New York: Routledge.

Halliday, M.A.K. (1978). *Language as Social Semiotic*. London: Edward Arnold.

Harris, M. 1968. *The Rise of Anthropological Theory: A History of Theories of Culture*. New York: T.Y. Crowell.

Harris, M. 1976. History and significance of the emic/etic distinction. *Annual Review of Anthropology* 5: 329–350.

Harris, S. and Bargiela-Chiappini, F. (2003). Business as a site of language contact. *Annual Review of Applied Linguistics* 23: 155–169.

Haugen, E. (1959). Planning for a standard language in Norway. *Anthropological Linguistics* 1(3): 8–21.

Haugen, E. (1966). Linguistics and language planning. In W. Bright (ed.) *Sociolinguistics*, pp. 50–71. The Hague: Mouton.

Haugen, E. (1983). The implementation of corpus planning: Theory and practice. In J. Cobarrubias and J.A.Fishman (eds.) *Progress in Language Planning: International Perspectives*. Berlin: Mouton de Gruyter.

Haugen, E. (1972). The ecology of language. In A.S. Dil (ed.) *The Ecology of Language: Essays by Einar Haugen*, pp. 325–339. Stanford University Press.

Heath, S.B. (1976). A national language academy? Debate in the new nation. *International Journal of the Sociology of Language* 11: 9–43.

Heath, S.B. and Mandabach, F. (1983). Language status decisions and the law in the United States. In J. Cobarrubias and J.A. Fishman (eds.) *Progress in Language Planning: International Perspectives*, pp. 87–105. Berlin: Mouton de Gruyter.

Hebdidge, D. (1979). *Subculture: The Meaning of Style*. London and New York: Routledge.

Heller, M. (1999). *Linguistic Minorities and Modernity: A Sociolinguistic Ethnography.* London and New York: Longman.

Heller, M. (2006). *Linguistic Minorities and Modernity: A Sociolinguistic Ethnography.* 2nd edition. London: Ablex.

Herman, E.S. and Chomsky, N. (1988). *Manufacturing Consent: The Political Economy of the Mass Media.* New York: Pantheon Books.

Higham, J. (1955). *Strangers in the Land: Patterns of American Nativism, 1860–1925.* New Brunswick, NJ: Rutgers University Press.

Hill, R. and May, S. (2011). Exploring biliteracy in Mâori-medium education: An ethnographic Perspective. In T.L. McCarty (ed.) *Ethnography and Language Policy*, pp. 161–183. New York: Routledge.

Hill, R. and May, S. (2013). Non-indigenous researchers in indigenous language education: Ethical implications. *International Journal of the Sociology of Language* 219: 47–65.

Hirvonen, V. (2008). 'Out on the fells, I feel like a Sámi': Is there linguistic and cultural equality in the Sámi School? In N.H. Hornberger (ed.) *Can Schools Save Indigenous Languages? Policy and Practice on Four Continents*, pp. 15–41. Basingstoke and New York: Palgrave Macmillan.

Holmes, J. (1998). Women talk too much. In L. Bauer and P. Trudgill (eds.) *Language Myths*, pp. 41–49. London: Penguin Books.

Hornberger, N.H. (1987). Bilingual education success but policy failure. *Language in Society* 16(2): 205–226.

Hornberger, N.H. (1988). *Bilingual Education and Language Maintenance.* Dordrecht: Foris Publications.

Hornberger, N.H. (1994). Literacy and language planning. *Language and Education* 8: 75–86.

Hornberger, N.H. (ed.) (1997a). *Indigenous Literacies in the Americas: Language Planning from the Bottom Up.* Berlin: Mouton de Gruyter.

Hornberger, N.H. (1997b) Literacy, language maintenance, and linguistic human rights: Three telling cases. *International Journal of the Sociology of Language* 127: 87–103.

Hornberger, N.H. (1998). Language policy, language education, language rights: Indigenous, immigrant, and international perspectives. *Language in Society* 27: 439– 458.

Hornberger, N.H. (2002). Multilingual language policies and the continua of biliteracy: An ecological approach. *Language Policy* 1(1): 27–51.

Hornberger, N.H. (2005a). Opening and filling up implementational and ideological spaces in heritage language education. *The Modern Language Journal* 89: 605–609.

Hornberger, N.H. (2005b). Nichols to NCLB: Local and global perspectives on U.S. language education policy. *Working Papers in Educational Linguistics* 20(2): 1–17.

Hornberger, N.H. (2006a). Frameworks and models in language policy and planning. In T. Ricento (ed.) *An Introduction to Language Policy: Theory and Method*, pp. 24–41. Malden, MA: Blackwell Publishing.

Hornberger, N.H. (2006b) Voice and biliteracy in indigenous language revitalization: Contentious educational practices in Quechua, Guarani, and Maori contexts. *Journal of Language, Identity, and Education* 5(4): 277–292.

Hornberger, N.H. (ed.) (2008a). *Can Schools Save Indigenous Languages? Policy and Practice on Four Continents.* Basingstoke and New York: Palgrave Macmillan.

Hornberger, N.H. (2008b). Introduction. In N.H. Hornberger (ed.) *Can Schools Save Indigenous Languages? Policy and Practice on Four Continents*, pp. 1–12. Basingstoke and New York: Palgrave Macmillan.

Hornberger, N. H. (2009). Multilingual education policy and practice: Ten certainties (grounded in Indigenous experience). *Language Teaching* 42(2): 197–211.

Hornberger, N.H. and Hult, F.M. (2008). Ecological language education policy. In B. Spolsky and F.M. Hult (eds.) *The Handbook of Educational Linguistics*, pp. 280–296. Malden, MA: Blackwell.

Hornberger, N.H. and Johnson, D.C (2007). Slicing the onion ethnographically: Layers and spaces in multilingual language education policy and practice. *TESOL Quarterly* 41(3): 509–532.

Hornberger, N.H. and McKay, S.L. (eds.) (2011). *Sociolinguistics and Language Education*. Bristol: Multilingual Matters.

Hornberger, N.H and Johnson, D.C. (2011). The ethnography of language policy. In T.L. McCarty (ed.) *Ethnography and Language Policy*. London: Routledge.

Huebner, T. and Davis, K.A. (eds.) (1999). *Sociopolitical Perspectives on Language Policy and Planning in the USA*. Amsterdam/Philadelphia: John Benjamins Publishing Company.

Hult, F.M. (2003). English on the streets of Sweden: An ecolinguistic view of two cities and a language policy. *Working Papers in Educational Linguistics* 19(1): 43–63.

Hult, F.M. (2004). Planning for multilingualism and minority language rights in Sweden. *Language Policy* 3: 181–201.

Hult, F.M. (2005). A case of prestige and status planning: Swedish and English in Sweden. *Current Issues in Language Planning* 6(1): 73–79.

Hult, F.M. (2007). *Multilingual Language Policy and English Language Teaching in Sweden*. Ph.D thesis, University of Pennsylvania.

Hult, F.M. (2010a). Analysis of language policy discourses across the scales of space and time. *International Journal of the Sociology of Language* 202: 7–24.

Hult, F.M. (2010b). Swedish television as a mechanism for language planning and policy. *Language Problems & Language Planning* 34(2): 158–181.

Hult, F.M. (2012). English as a transcultural language in Swedish policy and practice. *TESOL Quarterly* 46(2): 230–257.

Hult, F.M. and Johnson, D.C. (eds.) (2013). *Research Methods in Language Policy and Planning A Practical Guide*. Hoboken, NJ: Wiley-Blackwell.

Hymes, D.H. (1962). The ethnography of speaking. In T. Gladwin and W.C. Sturtevant (eds.) *Anthropology and Human Behavior*, pp. 13–53. Washington, DC: Anthropological Society of Washington.

Hymes, D. 1964. Introduction: Toward ethnographies of communication. *American Anthropologist* 66(6): 1–35.

Hymes, D. (1972a). On communicative competence. In J.B. Pride and J. Holmes (eds.) *Sociolinguistics: Selected Readings*, pp. 269–293. Harmondsworth: Penguin Books.

Hymes, D. (1972b). Models of interaction of language and social life. In J. Gumperz and D. Hymes (eds.) *Directions in Sociolinguistics: The Ethnography of Communication*, pp. 35–71. New York: Holt, Rinehart, and Winston.

Hymes, D. (1990). Emics, etics, and openness: An ecumenical approach. In T.N. Headland, K.L. Pike, and M. Harris (eds.) *Emics and Etics: The Insider/Outsider Debate*, pp. 120–126. Newbury Park, CA: Sage Publications.

Iggers, G.G. (1997). *Historiography in the Twentieth Century: From Scientific Objectivity to the Postmodern Challenge*. Hanover, NH: Wesleyan University Press.

Imwinkelried, E.J. (2006). An extended footnote to 'statutory constructions not for the timid'. *The Champion*, May 2006.

Ivanič, R., Edwards, R., Barton, D., Martin-Jones, M., Fowler, Z., Hughes, B., Mannion, G., Miller, K., Satchwell, C., and Smith, J. (2009). *Improving Learning in College: Rethinking Literacies across the Curriculum*. London and New York: Routledge.

Jaffe, A. (1999). *Ideologies in Action: Language Politics on Corsica*. Berlin: Mouton.

Jaffe, A. (2011). Critical perspectives on language-in-education policy: The Corsican example. In T. McCarty (ed.) *Ethnography and Language Policy*, pp. 205–229. New York: Routledge.

Jaworski, A. and Coupland, N. (eds.) (1999). *The Discourse Reader*. London and New York: Routledge.

Jernudd, B. and Das Gupta, J. (1971). Towards a theory of language planning. In J. Rubin and B. Jernudd (eds.) *Can Language be Planned? Sociolinguistic Theory and Practice for Developing Nations*, pp. 195–215. Honolulu: The University Press of Hawaii.

Johnson, D.C. (2004). Language policy discourse and bilingual language planning. *Working Papers in Educational Linguistics* 19(2): 73–97.

Johnson, D.C. (2007). *Language Policy Within and Without the School District of Philadelphia*. Ph.D thesis, University of Pennsylvania.

Johnson, D.C. (2009). Ethnography of language policy. *Language Policy* 8: 139–159.

Johnson, D.C. (2010a). The relationship between applied linguistic research and bilingual language policy. *Applied Linguistics* 31(1): 72–93.

Johnson, D.C. (2010b). Implementational and ideological spaces in bilingual education language policy. *International Journal of Bilingual Education and Bilingualism* 13(1): 61–79.

Johnson, D.C. (2011a). Critical discourse analysis and the ethnography of language policy. *Critical Discourse Studies* 8(4): 267–279.

Johnson, D.C. (2011b). Implementational and ideological spaces in bilingual education policy, practice, and research. In. F.M. Hult and K.A. King (eds.) *Educational Linguistics in Practice: Applying the Global Locally and the Local Globally*. Bristol: Multilingual Matters.

Johnson, D.C. (2013a). Positioning the language policy arbiter: Governmentality and footing in the School District of Philadelphia. In J.W. Tollefson (ed.) *Language Policies in Education: Critical Issues*, 2nd edition. London and New York: Routledge.

Johnson, D.C. (ed.) (2013b). Thematic issue 'Ethnography of language policy: Theory, method, and practice.' *International Journal of the Sociology of Language*.

Johnson, D.C. and Freeman, R. (2010). Appropriating language policy on the local level: Working the spaces for bilingual education. In K. Menken and O. Garcia (eds.) *Negotiating Language Policies in Schools: Educators as Policymakers*. New York: Routledge.

Johnson, D.C. and Ricento, T. (2013). Conceptual and theoretical perspectives in language policy and planning: Situating the ethnography of language policy. *International Journal of the Sociology of Language* 219: 7–21.

Johnson, E.J. (2012). Arbitrating repression: Language policy and education in Arizona. *Language and Education* 26(1): 53–76.

Johnstone, B. (2008). *Discourse Analysis*, 2nd edition. Malden, MA: Blackwell Publishing.

Jones, K., Martin-Jones, M., and Bhatt, A. (2000). Constructing a critical, dialogic approach to research on multilingual literacy: Participants' diaries and diary interviews. In.M. Martin-Jones and K. Jones (eds.) *Multilingual Literacies: Reading and Writing Different Worlds*, pp. 319–351. Amsterdam: John Benjamins.

Kaplan, R. B. and Baldauf, R. B. (1997). *Language Planning: From Practice to Theory.* Clevedon: Multilingual Matters.

Karam, F.X. (1974). Toward a definition of language planning. In J.A. Fishman (ed.) *Advances in Language Planning*, pp. 103–124. Berlin: Walter de Gruyter.

Kemmis, S. and McTagart, R. (1988). *The Action Research Planner*, 3rd edition. Geelong: Deakin University Press.

King, K.A. (2001). *Language Revitalization Processes and Prospects: Quichua in the Ecuadorian Andes.* Clevedon: Multilingual Matters.

King, K. and Fogle, L. (2006). Bilingual parenting as good parenting: Parents' perspectives on family language policy for additive bilingualism. *The International Journal of Bilingual Education and Bilingualism* 9(6): 695–712.

Kloss, H. (1968). Notes concerning a language-nation typology. In J. Fishman, C. Freguson, and J. Das Gupta (eds.) *Language Problems of Developing Nations*, pp. 69–85. New York: John Wiley & Sons.

Kloss, H. (1969). *Research Possibilities on Group Bilingualism: A Report.* Quebec: International Center for Research on Bilingualism.

Kloss, H. (1977/1998). *The American Bilingual Tradition.* Washington, DC: Center for Applied Linguistics.

Krashen, S.D. (1985). *The Input Hypothesis: Issues and Implications.* New York: Longman.

Krashen, S.D. (1996). *Under Attack: The Case Against Bilingual Education.* Culver City, CA: Language Education Associates.

Krashen, S.D. (2012a, June 1). Put to the test. *Santa Monica Daily Press.* Retrieved: http://atthechalkface.com/2012/06/01/report-from-the-50th-assembly-district/

Krashen, S.D. (2012b, June 4). More news from the 50th district CA: I will vote for Tori Osborn. [Web log comment]. Retrieved from http://atthechalkface.com/2012/06/04/more-news-from-the-50th-district-ca-i-will-vote-for-tori-osborn/

Krauss, M. (1992). The world's languages in crisis. *Language* 68(1): 4–10.

Kress, G. (2001). From Saussure to critical sociolinguistics: The turn towards a social view of language. In M. Wetherell, S. Taylor, and S. Yates (eds.) *Discourse Theory and Practice*, pp. 29–38. London: Sage.

Kristeva, J. (1986). Word, dialogue, and novel. In T. Moi (ed.) *The Kristeva Reader*, pp. 34–61. Oxford: Basil Blackwell.

Krzyżanowski, M. (2011a). Ethnography and critical discourse analysis: Towards a problem-oriented research dialogue. *Critical Discourse Studies* 8(4): 231–238.

Krzyżanowski, M. (ed.) (2011b). Thematic issue 'Ethnography and Critical Discourse Analysis.' *Critical Discourse Studies* 8(4).

Kymlicka, W. and Patten, A. (2003a). Language rights and political theory. *Annual Review of Applied Linguistics* 23: 3–21.

Kymlicka, W. and Patten, A. (eds.) (2003b). *Language Rights and Political Theory.* Oxford: Oxford University Press.

Labov, W. (1972a). *Language in the Inner City: Studies in the Black English Vernacular.* University of Pennsylvania Press.

Labov, W. (1972b). The study of language in its social context. In J.B. Pride and J. Holmes (eds.) *Sociolinguistics: Selected Readings.* Harmondsworth: Penguin Books.

Labov, W. (1982). Objectivity and commitment in linguistic science: The case of the Black English trial in Ann Arbor. *Language in Society* 11(2): 165–201.

Laing, D. (1985). *Once Chord Wonders: Power and Meaning in Punk Rock.* Milton Keynes: Open University Press.

Landsheere, G. de (1982). *Empirical Research in Education.* Paris: United Nations Educational, Scientific and Cultural Organization.

Layder, D. (1993). *New Strategies in Social Research: An Introduction and Guide.* Cambridge: Polity Press.

Leibowitz, A. H. (1984). The official character of language in the United States: Literacy requirements for immigration, citizenship, and entrance into American life. *Aztlan* 15(1): 25–70.

Lemke, J. (1995). *Textual Politics: Discourse and Social Dynamics.* Abingdon: Taylor and Francis.

Levinson, B.A.U. and Sutton, M. (2001). Introduction: Policy as/in practice – a sociocultural approach to the study of educational policy. In B.A.U. Levinson and M. Sutton (eds.) *Policy as Practice: Toward a Sociocultural Analysis of Educational Policy,* pp. 1–22. London: Ablex Publishing.

Levinson, B.A.U., Sutton, M., and Winstead, T. (2007) Education policy as a practice of power: Ethnographic methods, democratic options. Paper presented at the 28th Annual Ethnography in Education Research Forum. Philadelphia, PA.

Levinson, B.A.U., Sutton, M., and Winstead, T. (2009). Education policy as a practice of power: Theoretical tools, ethnographic methods, democratic options. *Educational Policy* 23(6): 767–795.

Lewin, K. (1946). Action research and minority problems. *Journal of Social Issues* 2(4): 34–46.

Li Wei (2005). 'How can you tell?' Towards a common sense explanation of conversational code-switching. *Journal of Pragmatics* 37: 375–389.

Lightbown, P.M. and Spada, N. (2006). *How Languages Are Learned.* Oxford University Press.

Lin, A.M.Y. and Martin, P.W. (eds.) (2005). *Decolonisation, Globalisation: Language-in-Education Policy and Practice.* Clevedon: Multilingual Matters.

Linell, P. (1998). Discourse across boundaries: On recontextualizations and the blending of voices in professional discourse. *Text* 18(2): 143–157.

Lippi-Green, R. (1997). *English with an Accent: Language, Ideology, and Discrimination in the United States.* London and New York: Routledge.

Lo Bianco, J. (2008). Tense times and language planning. *Current Issues in Language Planning* 9: 155–178.

Lo Bianco, J. (2005). Including discourse in language planning theory. In P. Bruthiaux, D. Atkinson, W.G. Eggington, W. Grabe and V. Ramanathan (eds.) *Directions in Applied Linguistics,* pp. 255–263. Clevedon: Multilingual Matters.

Lopez, L.E. (2008). Top-down and bottom-up: Counterpoised visions of bilingual intercultural education in Latin America. In N.H. Hornberger (ed.) *Can Schools Save Indigenous Languages? Policy and Practice on Four Continents.* Basingstoke and New York: Palgrave Macmillan.

Lowth, R. (1762). *A Short Introduction to English Grammar with Critical Notes*. London: J. Hughs.

Luke, A. (2002). Beyond science and ideology critique: Developments in critical discourse analysis. *Annual Review of Applied Linguistics* 22: 96–110.

Macías, R.F. and Wiley, T. (1998). Introduction. In H. Kloss, *The American Bilingual Tradition*, pp. vii–xiv. Washington, DC and McHenry, IL: Center for Applied Linguistics and Delta System.

Madiscon, D.S. (2012). *Critical Ethnography: Method, ethics, and performance*, 2nd edition. Los Angeles: Sage.

Mann, S. (2011). A critical review of qualitative interviews in applied linguistics. *Applied Linguistics* 32(1): 6–24.

Marinova-Todd, S.H., Marshall, D.B., and Snow, C.E. (2000). Three misconceptions about age and L2 learning. *TESOL Quarterly* 34(1): 9–34.

Martin-Jones, M. (1995). Code-switching in the classroom: Two decades of research. In L. Milory and P. Muysken (eds.) *One Speaker, Two Languages: Cross-Disciplinary Perspectives on Code-Switching*, pp. 90–111. Cambridge University Press.

Martin-Jones, M. (2009). From life worlds and work worlds to college: The bilingual literacy practices of young Welsh speakers. *The Welsh Journal of Education* 14(2): 45–62.

Martin-Jones, M. (2011). Languages, texts, and literacy practices: An ethnographic lens on bilingual vocational education in Wales. In T. McCarty (ed.) *Ethnography and Language Policy*, pp. 231–253. London and New York: Routledge.

Martin-Jones, M., Hughes, B., and Wiliams, A. (2009). Bilingual literacy in and for working lives on the land: Case studies of young Welsh speakers in North Wales. *International Journal of the Sociology of Language* 195: 39–62.

Matheson, D. (2005). *Media Discourses: Analysing Media Texts*. Maidenhead: Open University Press.

May, J. (2006). Statutory construction: Not for the timid. *The Champion*. Retrieved from: http://www.nacdl.org/Champion.aspx?id=1539.

May, S. (2001). *Language and Minority Rights: Ethnicity, Nationalism, and the Politics of Language*. Harlow: Longman.

May, S. (2005a). Introduction: Bilingual/immersion education in Aotearoa/New Zealand: Setting and context. *The International Journal of Bilingual Education and Bilingualism* 8(5): 365–376.

May, S. (ed.) (2005b). Thematic issue 'Bilingual/immersion education in Aotearoa/New Zeland.' *The International Journal of Bilingual Education and Bilingualism* 8(5).

May, S. (2013). Interpreting language policy using political theory. In F.M. Hult and D.C. Johnson (eds.) *Research Methods in Language Policy and Planning: A Practical Guide*. Hoboken, NJ: Wiley-Blackwell.

May, S and Hill, R. (2005). Maori-medium education: Current issues and challenges. *International Journal of Bilingual Education* 8(5): 377–403.

McCarty, T.L. (2002). *A Place to be Navajo: Rough Rock and the Struggle for Self-Determination in Indigenous Schooling*. Mahwah, NJ: Lawrence Erlbaum.

McCarty, T.L. (2009). Schools as strategic tools for Indigenous language revitalization: Lessons from Native America. In N.H. Hornberger (ed.) *Can Schools Save Indigenous Languages? Policy and Practice on Four Continents*, pp. 161–179. Basingstokeand New York: Palgrave Macmillan.

McCarty, T.L. (ed.) (2011a). *Ethnography and Language Policy.* London: Routledge.

McCarty, T.L. (2011b). Introducing ethnography and language policy. In T.L. McCarty (ed.) *Ethnography and Language Policy*, pp.1–28. London: Routledge.

McCarty, T.L. (2013). Ethnographic research. In F.M. Hult and D.C. Johnson (eds.) *Research Methods in Language Policy and Planning: A Practical Guide.* Hoboken, NJ: Wiley-Blackwell.

McCarty, T.L., Collins, J., and Hopson, R.K. (2011). Dell Hymes and the new language policy studies: Update from an underdeveloped country. *Anthropology and Education Quarterly* 42(4): 335–363.

McGroarty, M. (2006). Neoliberal collusion or strategic simultaneity? On multiple rationales for language-in-education policies. *Language Policy* 5: 3–13.

McGroarty, M. (2011). Home language: Refuge, resistance, resource? *Language Teaching* 45(1): 89–104.

McGroarty, M. (2013). Mapping language ideologies. In F.M. Hult and D.C. Johnson (eds.), *Research Methods in Language Policy and Planning: A Practical Guide.* Hoboken, NJ: Wiley-Blackwell.

McKay, S. and Chick, K. (2001). Positioning learners in post-Apartheid South Africa schools: A case study of selected multicultural Durban schools. *Linguistics and Education* 12(4): 393–408.

McKay, S.L. and Weinstein-Shr, G. (1993). English literacy in the US: National policies, personal consequences. *TESOL Quarterly* 27(3): 399–419.

Menken, K. (2008). *English Learners Left Behind: Standardized Testing as Language Policy.* Clevedon: Multilingual Matters.

Menken, K. and García, O. (eds.) (2010). *Negotiating Language Policies in Schools: Educators as Policymakers.* New York: Routledge.

Mertz, E. (1982). Language and the mind: A Whorfian folk theory in United States language law. *Duke University Sociolinguistics Working Paper* 93.

Mitchell, N. (2002, Nov. 6). Colorado hands English immersion backer his first loss. *Rocky Mountain News,* p. 29A.

Mitchell, D.E., Crowson, R.L., and Shipps, D. (eds.) (2011). *Shaping Education Policy: Power and Process.* New York: Routledge.

Mohanty, A. Panda, M., and Pal, R. (2010). Language policy in education and classroom practices in India: Is the teacher a cog in the policy wheel? In K. Menken and O. Garcia (eds.) *Negotiating Language Policies in Schools: Educators as Policymakers.* New York: Routledge.

Mortimer, K. (2013). Communicative event chains in an ethnography of Paraguayan language policy. *International Journal of the Sociology of Language* 219: 67–99.

Murray, L. (1795). *English Grammar.* York: Printed and Sold by Wilson, Spence, and Mawman.

Myers-Scotton, C. (1993). *Social Motivations for Codeswitching: Evidence from Africa.* Oxford: Clarendon Press.

Nahir, M. (1984). Language planning goals: A classification. *Language Problems and Language Planning* 8: 294–327.

Nettle, D. and Romaine, S. (2000). *Vanishing Voices: The Extinction of the World's Languages.* Oxford University Press.

Neustupny, J.V. (1974). Basict types of treatment of language problems. In J. Fishman (ed.) *Advances in Language Planning,* pp. 37–48. The Hague: Mouton.

Ochs, E. and Schieffelin, B. (1983). *Acquisition of Conversational Competence.* London: Routledge.

Ottosson, D. (2008). *State-Sponsored Homophobia: A World Survey of Laws Prohibiting Same Sex Activity Between Consenting Adults*. International Lesbian and Gay Association.

Padres Unidos (2003). Colorado upholds the right to bilingual education. *Rethinking Schools Online* 17(3).

Pan, L. (2011). English language ideologies in the Chinese foreign language education policies: A world-system perspective. *Language Policy* 10: 245–263.

Pedraza, J.S. (1997). Saving and strengthening indigenous Mexican languages: The CELIAC experience. In N.H. Hornberger (ed.) *Indigenous Literacies in the Americas: Language Planning from the Bottom Up*, pp. 171–187. Berlin: Mouton de Gruyter.

Pennycook, A. (2004). Language policy and the ecological turn. *Language Policy* 3: 213–239.

Pennycook, A. (2002). Language policy and docile bodies: Hong Kong and governmentality. In J.W. Tollefson (ed.) *Language Policies in Education: Critical Issues*, pp. 91–110. Mahwah, NJ: Lawrence Erlbaum Associates.

Pennycook, A. (2006). Postmodernism in language policy. In T. Ricento (ed.) *An Introduction to Language Policy: Theory and Method*, pp. 60–76. Malden, MA: Blackwell Publishing.

Phillipson, R. (1992). *Linguistic Imperialism*. Oxford University Press.

Phillipson, R. (2003). *English-Only Europe? Challenging Language Policy*. London and New York: Routledge.

Phillipson, R. and Skutnabb-Kangas, T. (1996). English only worldwide or language ecology? *TESOL Quarterly* 30(3): 429–452.

Pike, K.L. (1954). *Language in Relation to a Unified Theory of the Structures of Human Behavior*. The Hague: Mouton.

Piller, I. (2001). Naturalization language testing and its basis in ideologies of national identity and citizenship. *International Journal of Bilingualism* 5(3): 259–277.

Pinker, S. (1994). *The Language Instinct: How the Mind Creates Language*. New York: William Morrow and Company.

Porter, R.P. (1990). *Forked Tongue: The Politics of Bilingual Education*. Transaction Publishers.

Powell, R. (2009). The role of English in Southeast Asian legal systems. In T. Hoffman and L. Siebers (eds.) *World Englishes – Problems, Properties and Prospects: Selected Papers from the 13th IAWE Conference*, pp. 155–178. Amsterdam: John Benjamins Publishing Company.

Prucha, F.P. (2000). *Documents of United States Indian Policy*, 3rd edition. University of Nebraska Press.

Rabin, C. (1971). A tentative classification of language planning aims. In J. Rubin and B. Jernudd (eds.) *Can Language be Planned? Sociolinguistic Theory and Practice for Developing Nations*, pp. 277–279. Honolulu: East-West Center and University of Hawaii Press.

Ramanathan, V. (2005). Rethinking language planning and policy from the ground up: Refashioning institutional realities and human lives. *Current Issues in Language Planning* 6(2): 89–101.

Rampton, B. (2007). Neo-Hymesian linguistic ethnography in the United Kingdom. *Journal of Sociolinguistics* 11(5): 584–607.

Ricento, T. (2000a). Historical and theoretical perspectives in language policy and planning. *Journal of Sociolinguistics* 4(2): 196–213.

Ricento , T. (ed.) (2000b). Ideology, politics, and language policies: Focus on English. Amsterdam/Philadelphia: John Benjamins Publishing Company.

Ricento, T. (ed.) (2006a). *An Introduction to Language Policy: Theory and Method.* Malden, MA: Blackwell Publishing.

Ricento, T. (2006b). Language policy: Theory and practice – an introduction. In T. Ricento (ed.) *An Introduction to Language Policy: Theory and Method*, pp. 10–23. Malden, MA: Blackwell Publishing.

Ricento, T. and Hornberger, N.H. (1996). Unpeeling the onion: Language planning and policy and the ELT professional. *TESOL Quarterly*, (30)3: 401–427.

Richards, J.C. and Rodgers, T.S. (2006). *Approaches and Methods in Language Teaching.* 2nd edition. Cambridge University Press.

Richardson, J.E. and Wodak, R. (2009). Recontextualising fascist ideologies of the past: Right-wing disocurses on employment and nativism in Austria and the United Kingdom. *Critical Discourse Studies* 6(4): 251–267.

Rickford, J.R. (1999). The Ebonics controversy in my backyard: A sociolinguist's experiences and reflections. *Journal of Sociolinguistics* 3(2): 267–275.

Rogers, R. (2003). *A Critical Discourse Analysis of Family Literacy Practices*, Mahwah, NJ: Lawrence Erlbaum

Rolstad, K., Mahoney, K., and Glass, G.V. (2005). The big picture: A meta-analysis of program effectiveness research on English language learners. *Educational Policy* 19(4): 572–594.

Romaine, S. (2006). Planning for the survival of linguistic diversity. *Language Policy* 5: 441–473.

Roman, L.G. (1993). Double exposure: The politics of feminist materialist ethnography. *Educational Theory* 43(3): 279–308.

Roosevelt, T. (1917). The children of the crucible. In *Annals of America, 14, 1916–1928.* Chicago: Encyclopedia Britannica, 1968.

Rossel, C. and Baker, K. (1996). The educational effectiveness of bilingual education. *Research in Teaching of English* 30(1): 385–419.

Rubin, J. (1971). Evaluation and language planning. In J. Rubin and B.H. Jernudd (eds.) *Can Language Be Planned? SociolinguisticTheory and Practice for Developing Nations*, pp. 217–252. Honolulu: The University Press of Hawaii.

Rubin, J. (1977). Bilingual education and language planning. In B. Spolsky and R.L. Cooper (eds.) *Frontiers of Bilingual Education.* Rowley, MA: Newbury House Publishers.

Rubin, J. and Jernudd, B.H. (eds.) (1971). *Can Language Be Planned? Sociolinguistic Theory and Practice for Developing Nations.* Honolulu: The University Press of Hawaii.

Rubin, J., Jernudd, B.H., Das Gupta, J., Fishman, J.A., and Ferguson, C.A. (1977). *Language Planning Processes.* The Hague: Mouton Publishers.

Ruiz, R. (1984). Orientations in language planning. *NABE Journal* 8(2): 15–34.

Rumsey, A. (1990). Wording, meaning, and linguistic ideology. *American Anthropologist* 92: 346–361.

Samway, K.D. and McKeon, D. (2007). *Myths and Realities: Best Practices for English Language Learners*, 2nd edition. Portsmouth, NH: Heinemann.

Sarangi, S. (2007). Editorial: The anatomy of interpretation: Coming to terms with the analyst's paradox in professional discourse studies. *Text & Talk* 27(5–6): 567–584.

Sarangi, S. and Candlin, C. (2003). Editorial: Trading between reflexivity and relevance: New challenges for applied linguistics. *Applied Linguistics* 24(3): 271–285.

Sarangi, S. and Candlin, C. N. (2010) Editorial: Applied linguistics and professional practice: Mapping a future agenda. *Journal of Applied Linguistics and Professional Practice* 7(1): 1–9.

Sarangi, S. and Candlin, C. (2011). Professional and organisational practice: A discourse/communication perspective. In C. Candlin and S. Sarangi (eds.) *Handbook of Communication in Organisations and Professions*, pp. 3–58. Berlin: Mouton De Gruyter.

Savage, J. (2002). *England's Dreaming: Anarchy, Sex Pistols, Punk Rock, and Beyond.* New York: St. Martin's Griffin.

Saville-Troike, M. (1996). The ethnography of communication. In S.L. McKay and N.H. Hornberger (eds.) *Sociolinguistics and Language Teaching*, pp. 351–382. Cambridge University Press.

Schegloff, E. (1997). Whose text? Whose context? *Language in Society* 8: 165–187.

Schiffman, H. F. (1996). *Linguistic Culture and Language Policy.* London: Routledge.

Schiffman, H.F. (2010). South and Southeast Asia. In J.A. Fishman and O. García (eds.) *Handbook of Language and Ethnic Identity: Disciplinary and Regional Perspectives.* Vol. 1, 2nd edition, pp. 452–469. Oxford University Press.

Schmid, C.L. (2001). *The Politics of Language: Conflict Identity, and Cultural Pluralism in Comparative Perspective.* New York: Oxford University Press.

Schmidt, Sr., R. (2002). Racialization and language policy: The case of the U.S.A. *Multilingua* 21: 141–161.

Schmidt, Sr., R. (2006). Political theory and language policy. In T. Ricento (ed.) *An Introduction to Language Policy: Theory and Method*, pp. 95–110. Malden, MA: Blackwell Publishing.

Schissel, J. (2009). Narrative self-constructions of Senator Ralph Yarborough in the 1967 congressional hearings on the Bilingual Education Act. *Working Papers in Educational Linguistics* 24(1): 79–99.

Searle, J. R. (1969) *Speech Acts. An Essay in the Philosophy of Language.*Cambridge University Press.

Seedhouse, P. (2004). *The Interactional Architecture of the Language Classroom: A Conversation Analysis Perspective.* Malden, MA: Blackwell.

Shohamy, E. (2006). *Language Policy: Hidden Agendas and New Approaches.* London and New York: Routledge.

Shohamy, E. and Gorter, D. (eds.) (2009). *Linguistic Landscape: Expanding the Scenery.* New York and London: Routledge.

Shuibne, N.N. (2013). Legal research and analysis. In F.M. Hult and D.C. Johnson (eds.) *Research Methods in Language Policy and Planning: A Practical Guide.* Hoboken, NJ: Wiley-Blackwell.

Shulman, S. (2006). *Undermining Science: Suppression and Distortion in the Bush Administration.* Berkeley: University of California Press.

Shuy, R. (2001). Discourse analysis in the legal context. In D. Schiffrin, D. Tannen, and H. Hamilton (eds.) *The Handbook of Discourse Analysis*, pp. 437–452. Oxford: Blackwell.

Silverstein, M. (1985). Language and the culture of gender: At the intersection of structure, usage, and ideology. In E. Mertz and R. Parmentier (eds.), *Semiotic Mediation: Sociocultural and Psychological Perspectives*, pp. 219–259. Orlando, FL: Academic Press.

Skilton-Sylvester, E. (2003). Legal discourse and decisions, teacher policymaking and the multilingual classroom: Constraining and supporting Khmer/English biliteracy in the United States. *International Journal of Bilingual Education and Bilingualism* 6(3&4): 168–184.

Skutnabb-Kangas, T. (2000a). Linguistic human rights and teachers of English. In. J.K. Hall and W.G. Eggington (eds.) *The Sociopolitics of English Language Teaching*, pp. 22–44. Clevedon: Multilingual Matters.

Skutnabb-Kangas, T. (2000b). *Linguistic Genocide in Education—Or Worldwide Diversity and Human Rights?* Mahwah, NJ: Lawrence Erlbaum Associates.

Smith, Graham. 1997. *Kaupapa Maori as Transformative Practice.* Ph.D thesis, University of Auckland.

Spolsky, B. (2003). Religion as a site of language contact. *Annual Review of Applied Linguistics* 23: 81–94.

Spolsky, B. (2004). *Language Policy.* Cambridge University Press.

Spolsky, B. (2009). *Language Management.* Cambridge University Press.

Spolsky, B. and Shohamy, E. (1999). *The Languages of Israel: Policy, Ideology and Practice.* Clevedon: Multilingual Matters.

Sridhar, K.K. (1996). Societal multilingualism. In S. L. McKay and N. H. Hornberger (eds.) *Sociolinguistics and Language Teaching*, pp. 47–70. Cambridge University Press.

Stewart, W. (1968). A sociolinguistic typology for describing national multilingualism. In J.A. Fishman (ed.) *Readings in the Sociology of Language*, pp. 531–545. The Hague: Mouton.

Stritikus, T. (2002). *Immigrant Children and the Politics of English-only.* New York: LFB Scholarly Publishing LLC.

Stritikus, T.T. and Weise, A. (2006). Reassessing the role of ethnographic methods in education policy research: Implementing bilingual education policy at local levels. *Teachers College Record* 108(6): 1106–1131.

Talbot, M. (2007). *Media Discourse: Representation and Interaction.* Edinburgh University Press.

Talmy, S. (2011). The interview as collaborative achievement: Interaction, identity, and ideology in a speech event. *Applied Linguistics* 32(1): 25–42.

Talmy, S. and Richards, K. (eds.) (2011a). [Special issue]. Qualitative interviews in applied linguistics: Discursive perspectives. *Applied Linguistics* 32(1).

Talmy, S. and Richards, K. (2011b) Theorizing qualitative research interviews in applied linguistics. *Applied Linguistics* 32(1): 1–5.

Tauli, V. (1974). The theory of language planning. In J.A. Fishman (ed.) *Advances in Language Planning*, pp. 69–78. The Hague: Mouton.

Thomas, W.P. and Collier, V.P. (1997). *School Effectiveness for Language Minority Children.* Washington, DC: National Clearinghouse for Bilingual Education.

Tieken-Boon van Ostade, I. (2010). Lowth as an icon of prescriptivism. In R. Hickey (ed.) *Eighteenth-Century English: Ideology and Change*, pp. 73–88. Cambridge University Press.

Tollefson, J.W. (1991). *Planning Language, Planning Inequality: Language Policy in the Community.* London: Longman.

Tollefson, J.W. (2000). Policy and ideology in the spread of English. In J.K. Hall and W.G. Eggington (eds.) *The Sociopolitics of English Language Teaching*, pp. 7–21. Clevedon: Multilingual Matters.

Tollefson, J.W. (ed.) (2002a). *Language Policies in Education: Critical Issues*. Mahwah, NJ: Lawrence Erlbaum Publishers.

Tollefson, J.W. (2002b). Introduction: Critical issues in educational language policy. In J.W. Tollefson (ed.) *Language Policies in Education: Critical Issues*. Mahwah, NJ: Lawrence Erlbaum Publishers.

Tollefson, J.W. (2002c). Language rights and the destruction of Yugoslavia. In J.W. Tollefson (ed.) *Language Policies in Education: Critical Issues*. Mahwah, NJ: Lawrence Erlbaum Publishers.

Tollefson, J.W. (2006). Critical theory in language policy. In T. Ricento (ed.) *An Introduction to Language Policy: Theory and Method*, pp. 42–59. Malden, MA: Blackwell Publishing.

Tollefson, J.W. (ed.) (2013a). *Language Policies in Education: Critical Issues*, 2nd edition. London and New York: Routledge.

Tollefson, J.W. (2013b). Language policy in a time of crisis and transformation. In J.W. Tollefson (ed.) *Language Policies in Education: Critical Issues*, 2nd edition, pp. 11–32. London and New York: Routledge.

Tollefson, J.W. and Tsui, A.B.M. (2003). *Medium of Instruction Policies: Which Agenda? Whose Agenda?* Mahwah, NJ: Lawrence Erlbaum Associates.

Tse, L. (2001). *Why don't they learn English? Separating Fact from Fallacy in the U.S. Language Debate*. New York: Teachers College Press.

U.S. D.O.S. (2012). Background Note: Equatorial Guinea. Retrieved from http://www.state.gov/r/pa/ei/bgn/7221.htm.

Vaishnav, A. (2003, Dec. 26). English immersion is slow going: State's time frame for immigrant children to master English is tough to meet. *Boston Globe*, pp. b1.

Valdez, E.O. (2001). Winning the battle, losing the war: Bilingual teachers and post-Proposition 227. *The Urban Review* 33: 237–253.

Valdiviezo, L. (2013). Vertical and horizontal approaches to ethnography of language policy in Peru. *International Journal of the Sociology of Language*, 219: 23–46.

Walford, G. (2002). When policy moves fast, how long can ethnography take? In B.A.U. Levinson, S.L. Cade, A. Padawer, and A.P. Elvir (eds.) *Ethnography and Education Policy Across the Americas*. London: Praeger.

Warhol, L. (2011). Native American language education as policy-in-practice: An interpretive policy analysis of the Native American Languages Act of 1990/1992. *International Journal of Bilingual Education and Bilingualism* 14(3): 279–299.

Wedin, A. (2005). Language ideologies and schooled education in rural Tanzania: The case of Karagwe. *International Journal of Bilingual Education and Bilingualism*, *8*(6): 568–587.

Widdowson, H.G. (1995). Discourse analysis: A critical view. *Language and Literature* 4(3): 157–172.

Widdowson, H.G. (1998). Review article: The theory and practice of Critical Discourse Analysis. *Applied Linguistics* 19(1): 136–151.

Wiese, A.M. (2001). *To meet the needs of the kids, not the program: Teachers Cconstructing Policy, Program, and Practice in a Bilingual School*. Ph.D thesis, Graduate School of Education, University of California, Berkeley.

Wiese, A.M. and Garcia, E.E. (2001). The Bilingual Education Act: Language minority students and US federal educational policy. *International Journal of Bilingual Education and Bilingualism* 4(4): 229–248.

Wiley, T.G. (1999). Comparative historical analysis of U.S. language policy and language planning: Extending the foundations. In T. Huebner and K.A. Davis (eds.) *Sociopolitical Perspectives on Language Policy and Planning in the USA*, pp. 17–37. Amsterdam/Philadelphia: John Benjamins Publishing Company.

Wiley, T.G. (2002). Assessing language rights in education: A brief history of the U.S. context. In J.W. Tollefson (ed.) *Language Policies in Education: Critical Issues*. Mahwah, NJ: Lawrence Erlbaum Publishers.

Wiley, T.G. and Wright, W.E. (2004). Against the undertow: Language-minority education policy and politics in the "age of accountability". *Educational Policy* 18(2): 142–68.

Wodak, R. (1996). *Disorders of Discourse*. London: Longman.

Wodak, R. (2000). Recontextualization and the transformation of meanings: A critical discourse analysis of decision making in EU meetings about employment policies. In. S. Sarangi and M. Coulthard (eds.) *Discourse and Social Life*, pp. 185–206. Harlow: Pearson Education Limited.

Wodak, R. (2006). Linguistic analyses in language policies. In T. Ricento (ed.) *An Introduction to Language Policy: Theory and Method*, pp. 170–193. Malden, MA: Blackwell Publishing.

Wodak, R. and Fairclough, N. (2010). Recontextualizing European higher education policies: The cases of Austria and Romania. *Critical Discourse Studies* 7(1): 19–40.

Wolfram, W. (1998). Black children are verbally deprived. In L. Bauer and P. Trudgill (eds.) *Language Myths*, pp. 103–112. London: Penguin Books.

Woolard, K.A. (1992). Language ideology: Issues and approaches. *Pragmatics* 2(3): 235–249.

Woolard, K.A. and Schieffelin, B.B. (1994). Language ideology. *Annual Review of Anthropology* 23: 55–82.

Wortham, S. (2005). Socialization beyond the speech event. *Journal of Linguistic Anthropology* 15(1): 95–112.

Yanow, D. (2000). *Conducting Interpretive Policy Analysis*. Thousand Oaks, CA: Sage Publications.

Yitzhaki, D. (2010). The discourse of Arabic language policies in Israel: Insights from focus groups. *Language Policy* 9: 335–356.

Zhou, M. (2013). Using census data and demography in language policy analysis. In F.M. Hult and D.C. Johnson (eds.) *Research Methods in Language Policy and Planning: A Practical Guide*. Hoboken, NJ: Wiley-Blackwell.

Index

acquisition planning, 33, 37, 122
action research
  definition of, 171
  fundamental aspects, 172
  language policy action research, 174–180
advocacy and activism, 190–213
African American English (AAE)
  and the media, 198–200
  Ann Arbor School District Court Case, 197–198
  Oakland School Board policy, 141
Amendment 31 (Colorado), 200–202
appropriation (vs. implementation), 96–97
arbiter (of language policy), 100–101

bilingual education
  and ethnography, 43
  and reversing language shift, 48
  and Ruiz' framework, 36–38
  Wales, 60–64
  Mozambique, 64–69
bottom-up/top-down distinction, 6, 10–11, 108
business language policy, 20–24, 217–220

citizenship, 129, 133–137, 238
code-switching, 72–74
communicative competence, 30–31
conversation analysis (CA), 72
corpus analysis, 88–91
corpus planning
  example of, 12–16
  in early language planning research, 27–30, 123–124
covert/overt distinction, 10–11
critical discourse analysis (CDA), 154–158
  criticism of, 164–166
critical language policy (CLP), 39–43
  and critical discourse analysis, 158
  definition, 40
critical linguistics, 32–33

de jure/de facto distinction, 10–12
discourse-historical approach, 157–158

ecology of language (ecological linguistics), 51–52
educational language policy, 52–55
  and action research, 170–214
  and language policy orientations, 38
  definition, 54
egalitarian discourse community, 184, 209
emancipatory leader, 189
engagement, 191
ethnography (of language policy)
  and critical discourse analysis, 163, 165–166
  method, 144–151
  theory, 43–47, 61
ethnography of speaking/communication, 148–149
explicit/implicit distinction, 10–11

footing, 100, 175, 207

governmentality, 41–42

historical-structural approach, 39
historical-textual analysis
  definition of method, 250–251
  overview, 124–128

ideology
  and immigration, 88–91
  and language policy, 111–113
  English and ideological hegemony, 84
  language ideology defined, 112
  one nation-one language, 135–136, 231–232

Spolsky's language policy definition, 5–6
implementational and ideological spaces, 99, 104
instantiation, 107–108
intentionality, 114
interdiscursivity, 158–164
defined, 160
interdiscursive analysis in language policy, 249–250
intertextuality, 158–164
intertextual analysis in language policy, 246
interviews, 239–242

judicial decisions, 129–132

Kaupapa Māori, 186–188

language as problem/right/resource (Ruiz)
analyzing orientations in education, 244–245
definition, 36

language contact, 13
language planning
defined, 27
early language planning scholarship, 27–30
vs. language policy, 3
language revitalization, 48–49
Māori, 186–188
Native American, 195–196
Lau v. Nichols, 104, 129–130
law (and language policy), 128–140
linguistic anthropology, 166–168
linguistic culture, 4–5
linguistic ethnography, 147
linguistic imperialism, 49–51

media
and language ideology, 88–91
and language policy, 140–144
and language policy activism, 198–206

nativism, 127
No Child Left Behind (NCLB), 104, 113–116, 139, 211, 229–230, 257–258
norms of interaction, 8, 74–75

originalism vs. pragmatism, 138–139

participant-observation, 247–248
participation framework, 100, 175
policy as discourse/text, 101–102
policy as practice, 71
political theory, 128–140
positionality, 147, 220–224
post-modernism, 42–43
post-structuralism, 32, 114–115
PRAESA (Project for the Study of Alternative Education in South Africa), 180–184
probability sampling, 142–143
Proposition 203 (Arizona), 89, 110
Proposition 227 (California), 98

Question 2 (Massachusetts), 141–142

recontextualization, 158–164
definition, 161–162
reversing language shift, 47–49

speech chains, 167–168
status planning, 27–29
statutory interpretation, 137–140

testing (and citizenship), 133–134

CPSIA information can be obtained
at www.ICGtesting.com
Printed in the USA
LVOW01s1541190116
471354LV00021B/1567/P